Automating Finance

Trading floors are a thing of the past. Thanks to a combination of computers, high-speed networks, and algorithms, millions of financial transactions now happen in fractions of a second. This book studies the automation of stock markets in the United Kingdom and the United States of America, identifying the invisible actors, devices, and politics that were central to the creation of electronic trading. In addition to offering a detailed account of how stock exchanges wrestled with technology, the book also invites readers to rethink the nature of markets in modern societies. Markets, it argues, are sites for the creation of relations, and in studying how these relations changed through technology, the book highlights the sources, dynamics, and consequences of automation. In this respect, the book is both a history of automation in finance and a sociological analysis of the way in which automation gradually changed the lives and work of key financial actors.

JUAN PABLO PARDO-GUERRA is Assistant Professor in Sociology at the University of California, San Diego. Building on an early interest in econophysics and artificial financial markets, his work covers the history of technology in financial markets, the sociology of art markets, and the use of computational methods in social science.

Automating Finance

Infrastructures, Engineers, and the Making of Electronic Markets

JUAN PABLO PARDO-GUERRA

University of California, San Diego

CAMBRIDGE
UNIVERSITY PRESS

University Printing House, Cambridge CB2 8BS, United Kingdom

One Liberty Plaza, 20th Floor, New York, NY 10006, USA

477 Williamstown Road, Port Melbourne, VIC 3207, Australia

314–321, 3rd Floor, Plot 3, Splendor Forum, Jasola District Centre, New Delhi – 110025, India

79 Anson Road, #06–04/06, Singapore 079906

Cambridge University Press is part of the University of Cambridge.

It furthers the University's mission by disseminating knowledge in the pursuit of education, learning, and research at the highest international levels of excellence.

www.cambridge.org
Information on this title: www.cambridge.org/9781108496421
DOI: 10.1017/9781108677585

First published 2019

Printed in the United Kingdom by TJ International Ltd. Padstow Cornwall

A catalogue record for this publication is available from the British Library.

Library of Congress Cataloging-in-Publication Data
Names: Pardo-Guerra, Juan Pablo, author.
Title: Automating finance : infrastructures, engineers, and the making of electronic markets / Juan Pablo Pardo-Guerra, University of California, San Diego.
Description: Cambridge, United Kingdom ; New York, NY : Cambridge University Press, 2019. | Includes bibliographical references and index.
Identifiers: LCCN 2018057972 | ISBN 9781108496421 (hardback : alk. paper)
Subjects: LCSH: Finance–Technological innovations. | Securities–Data processing. | Electronic trading of securities. | Capital market.
Classification: LCC HG173 .P35 2019 | DDC 332.640285–dc23
LC record available at https://lccn.loc.gov/2018057972

ISBN 978-1-108-49642-1 Hardback

For Samuel and Nara

Contents

Figures

Preface

This book charts more than a decade of explorations around markets and technology. From my early curiosity of the history of the devices and machines that populated stock exchanges to a more recent turn to metaphors of kinship, community, and their political consequences, *Automating Finance* presents an evolving theoretical framework for thinking about the sources, dynamics, and consequences of computers and telecommunications in financial markets and capitalism at large.

Much of this book is motivated by a long-standing interest in the "ontology of markets," a term that I first encountered in the work of John Lie but that describes my fascination with how situations of trading, valuation, and exchange are produced in contemporary societies. This explains the overlapping themes of the book. One, for example, concerns the idea of market makers, a term often used to designate a particular type of financial intermediaries that can also be mobilized more broadly to think about the people and institutions that create and constitute markets. While we often think of markets through their front stage – the stall in the winding, cobbled street, the carefully calculated supermarket aisles, the trading floors populated by interested financiers, or the abstract fictions of economists – markets are complex sociotechnical achievements that require vast crews for their manufacture, maintenance, and reinvention. These crews constitute the *other* market makers, namely, agents, who despite their invisibility are central to the reproduction of the market.

A second theme refers to the organizational nature of markets. An important moment for this project was the realization that markets are always tied to specific organizational forms. Sociologists and economists have noted this to differing degrees, placing attention on how states, courts, firms, and other institutions define the boundaries of markets and exchange. The finding that inspired much of *Automating Finance* was slightly different, though: markets critically depend on the mundane routines, everyday practices, and lowly politics of messy organizations. They do not exist in opposition to hierarchies, but rather almost as ephemeral, performed surfaces of deeper, highly located bureaucracies rich in cultures, tensions, moralities, and contradictions. I find this theoretical shift useful for illuminating the difficulties of taming markets, but also for showing the unexpected sources of innovation that can upend relations of power in less than a generation. Half a century ago, stock exchanges were mostly mutualized organizations controlled by their members; today, they are publicly listed corporations devoted primarily to developing software and information infrastructures. This shift was not caused by technology but rather guided by the ever-changing ecologies of financial markets and the struggles, reactions, and utopias that they elicited within their organizations.

The third theme involves reconceptualizing markets through the optics of kinship. Here, I use several metaphorical resources to stress the possible connections between markets, often thought of as ephemeral situations, and communities, usually conceptualized in languages of durability and density. These metaphors include the fortuitous identification of the London Stock Exchange with "a house," discussions about relations and infrastructures derived from science and technology studies, and a more significant literature in anthropology that questions the nature of social relations. My argument is not that markets are exactly like kinship: this would be naïve and analytically incorrect. I do contend, however, that thinking about the communities and ethical commitments created with markets offers a way of reconceptualizing their political salience in contemporary societies. The issue is not whether markets are net "positive" or "negative," but rather assessing how specific arrangements create relations of dependence, exclusion, exploitation, and mutual responsibility.

The three themes that I explore in this book overlap, yet are separable. *Automating Finance* can be read as a history of infrastructures, a study of organizations, or a reflection of relations in markets. As an exploration, this book does not provide definite answers but pilots the terrain and incites the reader's imagination. This is what it's all about: rethinking markets from our past for our collective future.

Acknowledgments

Books often have few authors but are necessarily the products of many hands. Philip Good and Tobias Ginsberg from Cambridge University Press provided tremendous support and enthusiasm for this project. I was fortunate to have received funding over the years from several organizations to conduct research used in this volume, including the Consejo Nacional de Ciencia y Tecnologia, the Economic History Society, the LSE Suntory and Toyota International Centre for Economics and Related Disciplines, and the European Research Council under the European Union's Seventh Framework Programme (fp7/2007–2013)/ERC grant agreement no. 291733. A book like this would simply be impossible without the generous gift of informants like Richard Atkins, Richard Balarkas, Robert Barnes, Peter Bennett, John Cheine, Peter Cox, Elroy Dimson, Scott Dobbie, Dugald Eadie, Wolfgang Eholzer, Dame Clara Furse, Pete Harris, George Hayter, David Hobbs, Sir Michael Jenkins, Michael Johnstone, Christopher Keith, David Manns, Ian McLelland, Patrick Mitford-Slade, Michael Newman, Barry Riley, Graham Ross Russell, John Scannell, Daniel Sheridan, David Steen, Nic Stuchfield, Michael Waller-Bridge, Steven Wunsch, Stanley Young, and other unnamed interviewees. I am particularly grateful to Bennett, Hayter, Scannell, and Waller-Bridge for their comments on drafts of several chapters and for providing some of the images presented in the book. Marcel Mauss famously wrote of gifts as reciprocal ties that constitute larger collectives. I can only hope that, in my use of the informants' stories, I have rewarded their gifts and contributed to a different understanding of finance and its technologists.

At the University of Edinburgh, where I took the first steps in this project, I found endless support and countless formative conversations in David Bloor, John Henry, Gethin Rees, Pablo Schyfter, Steve Sturdy, and other residents of the Science Studies Unit on Buccleuch Place. In this space, my sight was shaped by a shared sensibility to the history and politics of knowledge and technology, central themes to early iterations of this book. During this time, Bernardo Batiz-Lazo introduced me to the literature on technological innovation in finance and banking that also provided an important pivot for rethinking the automation of stock exchanges.

The London School of Economics and Political Science provided tremendous colleagues in Daniel Beunza, Carrie Friese, Michael McQuarrie, Yuval Millo, Judy Wajcman, and Leon Wansleben, among many others. Through numerous conversations, coffees, and pints, they too shaped my thinking for this book, training the sensitivity toward the politics at play in financial automation. An important part of the argument that I develop was inspired at the Museu Nacional de Rio de Janeiro in 2014, where I was hosted by the Núcleo de Pesquisas em Cultura e Economia. My discussions with Eugênia Motta, Federico Neiburg, Gustavo Onto, Fernando Rabossi, and André Vereta Nahoum introduced all sorts of anthropological problems that became grounds for reimagining markets and their organizations. More recently, at University of California, San Diego, I found a welcoming environment for finishing this project supported by collegiality and friendship of Abigail Andrews, Amy Binder, Claire Edington, Cathy Gere, Lilly Irani, Kevin Lewis, Kerry McKenzie, Daniel Navon, Danielle Raudenbusch, Vanesa Ribas, Akos Rona-Tas, and April Sutton.

Of course, many other scholars influenced my work. I am grateful to Nina Bandelj, Claudio Benzecry, Bruce Carruthers, Michael Castelle, Ursula Dalinghaus, Andrew Deener, Fernando Dominguez Rubio, Marion Fourcade, Paul du Gay, Karin Knorr Cetina, David Lubin, Bill Maurer, Liz McFall, Fabian Muniesa, Taylor Nelms, Jose Ossandon, Mike Power, Susan Scott, Zsuzsanna Vargha, and Frederick Wherry for their insights, though I am surely missing many from this admittedly brief list. Throughout the years, Donald MacKenzie and Alex Preda provided ample, generous advice and support; to them, I am infinitely indebted.

Finally, I thank Nara and Samuel, for their patience, courage, sacrifice, and love. I could not have written this book without them.

I Markets in Milliseconds

Changes in valuation are greatly increased and even often brought about by the flexible quality of money to express them directly. And this is the cause as well as the effect of the fact that the stock exchange is the centre of monetary transactions. It is, as it were, the geometrical focal point of all these changes in valuation, and at the same time the place of greatest excitement in economic life. Its sanguine-choleric oscillations between optimism and pessimism, its nervous reaction to ponderable and imponderable matters, the swiftness with which every factor affecting the situation is grasped and forgotten again – all this represents an extreme acceleration in the pace of life, a feverish commotion and compression of its fluctuations, in which the specific influence of money upon the course of psychological life becomes most clearly discernible.

Georg Simmel, *The Philosophy of Money*, 1900

In today's high-tech exchanges, firms can execute more than 100,000 trades in a second for a single customer. This summer, London and New York's financial centres will become able to communicate 2.6 milliseconds (about 10%) faster after the opening of a transatlantic fibre-optic line dubbed the Hibernia Express, costing US$300 million. As technology advances, trading speed is increasingly limited only by fundamental physics, and the ultimate barrier – the speed of light.

Nature, 2015

It would take more than a century, but sociologist Georg Simmel eventually met physicist Albert Einstein, if not in the halls of an illustrious university, then metaphorically within the frenzied commotion of the electronic stock exchange. When Simmel wrote of stock exchanges as the capitalist nexus where values are "rushed through the greatest number of hands in the shortest possible time" (Simmel, 2004 [1900]: 506), he could not have foreseen just how short time could get. In the electronic systems that operate in most modern stock exchanges, the time of transactions is often measured in microseconds – roughly the same magnitude of time that it takes individual molecules of neurotransmitters to travel across the 20 nanometers of a synaptic cleft between neurons, itself less than 100,000th of the threshold of human perception. Financial transactions are so fast that relativity – not only of meaning, but also of space–time – must be accounted for when designing trading platforms for the market (see Wissner-Gross and Freer, 2010). For some, even light is too bulky, having to travel through optical fiber cables and microwave relays on the awkwardly spherical surface of the planet (Laumonier, 2014; Mac-Kenzie, 2018). If used to transmit information, weakly interacting neutrinos (or perhaps even the hypothetical reverse time-traveling particles known as tachyons) could cut directly through the earth's mantle and save a dozen or so milliseconds of latency for a new generation of ultra-high-speed traders[1]. This is where finance is today: caught between Simmel's nexus and Einstein's faster-than-light dreams.

In this book, I explore the histories of some of the technologies that accelerated stock markets over the past half century. My interests are both in the infrastructures that made speedy transactions possible and in the humble and largely invisible engineers that tinkered with and built the networks and machines of automated finance. This is a recent history. Just a few decades ago, well within the lifespan of most readers, stock exchanges were not the feverish spaces of electronic, algorithmic, automated activity that they are today. As Madonna topped the charts in the early 1980s, stock markets were relatively subdued spaces where, bar sporadic moments of great activity, most of the trading took the form of personal interactions and brisk

---

[1] Talking in 2015 at the Equity Market Advisory Committee meeting of the Securities and Exchange Commission (SEC) of the United States, renowned economists Andrew Lo of Massachusetts Institute of Technology (MIT) noted that as technology develops market participants transform their expectations of market temporalities. As an example, he noted: "a few years ago you may recall that an experiment out of Switzerland, the Large Hadron Collider, demonstrated erroneously that the existence of tachyons, faster-than-light particles, existed. The next day after the announcement, I received a phone call from an algorithmic trader, asking me to introduce him to a physicist engaging in tachyon research" (Securities and Exchange Commission, 2015).

conversations on the floors of century-old, club-like exchanges. Then and before, finance was a matter of bodies and voice, punctuated by the banter of the clerks and brokers, the clicking of keyboards, the striking of pencils, the crushing of paper, and the creaking of wooden floorboards. Perhaps best exemplified by the ground-breaking sociological work of Wayne Baker (1984) and Mitchel Abolafia (1996), stock and commodities markets at the time were densely social, communicative spaces. The cacophony of the marketplace and apparent randomness of trade was coordinated through shared norms and expectations, networks of competition and collaboration, and elaborate means for signaling, rewarding, and reprimanding the members of the trading floor's community. Fast-forward a mere 30 years. Madonna is still an active performer. Yet most trading floors have disappeared, replaced by what anthropologist Ellen Hertz (1998) calls a "community of effects" built through computers, screens, and cables scattered across inconspicuous locations throughout the world and where actions are not the result of a distinct collective intention but of the exercise of countless individual wills. In present-day financial markets, the logic is not one of coordinating interpersonal interactions but of managing the punctuated electronic signals that encode the orders from masses of anonymous investors. The art of finance is no longer about gazes and hand signals, but about toying with the nimble algorithms, sophisticated computer processors, hacked routers, and specialized telecommunication systems that are the material foundations of the contemporary stock exchange. Through technology, trading floors became an amalgam of cables and software; and through automation, rowdy human crowds were refashioned into silent and speedy electronic queues.

This book is not a conventional history of technology or automation: it does not care for the vision of leadership, the importance of careful planning, or the power of innovation as much as it does for the obduracy of bureaucracy, the potential of bricolage, and the significance of tinkering and maintenance on the sidelines of organizations. This book is also not about managers and their historically coherent institutions, jostling traders, interested politicians, and powerful financiers. In the following pages, there are neither Thomas Edisons nor John Pierpont Morgans. Rather, this book is about the workers and experts that make up financial institutions but that are seldom seen; it is a story of the vast sections of organizational hierarchies where change happens not necessarily through the power of authoritative control or the promise of revolution, but through the trials and tribulations of routine and surprise, the charm of performance, and the force of surreptitious standardization. This focus is decidedly important for understanding not only transformations in finance, but also markets, organizations, and automation more generally. Although scholars of technology have placed many efforts in reexamining the mythical figure of the lonely entrepreneur, images of automation as driven by heroic and radical inventors are still oddly persistent (a recent case in finance being the ruckus about the potentially revolutionary consequences of blockchain technologies; see Tapscott and Tapscott, 2016; Maurer, 2017). By examining the automation of finance, I want to stress the importance – and unpredictability – of the organizational middleware, the bulky center of market organizations that connects the public front office and the grueling and oftentimes obscured back office, the human software from the material hardware, the legacy systems from the technological vanguard. Change and stability are not created at the pinnacle of the organizational hierarchy but in the sometimes-tedious bureaucratic work of the vast middle. The historical implications are telling: financial automation was not entirely planned or designed, it just sort of happened.

1.1   WHY FINANCE?

At a time of great social and political upheaval, it might seem that investigating the automation of financial markets is an extravagant scholarly fancy. Why not, some have asked, expose automated finance as a more exacting form of capitalist activity? Why focus on the history of technologies rather than behaviors, on invisible workers rather than the thinkers and leaders that made financialized neoliberal societies possible?

I admit that this was the original motivation for this book. When I started research on financial markets more than a decade ago, my main interest was identifying the overt politics underlying these behemoths. Students of science and technology have demonstrated in countless occasions that artifacts and technological projects are never neutral, but are always the continuation of politics by other means. From speed bumps and bicycles to bridges and algorithms, devices and their associated practices always encode assumptions about how the social world *should* work.

These somewhat classical examples of how politics get built into artifacts are not the only possible narratives for technological projects. To say that financial automation was part of a coherent political project that leveraged technology to shape the world in particular ways would be an unfaithful, first degree approximation to the interviews and documentary materials that I collected in the field. For years, I looked for collective forms of manifest politics in the works of market managers and technologists, but these were simply not to be found. Intentional agency was elusive. What I encountered was not one but many fragmented projects, some involving the leadership of organizations though many others incubated in the invisible underbelly of the market. I sought ideologues but found (entrepreneurial) bureaucrats whose politics were fragile, disjointed, and eminently mangled with the effort of keeping the market in shape. This was not the story of a cunning and powerful urban planner who designed the world to crystallize dubious politics (Winner, 1980). Nor was it the story of how a single paradigm emerged to govern and discipline the field. No, this was a story of buildup, contingency, and unpredictability, and while politics certainly mattered, they did so in a rather more modest, mundane, lowly, and practical way.

This is precisely why studying finance matters: it offers a cautionary tale of the sources and messy politics of technology and automation that is lacking in contemporary public discourse. Consider the recent contributions by Erik Brynjolfsson and Andrew McAfee (2014), who argue that societies are now facing forms of automation that will displace workers in traditionally cognitively intensive industries such as law, medicine, and other services. At the heart of this argument sits the old language of David Ricardo's (1891) political economy, which presented "the substitution of machinery for human labor [as] very injurious to the interests of the class of laborers." The problem is not with Ricardo's theory of labor substitution, but with his metaphor of "the machine" as a punctual object, as an entity that emanates from the interests of the capitalist. Discrete technologies, we are often told, are what automate the workplace, whether in the form of the steam-powered looms of the nineteenth century, Harry Braverman's cybernetic data-processing-and-storing machines, or the ubiquitous robots that are prognosticated to displace employment into extinction. These are the mechanisms that, as Marx wrote, "after being set in motion, perform with its tools the same operation as the worker formerly did with the same tools" (MacKenzie, 1984). They are the very substance of automation.

But automation is a peculiar chimera: it conflates knowledge, devices, and organizations in intricate ways; it requires buildup, buy-in diffusion; it sits atop invisible platforms, standards, and gateways; it reconfigures cyborgs as much as novel and apparently independent machines. Automation is necessarily heterogeneous. The prevalent imagery of automating machinery deals poorly with such messiness: in finance, for example, there was not a single device or moment of transformation that heralded the arrival of automation; some devices mattered centrally, but only made sense when meshed within a network of practices, standards, platforms, and logics of action. If automation happened, it was as a long and contested historical process. Its boundaries were fuzzy; its meanings malleable; its participants heterogeneous; its politics numerous and contradictory. Automation emerged from the accumulation of legacy and the creation of the new as these were linked, wrangled, modified, and disconnected within organizations over time. To use the language of science and technology studies, automation was the product of extended *infrastructures* rather than of discrete machines – assemblages of practices, routines, standards, and devices that seamlessly fade into the background as if natural elements of our human environments (Bowker and Star, 1999; Edwards, 2003; Star and Bowker, 2006; Larkin, 2013).

I.2   INFRASTRUCTURES OF FINANCE

At a broad empirical level, this book makes a contribution to discussions about the history of the automation of finance within stock markets in Britain and America. Historians of financial markets have produced exceptionally clear and detailed accounts of the institutional evolution of the City of London and Wall Street – two epicenters of financial activity in the United Kingdom and the United States, respectively. A common feature of these histories is that they often conceptualize technology as something of a black box, closer to the machinery of Ricardo's metaphorical repertoire than to the messy narratives that characterize contemporary stories of infrastructures. Take the work of Ranald Michie (1999), who documents with tremendous assiduousness the history of the London Stock Exchange (LSE), the prime stock market in Britain. While Michie acknowledges the importance of technologies for the exchange, he does so by rendering their development a rational reaction to competitive threats and market opportunities instead of contested projects that transformed the organization and its logics from within. Market technologies, we read, were developed with apparently little effort and as required to meet to some external demand. This conceptualization of innovation as an exogenous process is also notable in the work of other historians of finance. For example, Youssef Cassis (2010) weaves an intriguing history of how global financial centers emerged over the last one and a half centuries, but he does not query the organizational dynamics that underpinned technological innovation. Charles Geisst's (2012) history of Wall Street recognizes the importance of technology in shaping modern American finance but asks few questions about the technologies that encroached the practices of the marketplace. Joel Seligman's (1982) several works also present a uniquely detailed story of the legal and institutional trajectories that forged American financial markets, recognizing the challenges of technological innovation to market participants; yet like other historians of finance, he does not delve into how technologies were assembled within organizations. Admittedly, we cannot ask financial historians to account for everything. But what is interesting about these and similar studies is the way technology and innovation are framed: not as something that happened and was fostered within the financial sphere but, rather, as an opportunistic appropriation from elsewhere (Cortada, 2003). Technology certainly matters, but only as an input rather than as an internal process.

Some economists and legal scholars have placed more attention on the technical and organizational minutiae of financial automation. For example, Ruben Lee's *What Is an Exchange?* (Lee, 1998; see also Lee, 2002) provides one of the best accounts of the strategic and managerial challenges faced by stock exchanges as digital technologies expanded throughout the financial services industry. For Lee, automation posed a series of important problems for the leadership of stock exchanges that required redefining the operational logic of their organizations: should they run as members-owned marketplaces as they did throughout most of their history, or should they become for-profit publicly traded corporations with a leadership voted in by anonymous shareholders? Should they cater to small retail traders, or should they work for larger institutional investors? Should they protect the interests of so-called market makers (agents that traditionally bought and sold securities on their accounts to provide liquidity to the market), or should they allow unfettered competition to take hold of the exchange? Lee explores these tensions in order to identify how competition drove stock exchanges down different paths of automation: some automated earlier while others were more cautions, depending on how they made sense of the institutional pressures of their local environments. Ian Domowitz and Benn Steil (1999; also

Domowitz, 2002) provide a similar analysis of the patterns of automation observed in financial markets during the 1980s and 1990s. By
identifying how automation was expressed in the various layers of the
market – from information dissemination to trading and settlement –
their work provides an important point of reference for thinking about
the global factors that shaped decisions on how to automate markets.
Although slightly more processual and cognizant of organizational
dynamics, a Ricardian explanation remains at the core of these
accounts: technology was introduced from the managerial outside to
make the economics of stock exchanges leaner and more efficient. As
Domowitz and Steil wrote in 1999, cost was "undoubtedly the most
significant factor driving the rapid expansion of automated trading in
the past several years."

The economics of machinery certainly contributed to automation but they were far from being the only factor that shaped
outcomes. As Lee's work demonstrates, automating an exchange is a
tremendous achievement that requires reengineering organizational
hierarchies, regulatory environments, creating interests, governance
structures, client relations, and operational practices *in addition to*
the technologies and devices of the marketplace. Automation is difficult because it implies a transformation of the market itself, and
while reducing costs certainly makes it more attractive, it necessitates inspiration beyond the logics of profit and thrift. To paraphrase
Bruno Latour (1992), something is missing that is central to the
dynamics of technological change: the organizational sections that
construct and maintain the infrastructures of the marketplace.

Some of these missing masses are found in the type of places
traditionally surveyed by students of science and technology. Think
here, for instance, of the seminal work of Karin Knorr Cetina (with
Bruegger, 2002) who studied the distributed, screen-based forms
of interaction that make coordination possible in global foreign
exchange markets. Think, too, of Caitlin Zaloom's (2006) accounts
of how traders in futures markets dealt with the transition from the
pits on trading floors to the anonymous screens of electronic trading

environments. Think, also, of Fabian Muniesa's (2003) study of how the creation of prices at the Paris Bourse was automated as part of a broader organizational reinvention. Or think of Alex Preda's (2006) work on how stock tickers profoundly transformed the cultures and temporalities of American finance. As members of a growing community of scholars interested in the imbrications between markets, technologies, and cultures, these authors recognize the stark materiality of finance, but they do so by stressing the contextual and interpretative nature of market technologies rather than their alleged intrinsic features.

Undoubtedly, the work of these and other authors contributed to uncovering what Donald MacKenzie (2008) calls the technicalities of finance, that is, the "systematic forms of knowledge deployed in markets [that are] social matters, and consequential ones." In studying finance, though, authors in this tradition have too often focused on devices defined in terms of their visibility: whether instant messaging systems that communicate traders, screens where information is appresented, controversial algorithms that determine closing prices, or analog devices that discern the ebbs and flows of market information, scholars have attended to perceptible technologies of finance that are intimately bound to the act of exchange.

What I do in this book is slightly different: to explore automation, I certainly look into the histories of some of the visible technologies that populate the front stage of markets – the trading screens, telephones, and controversial algorithms used to generate profits in fractions of a second (Muniesa and Callon, 2005). But importantly, I also focus on the less tended, slightly more invisible devices that operate beneath routine market action and that are deeply embedded in the bureaucracies of market organizations. These, I argue, are important "technicalities" when assessing the longer histories and trajectories of automation. As networks of devices, standards, and practices operating mostly in the background, they provide a stable frame of reference for action, cognition, and coordination, creating a sense of legitimacy, perhaps even inevitability, to automation. As perennial   sites   of   organizational   work,   these   less   visible infrastructures are also opportunities for the production of politics, moralities, alliances, and struggles that shape the market. Indeed, if there is a specter within finance, it is found not only in the polished steel, clear glass, and cold granite of the corporate front office; the specter is also conjured in the fractured and multiple politics that belie the infrastructures of the marketplace.

1.3   RETHINKING MARKETS, ORGANIZATIONS, AND TECHNOLOGIES

There are two broad consequences of shifting our analytical focus toward infrastructures. The first involves rethinking markets beyond a dominant transactional metaphor that privileges exchange as the cornerstone of the economy and its constitutive interactions. In addition to informing discussions about automation, the histories that I explore in this book have an ideational objective: to expand how we collectively imagine markets to include the infrastructural objects and forms of work that constitute communities of transactions and exchange. Emphasis on these is warranted for both theoretical and empirical reasons. For instance, despite a wealth of social-scientific studies of economies throughout the last century, relatively little has changed in our conception of what constitutes markets. And albeit apparent divergences in worldviews and political attitudes, sociologists, neoclassical economists, and scholars further afield share much of their conceptual terrain. For many social scientists (and publics at large), markets are first and foremost mechanisms of exchange and matter precisely because of how they provide a means for reallocating goods and services through monetized and impersonal bilateral transactions[2]. Firmly grounded on the economic literature of his time, for

---

[2] This is a view held primarily by neoclassical economists from the early twentieth century onward. Not all economists (or social scientists, for that matter) are neoclassical, of course. Classical political economists, for instance, had a much more inclusive conception of markets. The abstraction of markets as generalized mechanisms for exchange is a particular innovation that can be traced to the emergence of neoclassical theories in the late nineteenth and early twentieth centuries (Mirowski, 1988).

example, Max Weber saw markets as archetypes "of all rational social action ... a coexistence and sequence of rational consociations, each of which is specifically ephemeral insofar as it ceases to exist with the act of exchanging the goods" (Weber, 1978: 635). Weber's contemporary, Émile Durkheim (1976), similarly replicated an economistic definition, writing of markets as institutions geared primarily toward exchange. During the formative years of new economic sociology, Harrison White reproduced this paradigm by defining markets as "self-reproducing social structures among specific cliques of firms" (White, 1981). For White, markets are formed by agents that produce and exchange goods and services – that is, by actors whose identity is defined through exchange and transactions. Mark Granovetter (1985) echoed this transactional metaphor: his is not a challenge to the exchange-oriented conceptualization of markets but, rather, a proposal for explaining allocation outcomes in terms of "personal relations and networks of relations between and within firms." Note that his is a theory of the embeddedness of transactions in social relations, rather than a challenge to the classical conceptualization of markets as essentially transactional institutions. The concept is similar in Neil Fligstein's (2001) work, where markets are conceived as "situations in which some good or service is sold to customers for a price that is paid in money." Viviana Zelizer (2010) also presents markets as "institutionalized type[s] of social relations involving consumption, production and exchange." This account is consistent across sociological traditions. For Pierre Bourdieu (2005), markets are "the product of a twofold social construction ... the construction of supply ... and the construction of demand." Don Slater and Fran Tonkiss's (2005) review identifies markets as "the buyers and sellers of a particular good or service [comprised by] supply ... demand ... and price." And Patrik Aspers's (2011) recent work defines markets as social structures "for the exchange of rights in which offers are evaluated and priced, and compete with one another."

Richard Swedberg (2005) rightly indicates that sociology has "suggested new ways of conceptualizing how markets operate."

It has shown, through great empirical dexterity and theoretical rigor, that market transactions are embedded in, and shaped by, cultures, institutions, and interpersonal networks. But sociology, as other social sciences, has not entirely escaped what Bernard Barber (1977) memorably identified as the "absolutization" of the market – that is, an intellectual settlement that privileges the abstract, eminently exchange-oriented transactional market processes over the more mundane dynamics of the physical and material marketplace. By investigating the production of market infrastructures and their role in transforming finance, this book recovers some of this lost theoretical emphasis on the material, situated market*place*: even within finance's digital transactions, the materiality and obduracy of where exchanges occur matters fundamentally.

It would be too partial to focus solely on devices and the brute materialities of financial markets, of course. As noted above, automation was not only a product of technologies, but, as importantly, of the organizations where they came to matter. To use the language of Wanda Orlikowski and Susan Scott (2015), automation is a *sociomaterial* achievement. I aim to convey this sensibility about the intersections of infrastructures and organizations throughout this book. *Automating Finance* can be read as a "traditional" historical account of the automation of twentieth-century stock markets. But it can also be read as a broader argument about the relevance of the organizational middleware where much infrastructural work happens. This is largely because, unlike existing histories of finance, this book looks at a seldom studied category of actors that was arguably central to market automation: professionals of different backgrounds involved in designing, maintaining, and organizing the infrastructures of the marketplace. Unlike the recent sociological literature on technology and financial markets that has tended to emphasize a distinct professional group (economists) as key actors in performing the economy (Callon, 1998; MacKenzie, 2008, 2011; Fourcade, 2009), here I look at the role of a varied set of agents in the mundane construction and tinkering of market technologies. This group includes expert computer scientists and trained telecommunication engineers, but also self-trained electronics enthusiasts, industrialists with knowledge of computing, heterogeneous systems operators, and a wide gamut of individuals who, simply put, *make* things for the marketplace. Overall, the presence of these agents within capitalist organizations questions the way markets operate and are reproduced. In particular, they mirror the type of technical experts of whom Thorstein Veblen wrote in *The Engineers and the Price System*, his telling essay on the role of knowledge and management of the modern capitalist enterprise. For Veblen, the captains of industry cannot sustain the capitalist firm on their own. In addition to workers, the gears of industrial capitalism rely on "corps of technological production specialists, into whose keeping the due functioning of the industrial system has now drifted by force of circumstance" (Veblen, 1965). In tense collaboration with the owners of capital, these specialists – the "engineers" in Veblen's essay – make mass manufacture possible, determining "on technological grounds, what could be done in the way of productive industry, and to contrive ways and means of doing it." Note that these engineers are powerful in distinctively epistemic ways: while they may not own the means of production, they possess the cognitive instruments necessary for production to occur in an orderly manner; similarly, they directly facilitate entrepreneurialism both within and outside their organizations, combining techniques, knowledge, and devices in novel ways. (Admittedly, Veblen romanticized the image of the engineer, presenting her as driven by a more neutral quest for efficiency in contrast to the capitalists' interest in extracting profits through control and monopoly.) Following from Veblen, this book looks at the "engineers" of finance, the technical specialists that have contrived means for changing the way investors trade. So, while this is a book on infrastructures, it is also a study that compels us to think about the engineers or infrastructural workers that reconfigured and automated market organizations from within.

The studying of market "engineers" also offers an alternative way of thinking about the politics of markets. It would be tempting to consider market technologists as driven by a common cause, sharing particular affinities that made them a homogeneous group pursuing common ends through technological means. But as I explore in the following chapters, such an image reduces the richness and contingency of market making. Market engineers came for all walks of life – from elite universities to humble polytechnics, from the machinery of the war to the fields of Midwestern America. Their interests were varied, as were their politics. Perhaps the only thing they clearly shared was a belief in technology as a solution to problems, in the capacity to organize things through machines, and of the possibility of transforming markets into digital domains to some extent or another. This will be clear in the interviews and documentary materials that I present throughout this book, but it is also notable in the way technologists represented their future when automation was still a largely imagined horizon. One image is particularly striking: a poster produced by Peter Bennett, one of the main developers of the London Stock Exchange's electronic systems (Figure 1.1). Used in a

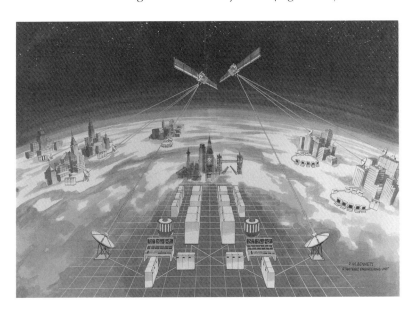

FIGURE 1.1 Poster by Peter Bennett, c. 1986/1987, representing the future of trading and stock exchanges. Reproduced with permission from the author.

presentation for the exchange's management in 1987, the image displays a world connected by technologies and devoid of human hands. The financial centers of Tokyo, London, and New York are connected by real-time satellite communications; in each, data is churned by locally networked supercomputers that serve as substitutes for the trading floor. The image is doubly powerful. On the one hand, it reinforces the invisibility of market engineers but foregrounds their objects of work: the satellites, computers, and data packages represented in the poster are designed, built, maintained, repaired, and upgraded. They are kept going and relevant by the unseen armies of technical experts that inhabit global finance. On the other hand, the image hints at what automation could ostensibly do to the social life of the markets. When applied to markets, the discrete architecture of computers and digital data transmission moved transactions from messy conversations on trading floors into ordered electronic queues. The sociology of markets changed not because of some political ideal, but because of the affordances of the devices that technologists introduced to the market.

1.4 MARKETS, KINSHIP, AND RELATIONS

The infrastructural turn advocated in this book is relevant for a second reason: it entices a different way of thinking about the permanence of the social in the face of great degrees of mechanization and automation. Let me explain this point in more detail.

A recurrent theme in the literature on financial markets involves condemning automation's role in dissolving social relations. Consider the fascinating and pernickety history of the City of London offered by David Kynaston (2001) – undoubtedly one of the most accomplished works on the social life of British banking and finance. In telling the numerous and tumultuous transformations of the city's institutions over the twentieth century, Kynaston conjures an almost melancholic image of a financial sector that was once a place of great sociality and that more recently succumbed to the humdrum rationalizing logic of mechanized globalization. In this, Kynaston is in illustrious company. In her path-breaking study, anthropologist Ellen Hertz also stresses a discontinuity in the stock markets of Shanghai, from being quite tangible, culturally dense, and relationally present communities of exchange to large techno-social assemblages "linked to [themselves] by a seemingly infinite network of computers … profoundly wrapped up in the process of imagining [what they mean]" (Hertz, 2000). Fiction writers also harnessed this trope to demonstrate the cultures lost to the machines (De Boever, 2018). I, too, have fallen to the allure of thinking about the end of culture and social control when caught within the virtual gears of information technologies. In a paper written with Daniel Beunza, Yuval Millo, and Donald MacKenzie (Beunza et al., 2011), we argued that automated markets are tied to the rise of a generalized culture of impersonal efficiency, that is, the idea that streamlining financial transactions and operations is best achieved by impersonal technical mechanism rather than social ties, eliminating the forms of interpersonal surveillance and control that were once a hallmark of the trading floor. This is not entirely far-fetched, for, after all, market participants themselves recall a mythical past when finance was about jovial conversations, long and lavish lunches, the smoke of cigarettes on the floor, and tight-knit relations that endured over time. Finance, we are told from multiple speakers, was simply more exciting, more emotional, more *social,* before computers took control.

This oppositional trope of humans/machines is not unique to finance. Quite the contrary, it is a contested yet foundational element of the intellectual project of modernity/anti-modernity (the reader can think of other relevant dichotomies: civilization/wilderness, society/nature, reason/emotion, machine/organism). But when studying automation, this trope is analytically counterproductive precisely because it obfuscates the modern categories of "the social" and "the machinic" as being obvious, stable and inherently opposed (Latour, 2012). By focusing on infrastructures and their location in organizations, I want to move away from this way of conceptualizing the world. Specifically, I highlight the continuities in what social relations mean to markets, automated or otherwise. If markets are more than simply sequences of transactions, if markets are indeed organizational achievements, then relations endure because of, rather than despite of, infrastructural change. Infrastructures and the knowledge complexes that they necessitate are *generative* of relations; they imply the production of connections, work, and communities rather than of disruption, isolation, and anomie.

The argument that automation does not dissolve "the social" but simply reconfigures modes of interaction and knowledge-making could be made through some of the existing theoretical repertoires of science and technology studies (think, in particular, of Bruno Latour and Michel Callon's tradition of actor-network theory, or literatures that incorporate users into the formation of meaningful sociotechnical worlds). For this book, I adopt a slightly oblique perspective: rather than thinking mainly about the super-symmetric ontologies of actor-network theory that distribute agency across humans and nonhumans, I resort to an anthropological metaphor that focuses explicitly on the status of relations and connectedness in order to understand what changes and what persists with the automation of finance. I think of markets and their organizations as kindred systems of relations, mediated as much by personal interactions and the density of meaning as by instruments and technologies that designate who is legitimately related to whom.

This shift turns to the work of anthropologist Marilyn Strathern, for whom the "relation" is not an obvious empirical fact, but rather a constantly produced designation. I find the idea of querying the status of (market) relations both intriguing and productive. In particular, it affords a vocabulary and conceptual framework that moves beyond both metaphors of markets as sequences of transactions and the reductive yet dominant metaphor of embeddedness often used by social scientists to understand market action. The second is particularly problematic, since conceptions of embeddedness assume a clear divisibility between otherwise distinguishable "spheres" (whether "the economic" or "the social"). This is troublesome, however, given the fact that market and social relations are difficult, if not impossible, to disentangle: for instance, the gift, as Mauss classically argued, transits a relation that is neither entirely social/emotional nor entirely economic/rational (Mauss, 2000). There is always some expectation of reciprocity in gifting and, while not monetary, it is market-like.

Rather than assuming the "social" embeddedness of "economic" transactions, I conceptualize markets as fundamentally relational systems. As Strathern rightly observes in her discussion of kinship, relations are not stable but constantly shift their boundaries and registers of application to reflect broader struggles in law, family practice, and scientific knowledge around parentage, siblinghood, relatedness, responsibility, and ownership more generally. This is why infrastructures matter: reconceptualizing markets as systems of kindred relations places attention on the invisible forms of knowledge and work that make market transactions legible, that allow buyers and sellers to be legitimately related to and then be rightfully quits (a matter cannot be "quits," or settled, if there was not a relationship in the first place!).

In the days of face-to-face trading on the floor, interpersonal knowledge and social skills played an important part in stock trading. Deals were tied to the social and organizational relations crafted between members of the exchange themselves inscribed in larger bureaucracies of administration and record keeping (or infrastructures, in a more general sense). Deals struck on the floor were processed and settled through a laborious and largely invisible machinery of clearing that required the use of special instruments and organizational expertise. Utterances only became trades when administered by these infrastructures: they *made* relations out of them. The relational work performed through infrastructures is not restricted to the markets produced on the old physical trading floors. Despite automation and the apparent disappearance of humans from the marketplace, the making and refashioning of relations persist in modern trading systems. Computer servers also converse and communicate, but their electronic exchanges only become legitimate transactions under the light of specific forms of knowledge (for instance, growing expertise in market microstructure that contrast with previous economic theories), operational standards (such as price-time priority), and legal agreements (such as sub-penny pricing, or order-routing rules set by the state); the relation can only be said to exist under certain circumstances, much in the same way as utterances on the trading floor only acquired meaning if properly registered by the relevant infrastructural bureaucracy. When these fail, relations cease to exist: after US markets crashed dramatically on May 10, 2010, in an event known as the "flash crash," trades conducted at abnormal prices were canceled. Although by all means technically reasonable market transactions, they were not considered legitimate and so were erased. Answering the question of how things are related shows the breaks and continuities in the historical development of financial markets. Rather than assuming that "the social" disappeared through automation, it focuses on identifying the boundaries of how legitimate relations were reinvented over time.

1.5   OVERVIEW OF THE BOOK

Because automation involves a gamut of technologies, this book covers the histories of devices and systems across different layers of stock markets, from the grueling clerical labor of the settlement back office to the more visible work of trading, order matching, and execution. I nevertheless admit that most of the narrative focuses on two types of systems that are particularly relevant to the forms of automated financial activity that we see today: data communication systems, which allow the orders from investors to travel across the world, and systems for matching and executing customer orders in an automated fashion. An important element of the narrative is the transition from trading floors to electronic order books – lists made up by the volumes and prices at which market participants are willing to trade specific financial instruments and that serve as the infrastructural gateways connecting the constituencies of the marketplace in a single electronic site of negotiation and exchange (without electronic order books, automated trading would not be possible in its current form). While immensely important operationally, economically, and sociologically, the history of order books has not yet been told and this is one of the tasks at hand in the remainder of the book.

The book is organized in two parts, tackling the conjoined trajectories of exchange, infrastructures, and relations. Thematically, the first corresponds to the market organization as a place of infrastructural change and deals with the transformations of a key institution of British financial markets, the London Stock Exchange. In particular, it examines how the makers of market infrastructures, largely invisible and subsumed within the stock exchange's old and traditional hierarchy, created systems and devices that captured finance and converted the marketplace to a digital, electronic form.

This first part starts in the next chapter, which asks the question of what changed with automation by exploring the early twentieth-century London Stock Exchange. A central concern is indicating how the predigital exchange operated as a distinct "market community," to use Max Weber's vocabulary. This vantage point is used to understand modifications induced by mechanization and automation. As a story of infrastructures, my emphasis is not so much on purely "social" forms (in a classical sociological sense), but on the distinct technologies that gave coherence to the market community on the trading floor. I call these "infrastructures of kinship" in order to allude to the way distinct social, technical, and organizational devices created relations in the market that defined the boundaries of the exchange as an organization and cultural entity and of the act of exchange itself as a relational form. As the chapter shows, automation did not start at the core of the community, but rather in its less visible underbelly, through the mechanization of some of the central devices (particularly those of clearing and settlement) that give markets their relational legitimacy. The kernel of automation was not the floor, I argue, but in the pipes, tubes, and number-crunching gears that gave credence to transactions in the marketplace.

Chapter 3 explores the roots and sources of financial automation between the mid-1960s and late 1970s within the London Stock Exchange by looking at how the mechanization of clearing and settlement spilled over into trading and data dissemination. A central theme of this chapter is the importance of the largely invisible cadre of workers that were responsible for the first wave of automation within the exchange. Relegated to the basements and alcoves of the organization and possessing expertise gained in developing and maintaining the exchange's early clearing and settlement systems, the initial generation of stock exchange technologists produced the first electronic price and quote visualization systems that would later transform trading practices across British finance. A condition for this process of capture was the invisibility of both the infrastructures and their makers that served as a powerful resource for surreptitiously reimagining the marketplace.

The theme of organizational change is continued in Chapter 4, exploring a period of rapid expansion of the stock exchange's technical teams and of their systems and devices. Propelled by regulatory constraints and a change in the structure of the British economy, LSE technologists seized the period between the mid-1970s and late 1980s to capture the normative and administrative core of their organization. During this time, they redefined what it meant to be an exchange. This chapter focuses on how the earlier generation of technologies coalesced into larger sociotechnical networks for the marketplace as the number of technologists ballooned into the thousands. As part of this process, I highlight a twist in the conceptions of stock exchange technologists from an interest in creating discrete stand-alone systems to developing all-encompassing platforms – that is, entities capable of supporting numerous tasks and monetizing services for their users. While bold and almost utopian, the platforms conceived by LSE technologists also demonstrated the dangers of capture and the hubris of rapid development. The chapter closes precisely with this theme, showing how growing too fast and large became a liabilty for LSE technologists as markets entered the uncertain and turbulent period after 1987. By 1992, most technologists had left the exchange.

When the LSE's technologists left the stock exchange in the early 1990s, they did not fade into darkness. Chapter 5 shows the consequences of the technological diaspora that followed the organizational changes and uncertainties produced by the 1987 market crash. By looking at the trajectory of a small group of leading technologists that broke away from the stock exchange in 1990, the chapter shows how infrastructural workers revolutionized the wider British securities markets rather than simply one of its (undoubtedly important) organizations. Critically, this involved developing and commercializing the first electronic limit order book in London. The challenges for technologists were not so much technical as social: they had to convince and convert a larger field that order books were the way of the future. As the chapter shows, the strategies of enrolling used by the technologists were ingenious: in addition to relying on the social and technological capital accrued in their tenure at the LSE, they resorted to the power of prophecy and charisma. Their strategy proved successful since their efforts were partly responsible for shifting British securities markets toward order books and electronic trading.

Whereas the first part of the book is concerned with engineers, infrastructures, and organizations, the second is preoccupied with the imbrications of national politics and infrastructural change. How do large infrastructural projects develop? And how do they crystalize political and moral struggles? Thematically, this second part moves from Britain to the United States with chapters that explore the creation of the National Market System.

Chapter 6 starts by looking at the problem of automation in American securities markets as a manifestation of a long-standing moral and political anxiety connected to the role of humans in the marketplace (particularly the New York Stock Exchange's specialists). Through the histories of some of the first efforts to automate stock markets in the United States, the chapter shows that projects of market automation were couched in moral and political terms, anchoring discussions of virtuosity upon a very specific device: the electronic limit order book. The chapter explores embryonic designs of the order book. One of these, a never-realized patent by Frederick Nymeyer, an American industrialist, amateur economist, and fervent Calvinist, demonstrated an overtly ethical concern in creating justice through automation. Contemporaneous with Nymeyer's work, the chapter also explores two other early experiments in market automation: on the one hand, those at Instinet, which sought a private solution to the problem of trading; and those of the Cincinnati Stock Exchange, one of the true pioneers of automation that tried to change the field for small investors amidst growing demand for retail investment.

Chapter 6 closes by looking at the consequences of electronic limit order books to the meaning and making of market relations. On trading floors, relations are almost sociologically and anthropologically obvious: buyer and seller are related through conversations, interaction, and exchange. But how does this apply to the electronic order book and the domain of automated trading that it makes possible? In the second part of the chapter, I argue that "relatedness" in modern finance depends on how distinct epistemic instruments are applied to resolve the existence or not of relations. By exploring some contemporary discussions on so-called spoofing (a practice that involves deceit in the market and connects to Nymeyer's moral concerns of the New York Stock Exchange's specialists), I show that the relations that seem to have been made meaningless through automation were recomposed by using novel forms of expert knowledge that shadow the logic of digital infrastructures. Specifically, I argue that the type of economic knowledge that matters changed in the transition from the floor to the computer server: whereas neoclassical financial economics was once the interpretative keystone, today the role is shifting to market microstructure theory, an area particularly attuned to the electronic fabric of modern exchanges.

From a discussion on how the first generations of electronic limit order books were designed and what they changed in our shared conceptions of finance, Chapter 7 moves on to identify how specific market designs propagated and colonized American stock markets. This involves dealing with the mechanism of infrastructures that compelled the simultaneous creation of institutional settings and technical environments that, once established, alter the distributions of what is possible, permissible, and imaginable. For infrastructures to emerge, actors must prepare terrains, create habits, and establish the boundaries required for infrastructures to work; once there, these terrains, habits, and boundaries both enable and constrain – to paraphrase Anthony Giddens (1984; see also Orlikowski, 1992), they "infrastructurate" the social world, creating restrictions and possibilities of action by means of the relations they entail between humans, categories, and things (Pipek and Wulf, 2009; Le Dantec and DiSalvo, 2013).

Empirically, the chapter explores the regulatory efforts by the US Congress and the Securities and Exchange Commission to incentivize markets toward a particular market design that spoke to their concerns about efficiency and access. Rather than fomenting a centralized solution that provided equality to all investors, regulators and government officials promoted a fragmented system of interconnected trading sites that, with time, became a fertile ground for the contentious practices of latency-sensitive trading. A key element of this process was an often-underappreciated episode in the history of the American financial system: the debate about how best to lay the common infrastructures for a national, internal stock market. As I argue in this chapter, the debate implied multiple political interests and worldviews but was part and parcel of a common dream, the creation of a national community – a financial democracy – that tied all citizens to financial markets and their fates.

Chapter 8 brings the book to a close by reflecting on three theoretical lessons from the automation of financial markets. It explores how changes to the infrastructures of exchange signaled a broader transformation within modern societies: that is, the emergence of systems based on queues that displaced crowds and their forms of collective deliberation. Rather than thinking of the automation of financial markets as a consequence of a deeper, murkier politics, I argue that stock markets condensed and amplified the ways societies reconstituted their lifeworlds through information technologies and rationalized organizations. As indicators, though, automated stock markets are telling: they offer insights into the quirky politics and uncanny moralities that inform the type of queues that, for better or for worse, increasingly shape the course of multiple domains of social life.

2　Infrastructures of Kinship

The 2009 independent documentary, *Floored*, captures what most people and quite a few market practitioners think of in connection to finance and automation. Probing the recent and dramatic history of Chicago's famous commodities trading pits, the documentary opens with words of contrast. "In 1997," it tells the audience, "more than 10,000 people traded on the floors. Later that year, computer trading emerged. Today, about 10% remain." Followed by images of rowdy trading pits, interviews with disgruntled clerks and traders, and videos of computer screens crashing on the ground, *Floored* distills a prominent trope about financial automation, namely, that computers somehow dissolved an activity that used to be thoroughly human and eminently social. In this chapter, I address this trope by thinking about what made stock exchanges so seemingly social, connected, club-like, and familiar. This is not in the interest of reinforcing images of automation as an astringent for socialization but rather to query their accuracy and stability. Did financial markets really change that much? Did social relations actually disappear within the circuitry of machines? What, if anything, changed with the automation of stock and commodities trading?

A valuable analytical strategy for addressing historical transformations is to show just how little the world has changed. This approach is valuable because it breaks with the myth of novelty. This is part of what I do in the following pages. Automation certainly implied changes to the structure of financial markets, but it also kept some things unchanged. Consider, as an illustration, two imaginary British investors separated by almost eighty years: one in the mid-twentieth century, the other in the present, both sitting comfortably somewhere west of London. Imagine, now, that both of these investors wish to buy stocks of a certain company. How do they proceed?

For our imaginary investor from the 1940s, buying and selling company shares was a task requiring disposition and a certain degree of capital, both financial and cultural. Share ownership in the United Kingdom was rare at the time, with only about 2.6 percent of the population having a footprint in stock markets. This small segment of the population (also disproportionately male: until the early 1970s, women could only sell stocks through an intermediary) was relatively sophisticated in its investment strategies. In contrast to their contemporaneous American peers who tended to concentrate on single stock ownership, British investors held diversified, if modest, portfolios (see Michie, 1999; Ott, 2011).

How did one buy stocks in 1941? If our imaginary investor were not tremendously wealthy, purchasing financial instruments of any type would have likely required a trip to the local branch of his bank where he would have initially spoken with the manager. The first issue at hand was determining the size and price of the purchase: how much was the investor willing to pay for, say, 100 shares of Imperial Chemical Industries, a popular company at the time? An indication of current prices could be gleaned by looking at the previous day's report in the *Financial Times*. Stock prices fluctuate throughout time, though, so our investor also needed to determine beforehand the maximum amount he was willing to pay for the shares. Having heard the decision, and after collecting some additional information and discussing the transaction with the investor, the branch manager would refer the order to the bank's stockbroker by telephone, cable, or post. Once in the offices of the stockbroker, a clerk checked and registered the order in the ledger to then transcribe it onto one of the firm's tickets that were forwarded by messenger to the firm's box on the edge of the trading floor at the stock exchange, a few streets away in the City of London. There, a broker confirmed the details of the order and sent it to the floor for execution. The process for conducting the trade then involved a bit of exercise, interpersonal skill, and some chance: ticket in hand, one of the firm's brokers would walk between the different dealers in Imperial Chemical Industries on the trading floor, asking each for a quote. The London Stock Exchange was organized around the principle of competition between dealers (then called jobbers), so the task for the broker was to find the best price in the market much in the same way as a consumer would walk between stalls in a street fair looking for the best deal. At times, demand was low, prices were adverse, and brokers would sit on the orders of investors over (a long) lunch, perhaps even overnight. But when a quote matched the client's request, the broker would agree with the appropriate dealer on a transaction. Dealer and broker then registered the purchase and submitted it for further processing in the back office of the stock exchange. At the close of trading, the clerks of brokers and jobbers collated and matched the transactions of the day to settle the deals struck on the floor – reconstructing, bit by bit, the activity of the market. A few days later, the transaction was cleared by exchanging cash for shares and updating the company's registrar with the investor's details – buying shares was, after all, a material exercise in corporate governance. The broker's firm then forwarded the (paper) share certificates to the bank's branch, charging them the purchase price plus a commission. Finally, several weeks or even months after the order was initiated, the investor received his shares upon clearing the final payment at his local branch.

Using current terminology, the latency of a trade for an ordinary investor in 1940s Britain – that is, the time it took from initiating the order to confirming its execution – was in the order of days. Aided by relatively expensive technologies – private telephone lines and dedicated access to stockbroking firms – wealthier private investors experienced slightly better latency, averaging days, perhaps even hours. The most sophisticated segment of the market, institutional investors such as mutual and pension funds, observed the lowest latencies: hours, perchance minutes, between submitting their order and receiving confirmation. And for these, the size of their trades translated into efficiency: in conversations with dealers and other brokers over lunch, orders to buy and sell large lots of shares were seamlessly unwound through the dense social networks of British finance. Indeed, for British stockbrokers, "the amount of personal trouble and worry that is caused [was] almost in inverse proportion to the wealth of the client" (A. Hamilton, 1986: 31–36). Markets then were large, gentle, opaque, and privileged.

Compare buying stocks in the 1940s with its equivalent in the present. Structurally, the process is much the same: an order is submitted to an intermediary (the broker); the broker seeks execution in the market; the order is matched; a confirmation is produced; and the transaction is settled. Technically, the process is quite different. For an idealized small investor sitting in West London today, buying a share in AkzoNobel (the company that bought the venerable Imperial Chemical Industries in 2008) takes minutes, perhaps even seconds. As in the past, an investor must procure a provider with access to the market. This may be her bank, but it may also be one of many online retail brokerage services offering investors direct access to the electronic marketplace, mirroring the privileged service that was given to wealthier investors in the past. In buying shares in AkzoNobel, our imagined investor would not need to see yesterday's closing prices in the *Financial Times*; rather, she would have access to real time quotes and prices from the market via her electronic retail broker – unlike her predecessors, she can "see" a good approximation of current prices as they change, and incoming orders to buy and sell as they arrive to the market. On selecting a price and volume, our investor submits her trade through either a dedicated computer program provided by her retail broker or some specialized online portal. Fractions of a second after being submitting, the order arrives in the servers of the retail broker where it is time-stamped and aggregated with other similar orders. Milliseconds later, the aggregated lot is broken up into smaller orders that are routed by algorithms to some of the several dozen electronic trading venues throughout the world – a convoluted combination of public stock exchanges, proprietary trading platforms, and so-called dark pools. (At the time of writing, for instance, the shares of AkzoNobel were traded on six public trading venues, five dark pools, a handful of proprietary trading systems, and numerous private over-the-counter transactions: in deciding where to submit individual market orders, algorithms analyze price differentials and execution costs across these markets and route trades accordingly.) A few hundred milliseconds after being sliced and distributed throughout the marketplace the order is executed and confirmation signals are sent back to the electronic retail broker. With this, records of ownership are revised, the client charged, her portfolio updated, and the final confirmation issued. Within seconds, our investor has traded. There was no movement of papers, no trading floors were visited, and no conversations took place. Markets today are fragmented, fast, cheap, and intimately electronic.

The differences between these two imagined scenarios seem entirely dictated by technology. This is only partly true. In addition to vastly different historical contexts – our first investor was likely an affluent citizen who could indulge in the luxury of speculation; our second investor was more likely a financialized subject who invested in the market as an uncertain strategy for securing her future – these two cases also represent different ways of connecting people through markets, both within and outside the stock exchange. Modern stock exchanges are certainly not the clubs that they once were, but this does not mean they have lost their role in producing particular types of "community." Rather than dissolving social bonds, automation implied new ways of knitting together individuals through the infrastructures of trading, communication, and settlement that make up the fabric of markets and their complex organizations. The automation of stock exchanges involved, in particular, altering the imagined structures of relations and community constituted on the trading floors through the introduction of new devices, techniques, and the human forms associated to their construction, maintenance, and repair. If we were to see financial organizations as kindred families, as tightly knit systems of human relations that are somehow structurally and functionally related, then electronic devices can be understood as having introduced unexpected, disruptive relatives into the community of conversations and exchange.

To make sense of how automation was a form of refashioning relations, I invoke the idea of the infrastructures of kinship of finance. By these, I am referring to the infrastructural elements of markets and market organizations that, while being largely invisible to the "front office" and often taken for granted among traders and dealers, are nevertheless central to creating forms of distinction, association, familial relationship, and hierarchies of worth within their imagined communities. These infrastructures are multiple, from physical devices that allow market participants to meet for exchange to less tangible institutional agreements about fairness and proper behavior that are often only invoked in moments of crisis and controversy. These infrastructures of kinship are a theme throughout the book, but in this chapter I examine how they operated during a critical period in the history of the paradigmatic London Stock Exchange. Whereas in the 1940s automated technologies and technical experts were relatively foreign to the stock exchange, by the early 1970s they had become taken for granted. In the late 1980s, the trading floor itself had disappeared, substituted by an army of technologists and distributed networks of screens and telephones where dealers left no footprints, "only the ghosts of electrons" (Grundfest, 1988). Today, the stock exchange is a publicly traded company operating not too far from its original site next to the Bank of England in the heart of the City of London. And while its elegant yet inconspicuous offices next to St Paul's Cathedral remain an important node of market making within global finance, they no longer echo the steps on the wooden trading floor or the terse conversations held in the relative privacy of the jobbers' pitches: rather, electronic trading activity takes place within sophisticated servers a few blocks away on Earl Street. If infrastructures are relational, as the scholar Susan Leigh Star argued, then studying the webs of market devices before the age of the machines provides a partial answer to what has changed with the automation of finance.

2.1   INTRODUCING THE LONDON STOCK EXCHANGE

The London Stock Exchange was certainly not the first organized financial marketplace in the City of London. Prior to the stock exchange's informal creation in the mid-eighteenth century, the Royal Exchange served as the city's main site for trade between "Merchants, Tradesmen, Factors and Brokers" (Glaisyer, 2006). Established by the merchant and financeer Thomas Gresham in 1571, the Royal Exchange was for a long time the heart of London's connections to international commerce, extolling the riches gained overseas through the exchange of wealth it produced at home. In its ornate courtyard surrounded by shops, patrons exchanged exceptional goods such as linen, spices, and tea through trades that reflected the breadth and scope of England's rapidly swelling empire and the rising power of its local economic elites.

The Royal Exchange was, nevertheless, a restricted space and in 1698 its owners expelled rowdy stockbrokers from trading within the precinct. As government debt and joint-stock companies grew in number resulting from England's expanded economic and military activities overseas, trade in financial instruments overflowed onto the streets and alleys of the ancient City of London. In this, and much like everyday street markets and fairs, finance was at the time a matter of space and location: it concentrated in sites that provided investors and speculators with the ability to meet counterparties for trade. And like street markets and fairs serving the public, these interstitial sites were often framed through the apparently dubious character of the crowds of stockbrokers and stockjobbers that congregated in them. As a member of the Royal Exchange complained in 1700,

> By the daily Resort and Standing of brokers and Stock-Jobbers in the ... Alley, not only the Common Passage to and from the Royal-Exchange is greatly obstructed, but Incouragement is given by the tumultuary Concourse of People attending the said Brokers, to Pick-Pockets, Shop-Lifters, and other Idle and Disorderly People to mix among them.

　　　　Volumes of financial transactions grew steadily throughout the eighteenth century – primarily around public debt – taking trade into pay-for-use coffee houses that flourished in the vicinities of Change Alley in the City of London. Among these, Jonathan's Coffee House commanded the greatest audiences, becoming one of the multiple laboratories for two key organizational innovations in finance. The first was patently physical and exemplified by John Castaing's production of a list of stock and commodities prices in 1698 and published under the title "The Course of the Exchange and Other Things" (similar lists would only emerge later in Europe). By publishing a periodical list of prices in ink and paper that traveled far beyond the voices and individual transactions of the city, Castaing's list gave an early informational structure to trade and contributed to the project of forming a public market outside the immediate scope of Change Alley, much in the same way as the printing press was implicated in the creation of the modern bourgeois public sphere, as famously argued by social theorist Jürgen Habermas. As a device that conveyed an admittedly delayed image of the state of share trading, "The Course of the Exchange" and other lists of prices created a mutually observant community of market users that, while sharing common institutional concerns and accepting broadly similar notions of control, was inclusive in its membership and participation.

　　　　The second organizational innovation involved the fabrication of legitimacy. Coffee houses and other sites of exchange were not populated by the traditional elites of English society (see Carruthers, 1999, who studies how the creation of stock markets was embedded in a larger political battle over the control and reconfiguration of the English state.). This is notable in the contrasts drawn between the Royal Exchange whose users were wealthy individuals tied to the merchant and political classes of the seventeenth and eighteenth centuries, and the relatively more "popular" crowds of stock and commodities traders that operated in the nooks and crannies of the City of London. Coffee houses were more porous than their privileged, regal counterparts: as described by George Gibson (1889), "there was no organization [within coffee houses], it being merely a common meeting-place without any restrictions or limitations whatever."

Prestige was desirable as both a source of outward legitimacy and internal control. Precisely because of their lack of professional demarcation and the leaky boundaries of their trading sites (anyone with a sixpence could access the market and call himself a broker, noted Gibson), stockbrokers and stockjobbers were a socially precarious group in eighteenth-century England, a situation amplified by their earlier involvement in public debacles, including the South Sea Bubble of the 1720s. A discussion in *The London Magazine* (also known as *Gentleman's Monthly Intelligencer*) from 1774 makes this clear. In the magazine, calls were made to put an immediate stop "to the most pernicious and infamous species of gaming, that of stock-jobbing" which were certainly corrupt because "all ranks and denominations of men have gotten into this method ... the very low class of tradesmen: and hence we may, in great measure, account for the many bankruptcies which are continually happening." Stockbrokers were not immune to such critical views for they were, as one commentator also argued in *The London Magazine*, "those pests to society" that have led so many gentlemen astray (Townsend, 1774: 66). What was needed to resolve such dire character was some form of social closure, a mechanism for creating legitimacy through the joint production of external boundaries and internal cohesiveness and status (Preda, 2009). The first attempt at this came in 1773 when a group of brokers built a new trading site beneath a coffee shop to substitute Jonathan's. The building, initially known as New Jonathan's, was then called the Stock Exchange Coffee House. To control access, they introduced a key organizational innovation: a membership or subscription that, in exchange for an annual fee, provided entry to an organized private space for the trading of stocks and bonds. Soon enough, the American Revolution provided a further catalyst for reinvention (wars sow the seeds of debt): growing trade in public debt meant that the Stock Exchange Coffee House "reached such a state of prosperity, and importance as to justify a new building" (Gibson, 1889). And so, in 1801, the London Stock Exchange was born.

There are many fine and detailed histories of the London Stock Exchange and it is not my purpose to review these in depth (notably, Michie, 1999; Kynaston, 2001). What matters to our story of infrastructures is the pivotal moment in the early nineteenth century when social closure was achieved partly through physical means. The creation of the modern stock exchange as a members-only community was certainly an important innovation within the organizational landscape of finance that bridged two apparently contradictory pressures: on the one hand, creating a public sphere for information and the trading of debt/property; on the other hand, establishing a restricted and legitimate place for exchange among respected citizens. The exchange was a new cultural formation that, with time, garnered great recognition among the dominant political and economic classes in Britain. Consider, for instance, the contrast between the above-mentioned *London Magazine*'s description of brokers and jobbers in 1774 and the findings of the Royal Commission on the London Stock Exchange a century later. By 1876, Parliament considered the stock exchange to have demonstrated acting "uprightly, honestly, and with a desire to do justice" in all matters financial (Royal Commission, 1878). Brokers and jobbers were no longer the "pests of society," as they had been written about a century earlier, but were now legitimate, even commendable actors within the broader landscape of the British class structures. Closure worked (Preda, 2009).

The cultural dynamics of the material "investments in forms" (Thevenot, 1984) required for producing the stock market's legitimacy and stabilizing the pressures of the public and the private are often less recognized in histories of finance. One such investment was particularly prominent in London: the building of the stock exchange itself, which served as both a physical and symbolic reference for the community of market participants trading instruments within its august if somewhat hodgepodge halls. A feature of the building is notable, namely, how the members of the exchange referred to it.

The stock exchange was not simply a trading floor or a club, though it acted as both. More importantly, it was an intimate space, warranting the alternative and widely used designation of "the House." To explore the forms of cultural and infrastructural change that were core to the automation of finance in London (and that are echoed elsewhere, from São Paulo and Shanghai to Toronto and New York), I want to play with the multiple valences of the term "house" and the notions of association, community, family, and kinship that are linked to it. While homes are sites for the production of kinship, houses are their material, infrastructural correlates. The task, then, is to understand how "the House" configured markets in London and in doing so brought to life the distinct social relations that permeated transactions in British finance.

2.2 THE HOUSE

The term "house" is has long been in the English language. Of probable Germanic provenance, it was originally associated to the act of hiding or taking cover from something or someone. As language evolved, the word "house" proliferated in meanings. Among the most prominent, it came to signify the physical building where people congregate, including those where families reside and homes are made – a place of dwelling. As a referent to material, bounded sites, "house" also came to represent other types of public and private meeting spaces including those where certain types of business occurred, such as the notorious coffeehouses of the seventeenth and eighteenth centuries where money and knowledge changed hands among patrons, the Houses of Parliament and Congress where legislations are voted, playhouses where entertainment is provided to a paying audience, and buildings where refreshments are offered such as public houses and restaurants where, on rare occasions, one still receives a small complement "on the house."

This synecdoche of "the house" is perhaps so pervasive because of the polyvalent meanings attached to houses in multiple cultures. The "house" indexes many, sometimes contradictory, concepts at once. For Claude Lévi-Strauss, it is an institution that combines opposing principles of social organization, a "fusion of categories which are elsewhere held to be in correlation with and opposition to each other, but are henceforth treated as interchangeable" (Lévi-Strauss, 1983). For others, houses are reflections of the selves that inhabit them. For some, they are sites of production where inputs are combined to create the varied yet stratified preferences of society (Becker, 2009). And yet for others, they are also locations that link individuals through some form of kinship – spaces where, as anthropologist Marilyn Strathern (2005: 9) writes, "one can imagine ... the relative of a relative, relationships between relationships." Thus, Shakespeare wrote of the Houses of Capulet and Montague while Poe wrote of the House of Usher; the Houses of York, Lancaster, Tudor, Stuart, and Hanover punctuate British history; and we often think of the Houses of Rothschild, Baring, and Morgan as having fundamentally shaped finance and banking in the nineteenth and early twentieth centuries. In all these cases, the term "house" stands as a placeholder for the intricate networks of blood connections, interpersonal obligations, symbolic resources, and mutual acknowledgments created by groups of people "naturally" related to one another. Houses are about relations, naturalized, imposed, contested, and produced.

The ambivalence between "places" and "relations" encoded in the several meanings of the word "house" is reflected in its usage with respect to the stock exchange. On the one hand, within British financial circles, "the House" referred to the physical building where the brokers and jobbers of the London Stock Exchange made markets. The House was a structure that, as Gibson (1889) wrote, had an exterior "inconsequential and almost undistinguishable from contiguous buildings. [It was a building with] no well-defined architectural purpose, so that its blind passageways, winding staircases, and narrow closed doorways make it something of a puzzle to a stranger." On the other hand, "the House" also referenced the market community as a set of individuals connected through their transactions and organizational identities; as Gibson also noted, "the House" denominated "the general membership of the exchange." The House, then, was a site for both the performance of markets and the reproduction of relations. What I want to do with this polyvalence is to think about these two aspects of the organization as linked domains: the reproduction of relations (of exchange, membership, and organizational identity) can be interpreted as being similar to a form of kinship tied not only to the enactment and reenactment of transactions (the making of market relations), but also to the existence of a specific physical infrastructure – the building known as "the House" (the infrastructure of the marketplace).

The idea of kinship that I work with alludes but is not directly related to "traditional" definitions based on "natural" biological relations within human groups. While marriage and bloodlines might have created bonds within the community of the stock exchange, these did not define the membership of the organization – on the contrary, as historian Ranald Michie explores (1998), the boundaries of finance in London were quite porous. These biological conceptualizations of kinship were certainly important in early anthropological discussions about culture, situating family structures, and their associated meanings at the center of broader social organization (e.g., Radcliffe-Brown, 1952). As Janet Carsten (2004) writes, "anthropologists confined their efforts to understanding the 'social' aspects of kinship, setting aside the pregiven and 'biological' as falling outside their expertise." New technologies such as those linked to assisted reproduction, however, queried these assumptions. Through artificial insemination, surrogacy, and donated gametes, the "recomposed" and "recombined" families of the contemporary world broke away from the nuclear idealizations that dominated previous anthropological theories. Bloodlines and familial relations are not a reflection of an external "nature," but are partly created from within social groups, for example, by experts – scientific and legal – that mobilize knowledge, expertise, and techniques. Our kin are not merely defined through "natural fact" but through considerations that intertwine the legal, genetic, and collective in everchanging ways.

Against this backdrop, kinship is best thought of as reflecting the "web of moral responsibilities" (Franklin and McKinnon, 2001; Strathern, 2005) that emerges with the relentless reenactment of "familial" communities. Kinship is not necessarily of bloodlines but about communities. And these may extend well beyond both the "traditional" and "recombined" families of early and contemporary anthropology as visible when considering the ways that we talk about groups of "related" individuals: Religious groups often speak through the authoritative logic of patriarchy and the affinities of siblinghood; American college students frequently organize in fraternities and sororities that, through strong rituals of membership, identity, and cohabitation, evoke brotherhood and sisterhood; and, since at least Shakespeare's time, groups of people fighting for a common cause are not armies of detached individuals but "bands of brothers" in fellowship. It is within these tightknit groupings where the different forms of kinship that I think of throughout this book are formed. Following Carsten (2004), this "processual understanding" places "greater experiential emphasis on the way kinship is '*lived*' as opposed to biologically 'given.'" Kinship is produced in multiple locations: it is made publicly in the contested arenas opened up by novel reproductive technologies, as Strathern suggests; but it is also recreated in smaller bounded loci like houses where familiarity is practiced and relationships are lived. Importantly, kinship is also made in organizations and markets, where defining, creating, and breaking relations and connections are constant elements of work.

Understanding the material contexts for familiarity allows studying the technologies that configure particular forms of kinship and community-making that structure the practices, hierarchies, and politics of organizational groups. What were, we may ask, the devices that create kindred relations in practice at the exchange? Carsten provides some suggestions. For instance, in *After Kinship*, Carsten (2004) evokes her "house memories" as focusing "on a large kitchen table at which not only cooking and eating but also most family discussions, communal homework, and many games took place." Note that kitchens, television dens, and even the "enormous and often chilly 'living rooms'" that are used mostly as ceremonial backdrops for receiving guests, are inhabited by numerous artifacts – from scuffed tables and busy countertops where meals are shared and school homework is completed, to "ill-assorted collection[s] of somewhat ponderous antique furniture and paintings" meant to entertain visitors – that are instruments for the reproduction of a sense of kinship and family in specific ways. Houses create familiarity, not only through cohabitation, but, critically, through the material production of a shared past and present (Miller, 2008).

We can say, then, that these "ill-assorted collections" are examples of the technologies or infrastructures of kinship that perform family relations as a lived experience recreated in daily interactions, exchanges, and memories. Like the mantelpiece in the living room, the coffee-stained desk in the parents' study, or the often-used kitchen table, these objects co-constitute the expectancies of familiarity within the household. And while sometimes practical, these technologies are also symbolic and affective – different dwellers will remember their houses in different ways, some seeing the kitchen table as a place of forced daily homework, others as a site of heated battles and disputes about curfews, and others as the spot where the family project was drawn to a close at the end of every day; devices and their usages thus encode hierarchies within the family.[1] But objects also extend relations beyond the immediate confines of the house: simple devices such as photos of relatives allow connecting house dwellers with other actors, creating a shared (if contested) imaginary of the relations that constitute the kindred group.

---

[1] As Carsten (2004: 55) writes, "Their very everydayness both suggests the importance of what goes on within their walls and also makes it liable to be dismissed as familiar and mundane. When we focus on this familiarity, we can see how the divisions of the house are simultaneously inscribed by often unarticulated social distinctions. In moving about the house, residents learn, embody, and convey differences of age, gender, and seniority. We have seen how houses provide anchors of stability."

Returning to the matter of stock exchanges, we should not confuse the metaphor of kinship with an internalist account of markets and their organizations. While it is true that focusing on the infrastructures that make exchange relations and markets communities possible might bracket larger structures and forces, we should not lose sight of how kinship is necessarily contextual, hierarchical, and intersected by key social processes. Like the types of relational work explored by Viviana Zelizer (2012) in other economic realms, the forms of kinship that I invoke in this book are necessarily asymmetric in power, gender, class, and race. Similarly, the forms of kinship that I refer to are only stable because they are legitimized by their broader historical contexts. For the automation of stock exchanges, much of this context involves the increasing levels of financialization of capitalist societies as seen in the rise and retreat of welfare states, the growing influence of investment and pension funds (Clark, 2000), and the encroachment of credit, debt, and financial logics into the habits of governments (Krippner, 2011), corporations (Lapavitsas, 2013; Davis and Kim, 2015), and households (Fligstein and Goldstein, 2015; Zaloom, 2018). Without these transformations, the refashioning of stock markets through automation would have been untenable.

Rather than constraining our analytical perspective, placing attention on the techniques and devices of kinship and familiarity that go into making the economy reveals important intersections between class, gender, politics, and everyday practices that are not altogether evident in the existing institutional or cultural accounts of contemporary capitalism. Sylvia Junko Yanagisako's work on Italian textile firms provides an excellent example. By studying how kinship mediates the organization of silk firms in Como, Yanagisako identifies the often-unacknowledged forms of work, loyalty, support, class, and familial competition that structure and reproduce capitalism through bloodlines and relations. Rather than reducing Italian family capitalism to an expression of an overarching culture, Yanagisako adopts a processual approach that understands kinship and family as constantly changing. To say that capitalism is void of kinship or is constrained by specific cultural templates would be a mistake, Yanagisako points out, for "people produce capitalism through culturally meaningful actions that at the same time produce families and selves with particular desires, sentiments, and identities" (Yanagisako, 2002). If capitalism is reproduced, it is in part because it is kindred in gendered and cultured ways. Identifying the technologies and devices implicated in the making of kinship and the economy better discerns the multiple roles of markets in tweaking and maintaining structures of capital.

What are the specific infrastructures of kinship of finance?[2] That markets are inhabited by technologies of valuation of numerous sorts is now a well-established claim (for classical examples, see Callon, 1998; Muniesa and Callon, 2005; MacKenzie, 2008). How these technologies configure forms of kinship and familiarity within the apparently ephemeral market situation is, however, a relatively understudied theme. The fact that both the building and membership of the London Stock Exchange were referred to as "the House" offers an interesting, if unique, opportunity for querying these devices and technologies. We can ask, in particular, what where the infrastructures of kinship of the community and market of the exchange? What devices made "the House" a site for the coproduction of market transactions and kin relations? As I explore below, there were three types of technologies that configured familiarity in the stock

---

[2] While my use of "kinship" is primarily as a metaphorical device to underscore technologies that made market relations and communities possible, kinship-as-intermarriage in the stronger, classical anthropological sense also mattered in the British financial world, though with varying degrees of strength. Early research by Tom Lupton and Shirley Wilson (1959), for instance, showed strong familial and membership linkages between the banking elites in London. Later research by Michael Lisle-Williams (1984a, 1984b) observed some evidence for intermarriage networks among merchant bankers. More recently, Ranald Michie (1998) offered some criticisms, finding the social and organizational boundaries of the City of London rather more permeable than what both folklore and sociological research on elites suggested. Overall, kinship-as-intermarriage mattered, but was certainly not the main mechanism of relation-making in the marketplace.

exchange's marketplace: technologies of consociation, technologies of honor, and technologies of belonging. It is to these technologies that I now turn, for it is in their transformation that the infrastructural changes associated to automation are best discerned.

2.2.1   *Technologies of Consociation*

For Max Weber, the emergence of modern capitalist markets was located in a long historical process whereby the economic activities of individuals formerly operating within households and traditional circuits of barter were decoupled and embedded in larger "communities of exchange." The resultant markets were remorseless, expanding "to include the totality of all civilized peoples" (Weber, 2000 [1894]: 307). Weber saw in these communities of exchanges "the most impersonal relationship of practical life into which humans can enter with one another" (Weber, 1978: 636). He argued that within markets action was driven not by individual personal orientations, but by the "rational, purposeful pursuit of interests." For Weber, then, markets are rational and calculative spheres of human action – a view that is consistent with other early sociological accounts of markets and their role in modernization (Simmel, 1972). Importantly though, Weber also stressed markets as associational spaces; they are, as he wrote a "coexistence and sequence of rational consociations" that allow a constellation of agents with diverging needs and concerns to engage in exchange.

That Weber used the term consociation (or, in one of its original appearances, *Vergesellschaftung*) to think of markets is particularly notable. Against accounts that positioned markets as antithetical to sociability (Giddens, 1971; Swedberg, 2003), Weber saw these as spaces for the production of fleeting, yet meaningful, associations between buyers and sellers. These, furthermore, were the product of a socializing process whereby market participants consensually oriented their mutual actions with the aim of engaging in exchange. In referring to consociation, Weber did not equate markets to traditional organizations defined through formal order – note that in English "consociation" can also refer to fellowships and joint endeavors where personal bonds matter fundamentally. Quite the contrary, Weber insisted that markets were unique since their distinguishing feature was an abject impersonal rationality centered on the pursuit of trade. After the exchange, the fleeting communion is dissolved, leaving the parties quits. In effect, if not opposed to "the social," markets diverged from the restrictions of traditional, hierarchical associations (for this classical theme on hierarchies and markets, see Williamson, 1983).

What happens if we think of markets as closer to the type of formal voluntary organizations that populate other domains of social life, by adopting only some of Weber's conceptual toolkit? Take the canonical example of stock exchanges – institutions that have for long been emblematic of rational economic calculation and impersonal transactions (Walras, 2003; Marshall, 2014 [1890]). These organizations are clearly both markets and market*places*. Yet they are also complex associations where a variety of agents cooperate to stabilize exchange while struggling in the pursuit of their own interests, as Mitchel Abolafia (1996) rightly showed in his classical study of the New York Stock Exchange. While markets, these are also organizations built and reproduced through strong interpersonal relationships and hierarchical, rationalized decision chains. Stock exchanges are positioned at the intersection between associations defined through formal order and membership, and the logics of impersonal consociations of transaction and exchange. In this, they recall the broader meaning of *vergesellschaftung* within a long-standing literature on sociation, one that allows us to consider the forms and devices of fellowship that, however putatively brittle, constitute the "communities of exchange" of the marketplace. These forms may not be brittle at all, as Jan Rehmann notes, Weber's original term *vergesellschaftung* conveys not only association but, critically, "the more encompassing meaning of 'making society,' in the sense of shaping and realizing social relationships on all levels" (Rehmann, 2013).

What technologies were involved in "making society" and markets within the London Stock Exchange? The first key device was membership. As noted above, membership was a particularly crucial innovation in financial markets: it afforded the possibility of closing market participation to individuals deemed financially, socially, and morally worthy of exchange. In the case of London, Weber himself identified the membership barriers as being particularly steep. As he wrote in his essay on stock and commodities exchanges in 1889, London's was a "plutocratic" exchange "requiring a significant amount of wealth and security deposits ... as preconditions for admittance to business" (Weber, 2000 [1894]). At this simple level, membership defined the boundaries of the organization, the market community, and its specific forms of governance: only full members could vote on the exchange's rules and regulations; only they could access the trading floor (with some important caveats); and only they could make markets. Through its inherently restrictive character, membership also forced conditions of familiarity: unlike the idealized anonymous markets of early sociological theories, transactions within stock exchanges took place among roughly the same group of known individuals; no one was ever anonymous; no one was ever really quits.

Membership made interpersonal knowledge within the exchange a fundamental element for sensemaking in the marketplace. A large organization formed by more than three thousand members throughout most of the nineteenth and early twentieth centuries, the stock exchange had a conspicuous absence of badges identifying the inhabitants of the house. For most of its history, those buying and selling stocks at the exchange were known through their names and faces – it was only in 1959 that the exchange's council mandated the use of badges, and not without considerable opposition. As historian David Kynaston tells, member broking firms complained that this would "entail the constant putting on and removal of Badges, as obviously it would not add to the dignity of the Stock Exchange as a whole were Members to be seen walking round the City wearing whatever form of Badge is finally decided upon" (Kynaston, 2001: 192). If people knew who their counterparties were, it was because they had been inducted into a dense, tight-knit community. Knowledge of this community – and the possibility of imagining relations within it – was greatly practical. Writing of his experience arriving at the exchange in 1933, former member David Cobbett (1986: 32) noted the difficulties of navigating the trading floor when doing business. The organization of floor at the time, he noted, was "ambiguously notional, and not ... physically structural." Most dealers, he recalled,

> assembled close around the walls and surrounding the massive pillars dividing the floor space irregularly into sections, had seating facilities, space to erect a price board, and improvised shelves for dealing books and other paraphernalia of the business. But a large number of [dealers] not conveniently disposed, particularly the small firms such as the one I joined, were compelled to take their stand on the open floor, with the surging crowds of brokers and their clerks passing through and around them.

"The only information available to us in those days," continued Cobbett, "was gleaned from a perfunctory tour of the floor by the senior waiter, a medal-bedecked personage who would marshal each batch of new boys at the main door for a privileged insight into the layout, with the tacit expectation of a little something slipped into the receptive palm." It is clear that the community of exchange hinged on a relatively detailed understanding of the relationships and personalities on the floor. A veil of anonymity may have been the initial impression for an outsider but soon vanished within the exchange – the patterns of activity through which brokers and dealers made markets in London were intensely interpersonal.

As a distinct innovation, membership also defined categories of agents in the marketplace – and with this, produced a hierarchy of actors linked to positions in the organization as well as to career structures within the broader stock trading industry in London. There were, in particular, two classes of members, each mirrored by specialized clerks (known as "blue buttons," who were allowed to trade but were not formally members of the exchange). One group of members consisted of brokers that worked on the basis of commissions and acted as the agents of investors seeking to buy and sell shares. A second group of members was composed by so-called jobbers, who dealt with brokers on the trading floor and made their living from setting the spread between bids and offers in the baskets of shares they traded. The two traded on the principles of competing dealers: jobbers would compete with each other by adjusting their spreads while brokers would compete to attract clients from the investing public. "Thus the broker feeds the jobber," wrote Francis Hirst in 1911, "much as the solicitor feeds the barrister. The broker takes a commission and the jobber his turn" (Hirst, 1911: 73). Membership encoded a key division of labor and authority within the marketplace: whereas brokers often accrued social capital and recognition outside the exchange (which mattered crucially for business: until the 1970s they were not allowed to advertise), jobbers provided liquidity to the market and so held a particularly powerful position within the organization. Although this division held informally throughout most of the nineteenth century, it was encoded in the rules of the exchange in 1909 when members and the firms they represented had to opt for one of the two activities. They either acted as brokers or as jobbers, with no possibility of combining roles either on or off the trading floor. This division, known as single capacity, prevailed until 1986 and defined competencies and individual career trajectories in the stock market throughout much of the twentieth century (Attard, 2000).

Membership mattered not only because of the status it accrued but, substantively, because it granted individuals with access to the site where stock prices were readily available and markets were made. As the location where the community of exchange congregated, the trading floor was the house's second key technology of consociation, representing the practical and symbolic core of the organization. The trading floor, like the building wherein it was contained, reflected the exchange's long and punctuated history. "The shape of the floor," wrote Gibson in 1889, "is shapeless," the consequence of "opportunism in architecture" and the changing needs of the market: the original trading floor from 1802 served well for the buying and selling of some joint-stock shares and the existing government debt, but it proved inadequate for handling the growth of assets associated to the industrialization and colonial expansion of nineteenth-century Britain. New shares of foreign corporations, colonial debt, and numerous private railroad ventures and commercial explorations, required more space for trade – much in the same way that a street market necessitates larger premises as the number of stalls and the variety of products increases. And so, in 1854 the original building from 1802 was demolished giving way to one that came to be known as the "Old House." Thirty years later and as markets grew even further, it was augmented with the "New House," "a structure of brick, roofed with wood, with ironwork in the piers and some of the beams, and [interiors] plastered with some elaborate ornament" (Duguid, 1913: 181). Much like the current search for speed and increased messaging capacity in contemporary automated financial markets, the logic of material expansion within the exchange was one of accommodating demand. As Charles Duguid wrote in 1913, "[e]ven as the architecture of a nation is an index of its character, that of the Stock Exchange is intimately related to its history of never-ceasing growth. Structural extension has always been going on in all directions; it is going on now at its centenary and presumably always will be going on" (p. 13).

The occasional expansion of the trading floor was a more dramatic manifestation of forms of bricolage that reproduced the marketplace. Throughout the years, armies of carpenters, masons, cleaners, waiters, clerks, and other infrastructural workers constantly maintained and tweaked the architectures of the stock exchange and its trading floor. Sometimes changes were esthetic. For instance, in 1886 the plastered interiors of the New House were substituted with marble, leading members to informally rename that section of the building as the Gorgonzola Hall owing to the "peculiar veining" of the new material (Duguid, 1913). Other changes were rather more inconspicuous. The floor, for example, was always in the making, kept, modified and updated as use made its brittle materiality clear:

initially covered in "oak two inches thick," the New House's floor was later changed to "teak, the oak having been worn down in places to a thickness of only a quarter of an inch in the course of ten years. A Stock Exchange floor does not always last as long as this. An interesting calculation shows that the members' boots convert into powder, which is swept up as dust, some 150 cubic feet of oak or teak in every year!" Far from being a carefully designed technology, the trading floor reflected sometimes-unpredictable forms of tinkering, maintenance, and change.

A product of contingency, piecewise modifications, tight and unpredictable budgets, and the relentless incorporation of surrounding properties, the trading floor served a practical purpose: it physically organized markets within the house. Whether government and municipal debt or the shares of banking, insurance, brewing, mining, shipping, and electrical companies, the buying and selling of stocks occurred in notionally discernible islands of trading within the large spaces of a house "dominated by [the] great echoing dome and broken through its length by rows of supporting columns" (Attard, 2000: 9; Thomas, 2016; see Figure 2.1). But the floor also organized how the instructions from investors located outside the exchange were processed. It formatted the way information was created, communicated, and acted upon by members of the stock exchange's community. Orders to buy and sell securities from the public were collected on the periphery of the trading floor in small rooms operated by broking firms – the so-called boxes that, by the 1940s, contained "a number of telephones direct to the firm's switchboard and to important clients, and in some cases telex machines or teleprinters for direct contact with provincial exchanges and other centers throughout the world" (J.D. Hamilton, 1968: 49). With the orders of investors in their hands, brokers would procure for the best prices in the market, much in the same way as a customer seeks the best deals in a street fair by walking and talking to vendors. Unlike a street market, the vendors in the stock exchange (known as jobbers) made a living out of buying and selling securities and making a profit (turn)

FIGURE 2.1 Etching of the interior of the London Stock Exchange, c. 1870. Originally printed in Walter Thornbury's "The Stock Exchange," in Old and New London (1878).

from the spread in prices. The durable character of the stock exchange's community is visible in how jobbers and brokers interacted as part of the market's mechanics of trade: on the trading floor, the prices of shares and bonds existed primarily as ongoing sequences of utterances – in the form of quotes that indicated the values at which jobbers were willing to buy and sell certain volumes of particular securities. In calm dealing conditions, these utterances were produced only at the request of brokers who had to approach jobbers and say something of the sort "What are BP?" (meaning: what is the quote for shares in British Petroleum?). Under the "Rules and Regulations" of the stock exchange, jobbers had to provide a quote without knowing – at least in theory – whether the broker was a buyer or a seller (reading faces and overhearing conversations on the floor was certainly a skill that some jobbers developed). To avoid losses, jobbers "adjust[ed] their prices in accordance with the flow of buying and selling orders from the investing public, tempered with intelligent anticipation" (Berman, 1963: 13). Upon a request from a broker, a jobber would reply with a quote, for instance, "five hundred to five" ("500–5"), indicating that the price at which he was willing to buy "a reasonable" number of shares was 500 pence (bid), and that the price at which he was willing to sell was 505 pence (ask). Once said, the quote was firm – it could not be changed. To his answer, the broker could take one of several paths. He could agree to buy at a volume pre-indicated by the client (that is, to execute the deal) by responding something of the sort "Take 500" (sell) or "Take 505" (buy). The broker could also mention that he was only quoting (that is, he was asked by his firm or client to find out prevailing market prices). Or the broker could simply walk away to another pitch, procuring for a better quote (The Stock Exchange, 1976). "The art of a good broker," wrote Berman (1963) in his review of investment, "is to know when to deal and when to hold his hand and try for a better price." It was, indeed, quite a fine art. As former jobber David Steen recalled in an interview, quotes were "bound to the circumstances and the situation, [to] how many shares you were long or short on the book, [to] how the rest of the firm [was] positioned." As such, they could change rapidly: "a broker who has gone to the telephone to quote a price to a client may find that in spite of the fact that there are telephone boxes inside the Stock Exchange the price has altered by the time he gets back into the market again" (Berman, 1963).

The market of the stock exchange was a community of conversations (Hertz, 1998) much more than a sequence of impersonal consociations. And of course, this could be a source of much ambiguity. While the stock exchange was meant to originate prices that reflected the value of the instruments traded on its floor (company valuations and tax calculations, for instance, hinged on the closing prices published in the daily stock exchange official list), dealings occurred within the relatively enclosed and opaque conversations between jobbers and brokers. For some early observers, the cacophony of the trading floor motivated great suspicion. As one critic wrote in the late eighteenth century,

> The noise of the screech-owl – the howling of the wolf – the barking of the mastiff – the grunting of the hog – the braying of the ass – the nocturnal wooing of the cat – the hissing of the snake – the croaking of toads, frogs, and grasshoppers – all these, in unison, could not be more hideous than the noise which these beings make in the Stock Exchange.
>
> *(Hales, 1795)*

To have legitimacy, the exchange needed more than membership and a trading floor. It required a vast assemblage for crafting and maintaining trust in its boisterous yet hermetic community.

The stock exchange was quite confident of the mechanics of its trading floor and, upon criticisms, offered two key arguments in its defense. One stressed the qualities of the membership as a genteel group worthy of managing the affairs of a national institution. Brokers and jobbers, argued the exchange's leadership, acted with great integrity and in the public's interest. As a pamphlet from 1951 noted, members traded in a restrained and controlled manner, with "standards imposed by the Stock Exchange [that had long been] more stringent than those of the Law itself. The Stock Exchange exists to serve the investing public, whether inexperienced or expert, big or small" (Council of the Stock Exchange, 1951). Another very different argument stressed the virtues of the trading floor itself as the best mechanism for guaranteeing equality within the local marketplace and British finance at large. Such equality was predicated, argued the exchange, on the trading floor's unique ability to make information on companies simultaneously available to the market's membership.

The trading floor was not simply a convenient meeting place; importantly, it was a moral technology. Reporting in 1957 on how company announcements were processed on the trading floor, for instance, the *Stock Exchange Journal* noted that

> Accurate information is just as important in Stock Exchange practices as in any military operation. Without a flow of early comprehensive and authentic company news, jobbers are unable to assess values, brokers are unable properly to advise their clients, and investors are unable to form correct conclusions as to company prospects ... There are ... three major requirements which have to be observed [in collecting and disseminating company news]:
> (1) *Accuracy and authenticity* – that is, all the information must be issued and sponsored by the company concerned or come from some other responsible and approved source; (2) *Promptitude* – that is, the news must be placed at the disposal of the House immediately, it is available; and (3) *Impartiality* – that is to say, it must be available to all members or at least to all interested members simultaneously.
>
> *(FSG, 1957: 104)*

What mattered was not only the allegedly virtuous character of brokers and jobbers but also the material process through which information was distributed on the floor: all news of traded companies were made collectively visible by posting then on announcement boards within the trading floor. For the stock exchange there was no better way for guaranteeing a market that allowed buying and selling shares "in the quickest, cheapest and fairest manner" (Council of the Stock Exchange, 1951). Even as late as 1974 when the first generations of data communication technologies had become widely adopted within the City of London, the stock exchange insisted in the moral superiority of its floor. In its official response to a critique from a parliamentary working party at the time, for example, the stock exchange stressed such an opinion. In their letter, the Council of the Stock Exchange wrote that they, [acknowledged] the reality that there is no way in which news can be received by all individuals simultaneously throughout the country. By requiring all company news to be published first at The Stock Exchange it insures that all Brokers have the information and are therefore able at least to prevent their clients acting in ignorance of it. Because the jobbers are also instantly apprised of the information and if necessary adjust the market price it is by definition impossible for any operator, however slick, to gain an advantage over any other once the news is published in the Market. Once an item of news has been announced the price in the Market at once reflects that news. If of course by whatever means the operator can anticipate the news this may be at the Jobber's expense and not at the small investor's.

(Council of the Stock Exchange, 1974)

The trading floor, then, was a decisive technology of consociation in multiple and subtle ways. By providing a bounded arena for congregation, it brought the members of the organization together around the act of exchange; by serving as a familiar space of business and socialization, it replicated modes of relatedness among the members; and by organizing the market and reproducing the division of labor entailed in membership, it formatted the dynamics of inter-action and exchange. The trading floor was the technology upon which multiple asynchronous and asymmetric relations and market-place conversations were bound, structured, and collectively under-stood. And it was quite unique: this was not the floor of the Chicago Board of Trade, where activity was coordinated within octagonal pits that promoted visual transparency and simultaneously embodied the principles of competition (Zaloom, 2006); it was also not New York's floors, where specialists made markets in their shares through their pitches and their power of monopoly (Abolafia, 1996). No: London's floor was quite different, encoding through materialities and organiza-tional routines the historically specific moral orders of the stock exchange and its community. It echoed, for instance, the long-standing market structure of wholesale dealers that formatted trading in the streets and alleys of the City of London in the late eighteenth century. But it also materialized the moral and cultural concerns of its users, being a space that privileged its participants symbolically while emulating forms of equality and responsibility.

If trade was mostly a conversational activity, the realization of exchange required a technology that grounded the agreements spoken on the floor in the physical swap of certificates for money. It is here that settlement, the third technology of consociation, becomes relevant. If they were to be of any economic significance, the fleeting agreements reached on the floor required a translation from the interpersonal spheres of private speech acts to the rational, legal, and public logics of paper trails and detailed administrative records. Settlement matters precisely because it makes finance "financial": as Millo et al. (2005) discuss: one of the etymological roots of the word "finance" is found in Middle French's "finer," which means to end or to pay. Settlement is the endpoint, the finalization of the trade through its ultimate payment. Through this, settlement also takes finance into the public: by making effective the transfer of money and the ownership of shares across the community of exchange, this critical practice not only allows the parties of transactions to be at quits, bringing their brief relation to an end, but also creates a public record of private transactions.

Settlement is not a sequential process. We often think of markets much in the same way as Weber did, as sequences of individual consociations, chains of dyadic relations bound by the fact that the parties involved in them are free before they move on to their next transaction. Thus, in our ideal markets, exchange and settlement are assumed as intertwined and co-temporal: like a buyer walking through the stalls in a street market, we think of negotiation and exchange as taking place simultaneously, while client and vendor converse, reach an agreement on a price, exchange money, and receive the goods.

But financial markets are structured by the temporal differences between floor transactions and the delivery of stocks and bonds.

Settlement and clearing are relatively laborious operations that outlive the utterances on the trading floor or the microsecond transactions in electronic matching engines: in the days of face-to-face trading, deals agreed on the floor between brokers and jobbers were just the starting point of longer and largely invisible organizational processes that required the tallying, comparing, matching, recording, and exchanging of money and legal rights across the market membership. These processes took not minutes or hours, but days and months (a note from 1961 indicates, for example, that investors could expect to receive their paper certificates through their brokers about three months after the relevant transaction had taken place; see *Investors Chronicle*, 1961). After reaching a deal with a broker, each jobber or his clerk would generate a "ticket" or record for the relevant transaction – containing the name of the broker, his firm, the agreed price, and the size of the deal (known on the floor as the "shape"). At the end of the trading day, specialized clerks for each jobbing firm collected all the tickets that had been generated on the floor and produced lists of the transactions for the session. The tickets and lists of deals were the type of "transactional things" that Bill Maurer and Lana Swartz call attention to within the broader economy: although ephemera (few examples remain of these devices), at the time of their making they crystalized the activity of the marketplace (Maurer and Swartz, 2017).

Because it involved processing this wealth of administrative market ephemera, settlement was an organizationally intensive activity. As Dundas Hamilton, former chair of the Council of the Stock Exchange, wrote in his detailed account of stockbroking practices in 1968, the process of settling deals and recording transactions was absolutely laborious and necessarily skilled:

> Sorting out the "shapes" in a jobber's office to match buyers and sellers most economically is a skilled job and one which lends itself to the use of the most sophisticated equipment. ... Each day, member firms submit to the Settlement Office a list of their transactions in clearing stocks. At the end of the account the

Settlement Office issues to each of firm of brokers a list of the "shapes" of the securities sold by them and the brokers to whom each number of shares should be delivered. At the same time a list of the "shapes" making up each of their purchases is given to buying brokers, showing the names of the brokers who will be delivering the securities, to whom they should issue their tickets.

(J.D. Hamilton, 1968: 62)

The intensity of settlement was only compounded by the fact that throughout most of its history, and well into the 1950s, clearing and matching transactions at the stock exchange was entirely manual. Such was the scale of this task that it quite literally enveloped the transactions on the floor: with the creation of the Settlement Department in 1880, the stock exchange added a Settling Room to the basement of the house occupying an area as large as the floor, "lined with oak paneling and glazed tiles" (Duguid, 1913: 304); in addition to this room, the department also occupied "three upper floors, 120 feet long" where deals were made sense of through the rationalizing logic of matching and recordkeeping (see Figure 2.2). Writing about the history of the exchange, Duguid (1913) also stressed this sense of importance, depth, and efficiency, noting that

although [settlement] has frequently been the subject of much grumbling, only at periods of exceptional strain ... has the Department really been unable to cope with its important work. Heavy indeed is the labour connected with the comparison of the clearing lists on the nights of settling days; it is of course all night work. To trace the stocks and shares that have been bought and sold during the fortnight's account, to find an ultimate buyer and seller, canceling transactions by cross entry, so that scores of payments which would otherwise be necessary are reduced to one – that is the work of the clearing clerks, who are brought from all quarters.

Paperwork and physical labor were aplenty in finance before automation: to reconstruct the trading patterns of the day, settlement

FIGURE 2.2 Etching of "The Clearing House" from Walter Thornbury's "The Stock Exchange," in *Old and New London* (1878). The image may represent what was later known as the Settlement Room of the London Stock Exchange.

and clearing clerks often spent countless hours "checking the bargains" to guarantee the veracity of the trades that had been reported to their department. "In the confusion of great activity in markets," wrote J.D. Hamilton, "mistakes can be made by either side, both in identifying the person with whom the deal has been made and in entering the correct details into the dealing book … Each morning clerks from the brokers' and jobbers' offices meet in the Settlement Room beneath the floor of The Stock Exchange and check the bargains of the previous day [giving members the opportunity] to correct any other occasional errors that may have occurred" (J.D. Hamilton, 1968).

There were advantages to such a laborious system. Rather than paying for individual transactions, aggregating deals in the marketplace reduced the volume of transfers between buyers and sellers. As Hamilton explained, settling the deals made over each 14-day accounting period (there were 22 accounting periods per working year) allowed the stock exchange's Central Stock Payment Office to guarantee that "each member firm receives only one cheque for all stocks delivered and pays only one cheque for all stocks received." This practice, commonly referred to as "netting," demonstrates settlement's role as an infrastructure of kinship, a technology that created and reproduced moral relations across the market community: netting organized debt, perhaps the most fundamental social relation involved in exchange (Mauss, 2000).

Consider a Maussian perspective on settlement as an organizational ritual of debt making and debt unmaking (Peebles, 2010). As temporal placeholders, accounting periods were not only practical ways of organizing payments and transfers across the membership of the exchange. Fundamentally, within these periods all active market participants became "related"; the act of settling implied making explicit private speech acts and connecting individuals through chains of mutual debt; it determined relations among relations, links among links, in order to discern who owed what to whom. Settlement operated on ongoing relations of debt, of credit, and on slow forms of liquidation that were reproduced, carried over, and echoed in the numerous cycles of clearing and matching that took place over the trading year. Settlement was generative rather than finalizing: before it could detach relations and bring transactions to an end, it had to create them through administrative means. Settlement tied together the "community of exchange," at the very least within each accounting period, where it created dependencies that, when challenged, posed moral dilemmas to the membership of the marketplace. Default, for instance, was considered gravely pernicious not just because it spoke of the failure of an individual, but, perhaps more importantly, because it generated a settlement hazard to the community at large. A member that defaulted on his payments would unravel his debts, creating ripples for those outside the polluted set of transactions. Default complicated settlement and forced the exchange to untie transactions of defaulters from those of the legitimate remainder.[3] This point remains important today, as demonstrated by Annelise Riles's (2011: 132) elegant discussions of bank settlement in modern Japan. In the early 2000s, she writes, workers of the Bank of Japan planned to introduce a gross settlement system that separated and accounted for each transaction sequentially and in real time. With real-time settlement, the asynchronous relationship between exchange and delivery is eliminated, making markets true successions of isolated transactions. Such innovation was predicated, in part, on the need to unwind the systemic risks posed by the potential default of one member of the payment system. In the imaginary of the bank's bureaucrats (or Sato, one of Riles's key informants), such a move isolated responsibilities and made risk calculable – bringing settlement in line with the forms of rationality that are often deemed paradigmatic of atomistic markets. This is precisely the trouble with settlement: it manifests the "web of moral responsibilities" underlying exchange.

The importance of settlement resides in its capacity to create the type of linkages that make financial markets relevant to society at large (and that, when undone without control, can have catastrophic consequences as demonstrated in times of crisis). In *Framing Finance*, Preda rightly points at the Weberian argument that stock exchanges are "necessarily institutions of power [that is exercised through] their capacity to create reciprocal obligations across society" (Preda, 2009). We may question, however, the conventional idea that these reciprocal obligations are created primarily on the trading floor – that they are solely "transactional" in a blunt sense. As the above discussion

---

[3] The situation is similar to the problem posed by unraveling kinship through technology: when the nature of a relation is questioned, it obligates the parties to query not only that instance but every other instance.

suggests, stock exchanges are not "just" marketplaces. They are intricate organizational arrangements structured by technologies that make consociation possible. The power of stock exchanges is certainly connected to their "control of [the] technological transaction systems" that populate trading floors, but it also hinges on the devices that make the community's relations visible and facts of law. Settlement is one such device. If fleeting relations are created in the market, they are only made knowable and exercisable through the techniques and processes of settlement, through the making and unmaking of ties; it is settlement that produces kin out of the trading floor's familiarity, public knowledge out of the multiple conversations that happen within the community of exchange.

2.2.2   Technologies of Honor

Let's return to Weber's discussion of markets. As Weber noted, mutual obligations and shared expectancies of behavior are necessary for rational market action to occur. Without them, uncertainty about the likelihood of transactions is great and the incentives to trade small. As he wrote:

> The partner to a transaction is expected to behave according to rational legality and, quite particularly, to respect the formal inviolability of a promise once given. These are the qualities that form the content of market ethics. In this latter respect the market inculcates, indeed, particularly rigorous conceptions. Violations of agreements, even though they may be concluded by mere signs, entirely unrecorded, and devoid of evidence, are almost unheard of in the annals of the stock exchange.
>
> *(Weber, 1978: 636–637)*

This passage provides an important clue about different types of technology that constituted relations within the communities of exchange of British finance. Although technologies of consociation made transactions within the conversational community of the marketplace, technologies of honor replicated and reinforced bonds of reciprocity within and outside "the house" providing legitimacy and stability to the business of the exchange.

Technologies of honor are associated to the essential tension of stock exchanges that had to balance the public and private through their marketplace. While financial markets are not "secret, sectarian activities," it is incorrect to say that they are institutions fully located in the public sphere. Like other trading venues, the stock exchange was a restricted space – effectively, a legally private space owned and regulated by its members and proprietors. And although the prices produced on its trading floor had a public dimension, they resulted from eminently private speech acts guided by private interests. How to balance the internal opacity of transactions with the public duties of the organization? And how to guarantee that the personal interests of the few did not outweigh the collective interests of the many? Technologies of honor were deployed to address these questions and were anchored on the constitution of the organization as a status group within finance and the broader class structure of nineteenth- and twentieth-century Britain. (It is useful to recall here that Weber characterized status groups as having "a specific, positive or negative social appreciation of 'honor,' related to common group characteristics.") While a relatively hermetic membership contributed to closure, the cultural dimensions of honor and status had to be fabricated materially, providing the community with both outward legitimacy and internal coherence. Technologies of honor afforded such qualities by providing the type of structural references that, as Jens Beckert (2009) indicates, "allow for relatively stable reciprocal expectations which actors have with regard to the behavior of relevant others and future events."

One important family of technologies of honor at the stock exchange worked by making the "social appreciation" of trading obligations visible on the floor in real time. As discussed above, default was an operational and social concern throughout most of the stock exchange's early history – particularly during its first decades when governance structures and jurisdictional demarcations between brokers and jobbers were still ambiguous (Ma and Van Zanden, 2011). During the early nineteenth century, for instance, members of the stock exchange "could run up large open positions with other members" that, upon rapid changes in prices, became impossible to cover. Making these defaults common knowledge on the floor was important for limiting damages against the broader marketplace community. And so, as Duguid (1913) wrote,

> The names of those who could not meet their liabilities and who refused to disclose the names of the principals through whom the losses were sustained were to be publicly exposed in the market. That day [in 1795] was originated the Stock Exchange blackboard. It was placed in a conspicuous part of the House, and for many, many years it was the spiteful practice to paint the defaulter's name upon it so that it should remain there to his permanent disgrace.

By 1833, the means for proclaiming defaulters changed: to inform members in the fastest manner possible, "all defaulters [were] declared by the Hammer" (Michie, 1999: 40; see Figure 2.3), with their names subsequently "affixed to the notice-boards of the House for a few hours only" (Duguid, 1913). Defaulting was consequential: members ceased to trade with a defaulter; and defaulters and their firms lost membership with no possibility of readmission.

Linked to market proclamations, the exchange also provided members with organizational supports that fostered cooperation within the competitive environment of the trading floor. Although one member's losses could potentially be another member's profits, the exchange had to limit opportunism and the effects of misfortunes that affected the members' collective interests to create a space conducive to orderly trading (such as a client's or stock issuer's default – events that were out of the control of brokers and jobbers; see Abolafia, 1996). Informing the membership about defaulters either through the hammer or notices posted in the house was one mechanism for creating these conditions, reinforced by the floor's dynamics of mutual surveillance and regulation. These technologies promoted

FIGURE 2.3 "Three taps with a hammer – Proclaiming a defaulter on
the London Stock Exchange." Originally published in Harper's Weekly,
February 9, 1874. © Illustrated London News Ltd/Mary Evans.

forms of "negative appreciation" among the community of the
exchange that reinforced shared notions of proper business behavior.
A second mechanism introduced in the early twentieth century, however, used "positive appreciation" and resembled a type of organizational welfare system that guarded the community from calamity. To
protect members from losing their means from defaults for which
they were not responsible, the stock exchange created a guarantee or
compensation fund to which affected members could recur (while
discussions on the fund started in the mid-1930s, it was only established in 1950 largely due to the difficulties of the war). Unlike the
hammering of defaulters' names that singled *out* individuals, the
Compensation Fund singled them *in* – it strengthened community
bonds by highlighting that failure had been a matter of chance rather
than improper conduct. Both technologies were predicated on
patently moral notions of virtues and responsibility: they were based
on collective ideas of what it meant to be a proper, honorable, and
disciplined member of the exchange.

Technologies of honor became increasingly common during the early twentieth century, a period when the very survival of the stock exchange as a private institution was at risk. Punctuated by wars, global financial turmoil, and the frequent threat of nationalization, the stock exchange made particularly intense and noticeable investments in honor, stressing the membership's worthy character and the institution's critical role in the British economy. Perhaps the most salient of such investments was the creation of the stock exchange's motto, *Dictum Meum Pactum* (My Word is My Bond), which first appeared in 1923 when the organization received its official coat of arms. While evoking a noble and apparently ancient past, the motto is conspicuously absent from nineteenth-century descriptions of the exchange – where the mechanics of business and stories of defaults and speculative manias were more frequent topics of discussion. As one of various other invented traditions at the exchange (Pryke, 1991; Ranger and Hobsbawm, 1992), the motto reproduced of a strong sense of community defined through duty and self-discipline rather than through the pursuit of pecuniary ends – money was merely the means for something greater, a national project. For example, it was quite counterproductive for the staff of broking and jobbing firms to request a pay rise to their superiors: "the prevailing culture of job immobility was such that [leaving a firm after a dispute over pay] was a black mark in the eyes of other potential employers" (Kynaston, 2001). Across the exchange's member firms, duty and honor reproduced an ordered "system of relationships," as the historian William Reed (1975: 85) wrote, dissociated from meritocratic structures, resulting in "an intimate, family-like working environment, knit together by seemingly inalienable ties of mutual trust and loyalty." This, too, constituted kinship-like relations in the marketplace by establishing the type of origin stories intimately connecting images of nobility with the exchange's moral deeds and its social organization (Yanagisako et al., 1995).

These devices of honor were important not only as promoters of intra-organizational loyalty but also as gateways to the classed imagery of British society, mediating the private transactions of the familiar community of the exchange and public notions of rights and responsibilities associated to established English class structures. Although admittedly a simple example, consider the tacit dress codes of the stock exchange, where having proper attire was and integral part of the cultural codes of membership. In his recollections from the 1930s, for example, David Cobbett noted that "suede shoes or a checky suit on a relaxed Saturday morning would bring down the displeasure of the market on the individualist" (Cobbett, 1986: 30). Strangers, continued Cobbett, were often identified precisely because of their departure from the expected dress and conduct of a member of the exchange. The "curious interloper" that occasionally "gate-crash[ed] the privacy of the sacred floor" (Cobbett, 1986: 28–29), he wrote, confronted a spectacular reception:

> An intruder, particularly in those days of strict conformity to the commercial style of attire, would often cry out for attention variously by wearing the wrong clothes, perhaps smoking a pipe, or merely looking about him in bewilderment. The first Houseman to spot the stranger would immediately raise the cry "Fourteen hundred!" ... [It] is said picturesquely to date from the latter part of the last century when for a long time the membership stuck at 1399, and consequently the presence of an outsider made up the round number. Nor was the stranger in those days allowed to slip away unacknowledged. A jostling crowd would at once form around him, impeding the efforts of the waiters, who by that time had arrived on the scene to escort the intruder off the premises. All this would take place to a polite but insistent chorus to "Sit down!": a quite impossible endeavor, anyway.

In the attire and poise of its membership, the stock exchange served as a stage for the reproduction of overtly classed performances (Crane, 2000). Top hats populated the trading floor in the early twentieth century differentiating members from clerks who wore the more middle-classed bowlers.[4] Long lunches where fine wines and port flowed were obligatory components of trading activity – moments where transactions could be unwound through genteel conversations. And through the "dinginess and the respectability of age" commanded by its building, the stock exchange conveyed a sense of "so much old wealth, such long traditions of caution and stability, so keen a sense of responsibility among those in command … that London, with its unequaled annual surplus or overflow of capital for export, should be reckoned rather as the capital city of banking and investment than as the chosen home of speculation" (Hirst, 1911). The resulting display presented a public image of institutional respectability that notionally reflected the quality of its membership. As Whyte wrote in 1924, the members of the stock exchange "are a fraternity all by themselves. They are essentially of a sporting and good-natured temperament, patriotic in sentiment and generous in disposition [and whose] record of public service on public bodies rendered by members of this group compares favorably with any other class in the community" (Whyte, 1924: 8). The exchange was not just "family-like," as Reader (1979) suggested. In its constantly reinvented public persona, it presented itself as a dynasty – an honorable brotherhood at the heart of the national economy.

2.2.3   Technologies of Belonging

Technologies of honor inflected the pecuniary interests of the exchange and its membership onto broader notions of rights and responsibilities compatible with the classed imagery of English society. In this, they were overtly oriented toward the market and its practices, providing a source of legitimacy within and outside the organization. But not all activities at the exchange concerned the marketplace. Some merely sought to promote fellowship by nurturing community based on the alignment of business interests with shared repertoires of what it meant to be a "gameworthy" member of the

---

[4] For relevant discussions, see Davison (2009), Morgan (2005), and Crane (2000).

group (Preda, 2009). Through rituals and devices, technologies of belonging created mutuality in the exchange much in the same way as households are produced, in Carsten's words, by "the commensality of those who live under one roof": through the intermingling of leisure and work and the projection of the exchange's identity onto the personal lives of its members, these technologies enabled a strong sense of familiarity to emerge in relation to the business of creating the transactional sphere of exchange.

The technologies of belonging of the exchange were multiple – and for a modern observer, quite simple. One set comprised members' societies organized around a number of activities. For instance, there was a Stock Exchange Choral and Orchestral Society founded in the late nineteenth century, which by the early twentieth century offered regular "smoking concerts" at Queens Hall – and that, as a review in *The Times* from 1907 noted, had an atmosphere "clouded by other influences besides tobacco smoke" (*The Times*, 1907: 4). There was, too, a Stock Exchange Art Society created for the centenary of the organization, where "the busiest men in the City [could] enjoy the most leisurely of all recreations" (though, as another review in *The Times* of the society's exhibition at Drapers' Hall cautioned, it was "evidently enough the work of amateurs, and of amateurs who cannot spend much time in the pursuit of art" (*The Times*, 1901: 13). The exchange's membership also practiced various sports through its societies, from archery, athletics, and boxing, to rowing, tennis, and wild fowling.[5] Additionally, the exchange maintained a busy schedule of luncheons and civic projects that had both local and national philanthropic aims.

These "technologies" or organizational devices brought the community together around leisure and entertainment – making the house more than merely a site of business (seen under this light, one wonders about the originality of Silicon Valley's all-inclusive offices, with massages, catering, and entertainment on site). There were,

[5] Members of the London Stock Exchange, 1923, *House on Sport*.

however, other more physical technologies that had the same effect. A prominent example was the *Stock Exchange Journal*, a quarterly in-house magazine published between 1955 and 1975 that was widely distributed among the organization's membership. The journal had a very practical orientation: it was a means for tempering and modernizing the stock exchange's public image at a time of relative distress.

That the journal was initially an attempt to address external audiences to garner legitimacy is clear from its very first page. In his foreword to the first issue, C.F. Cobbold, then governor of the Bank of England,[6] welcomed the stock exchange's decision to make "its doings better known to the general public." "Legends die hard," he wrote

> and there are still people who regard the City as a mysterious center on high finance and money-dealing divorced from real life. But these legends are dying and the public are increasingly coming to realize how closely the City is interwoven with everyday commercial and industrial life and what a vital part it plays.
>
> *(Cobbold, 1955)*

For the architects of the exchange's public relations strategy in the 1950s, the *Stock Exchange Journal* was a means for managing expectations, conveying a sense of modernity and "real life" within the organization that foregrounded both the innovations and traditions of British finance.

The journal never became a true instrument of public relations, so its capacity to dismantle legends was precarious to say the least. Rather, the journal performed the work of symbolically constituting an imagined community of finance within the exchange, rooted on the weight of tradition but aware of the challenges of the future. It created, rather than vanished, legends. This logic was certainly apparent in the organization of the magazine. The final section of each

---

[6] Along with the Treasury, the Bank of England was one of the most politically influential institutions in British finance; see Kynaston (1994).

issue, for example, adopted the genre of country club newsletters, devoting space to notices from the numerous cultural and sports societies active at the exchange. At the beginning of every issue, however, a section entitled "House Notes" appeared regularly, offering practical insights on the organization: from the availability of new information services and details about construction work in the house, to news on regulations and the elections of new councilmen.

Between these two extremes – the genres of the country club newsletter and that of the business firm's daily announcements – the *Stock Exchange Journal* engaged in a peculiar combination of business technicalities and lyrical interventions meant to anchor the organization on a clear set of imagined histories and traditions. The journal also contained miscellaneous notes including historical articles dealing with the City of London's Roman origins and the days of the coffee houses in Exchange Alley; reminiscences by past and current housemen that constructed a sense of collective nostalgia; and personal interventions on everyday matters of the house, where poetic license and calculated demonstrations of cultural capital were frequent. As a textual artifact, the journal created belonging by performing three distinct tasks. First, it created a space for presenting finance as a community joined not only through business, but also history and emotion; as Carsten writes of houses, "dislocations in space" and the uncertainty surrounding the fate of the institution were opportunities for evoking "past practice," giving the community a "stable location." Second, the journal articulated the exchange with broader and seemingly "traditional" cultural referents, acting as a medium for the invention of organizational traditions; in this, it connected and reinforced class categories within the exchange – the journal, for instance, once featured swimming pools and faux Tudor houses (also known as "stockbrokers Tudor"), innovations that were coupled to new ways of demonstrating affluence and tradition in twentieth-century British society (Strathern, 1992). And third, by dealing with the business technicalities, it provided members with a practical reference that also detailed possible sources of organizational change;

the journal was a barometer of the organization and its needs – it was more than simply a glossy magazine.

2.3   DISRUPTIVE RELATIONS

So what changed at the London Stock Exchange? And why? The three families of technologies mentioned above – technologies of consociation, honor, and belonging – shaped much of the early history of the exchange by enabling, creating, reproducing, shifting, shaping, and managing the fleeting relations forged during transactions in the marketplace. Membership circumscribed the "groupness" of the community to a selected few; the trading floor structured how relations happened by formatting the space of actions; settlement crystalized the agreements reached in private conversations into public and legally intelligible exchanges; defaulters' notices and guarantee funds reinforced notions of proper behavior; and the exchange's societies and its journal enabled imagined communities to come into being. The market was a Weberian *Vergesellschaftung*, a consociation that "made up society" both within the organization (market technologies co-created the social world they inhabited) and outside of it (through invented traditions and legitimizing strategies, these technologies also mediated the relations with a broader imagery of English elites). Above all, though, the society made up through the technologies of the marketplace was uniquely *familiar*. The stock exchange was an intricate, hierarchical brotherhood, a house where peculiar forms of kinship were forged through the transactions of the floor. This is not to say that the form of kinship created within the community of exchange of the house was a faithful reproduction of some prototypical manifestation of English kinship (Strathern, 1992: 29). As Strathern rightly notes, "[kin] lives are private lives, the home is an intimate place, and every family has its own conventions. Whether or not they are shared with others of like class or religion, or can be claimed for the nation, lives are lived according to specific domestic styles." The exchange and the different technologies that weaved relations within its walls had lives of their own, reflecting both the specificity of the marketplace in its transactional logic and the aspirations, anxieties, and backgrounds of its diverse inhabitants.

In its classed makeup and invented rituals recreating "generic traditions" of Englishness, or the "domestic style" of the early twentieth century, the stock exchange echoed the cultural logic of another key institution of modern Britain: the Edwardian country house. Based on a long lineage spanning to the days of Chaucer, argued T.H.S. Escott in his 1906 *Society in the Country House,* the country house of "the English gentleman" emerged historically "as a center of social or political life [that] fulfilled [the tasks performed] to-day by the newspaper, by the circulating library, or by more exclusive methods of information." It was a place where family and society met and elite politics were forged. Not only was the exchange a familiar site for congregating its reputable membership, but, much like the country house, the organization had long been a clearinghouse for both market transactions and financial information (as noted above, this was one of the main selling points of the trading floor, and an anchor for the legitimacy of the exchange's hermetic membership). And in its concrete materiality described by Gibson, Duguid, Whyte, and so many other early twentieth-century commentators, the house gave its particular style of Englishness "an architectural form" (Strathern, 1992). When the stock exchange indicated in 1956 that it was a "national institution," it was not exaggerating. Their command of the securities markets in Britain certainly put them in this category, but so did their reenactment of the cultural forms that gave elite Englishness its distinctive character, the country house included.

Much like the families inhabiting Edwardian country houses, the stock exchange's kin was, too, the result of tremendous yet largely invisible work (Musson, 2009; Evans, 2011). Technologies of consociation, honor, and belonging required armies of individuals "in service," much in the same way as the rituals of the middle and upper English classes that performed family and class within the household. Change was located here, in the classed and organized division between the spaces where transactions bonded the exchange's

membership, and those where administrative bureaucracies transformed conversations into legal artifacts. The location of the Settling
Room in the basement of the house next to the engines and the power
conduits of the house is almost poetic: the heart of the market was the
floor where action happened, but it was invisibly enveloped by this
necessary yet unsightly infrastructural gut. One cannot but recall
The Gentleman's House: Or, How to Plan English Residences, where
in 1864 Scottish architect Robert Kerr described, in fine detail, the
proper organization of a noble manor: the private spaces of the inhabitants mattered, but so did the layout of kitchens, washhouses, linen-
rooms, bakehouses, wine cellars, fruitstores, servants' bedrooms,
butlers' pantries and housekeepers' rooms among various others that
remained in the backstage of class performance (Kerr, 1864). These
spaces, mostly invisible to the everyday experience of family in the
house, were densely populated. Sìan Evans (2011) estimates that
between 1700 and 1900, about 15 percent of the working population
of England was "in service"; compare this with employment in the City
of London in 1939 when there were an estimated 13,646 workers. Just
the stock exchange's Settling Room employed 726 clerks or 5 percent
of the total city workforce. Clerical workers in London certainly surpassed the national statistic. (Clerks in banks, insurance firms, and
counting houses, as well as the support staff in numerous other financial
institutions, very likely made the number of nonelite workers well
above 15 percent.) Settlement was also, and particularly in the twentieth century, a highly gendered space. Constraints created by the First
and Second World Wars led to a feminization of the Settling Room – as
Michael Pryke observes, by 1961, "the proportion of women office
workers [in the City of London] was actually greater than the average
for England and Wales and even for Central London" (Pryke, 1991;
Thrift, 1996).

This was the location of the disruptive relations that changed
the market and that prepared the stage for the later automation of
British finance. After the Second World War, settlement became a
considerable economic burden for the stock exchange. As British

markets recovered from the hostilities and as institutional investors increased their activity, pressure grew on settlement and the other services offered by the exchange, including the trading floor, which required modernization to accommodate the needs of a membership culturally and mentally transformed by the experience of the war. The technologies of consociation that kept the community together were ripping at the seams; the house required an organizational refitting. Settlement was central to the problem, but views on how and what to change varied tremendously across the membership. Equipped with greater numbers of skilled personnel and deeper pockets, larger broking firms felt they could process their own bargains and opposed subsidizing the costly Settlement Department of the exchange. Less equipped and more vulnerable to the sways of the market, smaller firms could not and required the services of the house. In the end, the Council of the Stock Exchange opted for the welfare of the membership, subsidizing the Settlement Department that was used "largely by the smaller member firms from the fees paid by all" (Michie, 1999: 334).

To limit costs, the exchange implemented a series of laborsaving measures. Up to that point in time, paying for the more than 700 workers of the Settling Room was tremendously expensive yet seemingly unavoidable as matching orders was slow and cumbersome, requiring skills and tacit knowledge that could only be gained through on-the-ground training and practical experience. But settlement was also a very rational and rationalized process: it implied standardized practices of accounting, tallying, and comparing data, some of which could be taken over by computers. To control the spiraling costs associated to rising wages, the exchange acquired a Hollerith punched-card machine in 1949 with the aim of mechanizing its administrative back office.

The initial generation of mechanized calculators was not associated with a fundamental shift in the practices and structures of the stock exchange. Stockbrokers, for instance, soon grew accustomed to the use of "accounting typewriters – machines which combine the calculator and the typewriter, generally operating from one keyboard"

(Day, 1956: 13). Expensive equipment (in 1956 they were estimated to cost up to £1,500, roughly £34,000 in 2016 prices), these machines had an advantage over existing forms of typing because relatively junior staff could prepare a variety of records in one go. Stockjobbers similarly adopted their own punched-card systems through which

> details of bargains are, as in the past, written in the Dealer's Book; calculations of amounts are made in the normal way; names of Companies and Brokers, &c., are translated into a figure code. Thereafter a routine operator with a desk keyboard instrument taps out the various figures and perforates a card; this is checked by passing through another desk instrument ... The cards accumulate up to some desired point in the operations and are then passed to the next operation. From this point onwards the machine takes charge.
>
> (Day, 1956)

So, while operational innovations, this very early phase of mechanization during the 1950s largely blended into the existing structures of the house, fitting into the models and practices of the larger and better-capitalized brokers and jobbers.

Mechanization, however, made imagining a radically different future possible: complex calculations that previously required many staffed hours "can to-day be done electronically" wrote Mark Day in the *Stock Exchange Journal* in 1956,

> and as cogs and cams give place to transisters [*sic*], magnetic cores and vacuum tubes, and electrical impulses become the order of the day, the question of the applicability of the Electronic Computor [*sic*] to the Stock Exchange work is coming up for discussion and quite serious consideration.

Unlike mechanical tabulators, electronic computers allowed dreaming about crucial transformations in the practices of the exchange – they stood as metaphors of a possible future where finance was produced in a very different way. "If only jobbers could be persuaded to report bargains into [a centralized machine] as they were carried out," wrote M. Bennett (1959) in the *Stock Exchange Journal*,

> it would clear all stocks automatically and, not only that, it would give a running record of the dealing prices in every broker's office, reducing the staff required in boxes and order rooms and the House itself ... We might even reduce the costs to such an extent that small orders became profitable and the ideal of the Cloth Cap Investor at last became a reality.

Automation would not only cut costs and increase efficiencies in the back office; fundamentally, it also made the market more legitimate to the public at large, so argued its advocates, allowing for even small, working class investors to trade through the august systems of the stock exchange.

This is what made the first generation of digital computers different: they embodied, at least in the imagination of some members of the organization, the possibility of a profound transformation. The exchange implemented its first computers in the early 1960s, initially with the leasing and installation of an International Computers and Tabulators unit that could handle the automatic clearing of 140 stocks and up to 150,000 bargains in a single account (Abacus, 1962). Following this acquisition, an article in the *Stock Exchange Journal* pondered about the possibility of introducing even more ambitious systems that would comprehensively cover the market's administrative infrastructure. "Some sort of computer installation in the Stock Exchange itself," read the article, "could handle part, if not all, of the accounts and records at present kept in the offices of Members" (Anonymous, 1960). By 1964, the stock exchange purchased an IBM 360 that reduced processing of trades to a tenth of the original 876 person-hours.[7]

---

[7] See Michie (1999); the *Stock Exchange Journal* makes no allusion to this system, and the records of IBM place the first purchase of one of their systems (a Model 158) in 1973 (Grimm, 1977), the adoption of computers within British finance was well under way by the mid-1960s.

In March 1966, the stock exchange officially reported the installation of its first computer – an ICT 1903 – in the Settlement Office at
26 Austin Friars. An intriguing article accompanied the news of this
acquisition. "The bloodless technocrats," wrote Geraldine Keen, "have
found their way into this bastion of civilization. The dustbins of Throgmorton Street will be loaded with quill pens and thousands of lines a
minute will be clacking from the tasteful buff colored peripherals of an
ICT 1903" (Keen, 1966). The realities of the system proved modest.
The first account containing records for 170 stocks was fed into the
ICT 1903 on November 15, 1966, taking a mere 12 minutes to process;

> the computer then took approximately an hour to sort the pieced
> bargains into order for printing and 25 minutes to print out the
> result. Under punched card methods, this work would have taken
> the Department, plus part time staff, approximately 12 hours on an
> Account of this size.
>
> *(Anonymous, 1966)*

While seemingly another incremental innovation, the digital
computers acquired by the exchange brought about disruption in the
community's relations, in how kinship was made in the house and in
the market. The computers themselves, as any other form of technology, were not the disruptors. Change came, rather, from the human
appendages associated to their installation, operation, and maintenance
(Barley, 1986; Barley and Bechky, 1994; Yates, 2005). If computers
disrupted relations it was because they compelled the organization to
expand its membership, transform its kin. Although the exchange
leased most of its computers from vendors, it established small internal
maintenance crews to keep the novel electronic systems in order. But
as technical specialists trained in the operation of computers and
telecommunication systems, these technologists were socially, culturally, and organizationally distant from the gentlemanly brokers and
jobbers that controlled the exchange and its marketplace (Courtney
and Thompson, 1996; Michie, 1999). They were not settlement clerks,
or regular employees "in service" in the house: unlike these skilled yet

largely manual workers, the new technical specialists controlled systems that were esoteric and technically unintelligible to the existing membership. The specialists were also not akin to brokers or jobbers who derived their positions out of the careful cultivation of relationships with the outside world and on the trading floor. They were "invisible" outsiders that, as one confided during interview, were "sort of plebs" (Buck interview)[8] occupying roles far removed from the higher echelons of the organization's hierarchy. But they were, nevertheless, *within* the organization, carefully shaping the systems and devices that made the house's kin; they were the disruptive relatives that changed the fabric of transactions in the exchange and in doing so set in motion the gears for the later automation of finance.

Like the earlier tabulating technologies used for account keeping at the exchange, computers also had a second transformative effect: they created new possibilities for imagining the present and future of the membership and its market. In *The Closed World*, Paul Edwards elegantly shows how the first generations of digital electronic computers in the mid-twentieth century were both instruments and metaphors for the politics of command and control of the Cold War. The same can be said of computers in finance: as they meshed into the infrastructures of the organization by populating the Settlement Department, they effected an "imaginative reconstruction" of the marketplace, the membership, and its invented traditions. Computers fundamentally questioned the market relation and, consequently, the webs of moral responsibilities that constituted the kin of the house. Change came not through processing power, but through the imaginative potential of computers as symbols of how relations could be rekindled through the careful mechanisms of the machine.

2.4   CONCLUSIONS

As a quintessential capitalist field, finance is not often thought of in kindred terms. Money, competition, and pecuniary interests seem

---

[8] Interview with Peter Buck; Interview with Peter Bennett.

antithetical to the household, to the spaces of kinship and siblinghood where affectivity, memories, and relations are mortars of the social world (Zelizer, 2009). Yet if markets are consociations, as Weber suggests, they must also be communities, spaces where relations are forged in transactional chains where agents are never really quits. And if spaces of community, the structure and operation of marketplaces render anthropological metaphors of kinship and familiarity relevant instruments for thinking about the devices that configure and constitute the communities of finance. From membership and trading floors to settlement and internal magazines, the infrastructures of kinship of markets are multiple, making up a world where transactions are stable, knowable, and sensible.

Thinking about these devices calls for considering markets in their historical contexts. Infrastructures of kinship exist in relation to particular places and moments, and studying their transformation offers a partial answer to the question of what changes with the automation of finance. Yet as "relational properties," a discussion of infrastructural change conjures the anthropological concept of the relation itself: like infrastructures, the relation is a product of work and knowledge produced in the act of making community, of locating similarity and difference, of tracing some connections while erasing (or ignoring) others. Automation is, hence, not a story of self-governing technology run amok, but of how knowledge and technologies were refashioned in everyday practice, linking buyers and sellers through novel mechanisms. As I explore in the next chapter, and not unlike the controversies surrounding reproductive technologies that percolated the reinvention of kinship in late twentieth-century Western societies (Franklin and McKinnon, 2001), the forms of knowledge and work reconstituting relations at the exchange were largely imperceptible to the transactional core of the marketplace, to its relevant and symbolically powerful community of exchange. If anything, relations were refashioned through the power of invisibility and the taken-for-grantedness of technological infrastructures. Just as genetic and reproductive technologies produced at the edges of the public sight were imbricated in the transformation of kinship in the late twentieth century, infrastructural changes imperceptible to the marketplace transformed what it means to "make markets" today. This story, which foregrounds lowly engineers rather than honorable members, is the one I now turn to in Chapter 3.

3   The Power of Invisibility

For a long time, finance in London was explicitly a matter of thick and sticky social relations. Consider the London Stock Exchange, historically the preeminent site for trading stocks and bonds in Britain. While a marketplace and national institution, the walls of its building also contained a tight-knit brotherhood that through rituals, technologies, and practices of different sorts created and articulated the transactions of the market. Even as late as 1971, the *Stock Exchange Official Yearbook* contained a preface that would now seem anachronistic, almost politically inadequate. "[The] best way for a member of the public to get into touch with a Broker," read the introductory notice to "the would-be investor," "is by personal introduction" (Stock Exchange, 1970). As Whyte suggested almost half a century earlier, British finance may well have been an activity where material resources were scarce and few; but it was simultaneously a sphere where connections and community were notably dense and practically important (Whyte, 1924).

If finance was so culturally thick, if it constituted such a strong form of life, binding transactions to the social and organizational positions of stock exchange members, we can ask: what compelled market automation? As organizations traditionally owned by their user-members, the adoption of automated market devices in stock exchanges challenged the interests of an important and powerful category of market actors: in particular, it questioned the need for market makers who, like London's jobbers and New York's specialists, stood at the center of exchange and made their livelihoods from this privileged structural position. Why did markets change against the cultural and economic interests of their controlling members?

The most common answer to this question is that the potentially large impacts of information technologies on productivity were obvious incentives for exchanges to adopt systems that, with time, substituted the brokers on the floor and the jobbers in their pitches with algorithms and automated execution systems. Financial economists, for instance, understand automation and broader forms of financial innovation as the result of strategies that sought to grow profits within the increasingly competitive environments of twentieth-century capital markets. By reducing operational costs in mechanical tasks such as order matching, information dissemination, and settlement, automation allowed financial intermediaries to expand their market share – or, at the very least, to control the impacts of competition on their everyday activities (see Lee, 1998).

Subordinating technical change to the rational imperatives of market signals, this reading of history ignores the interests, cultures, and institutional tensions vested within the relations of finance. If markets were communities that created their social worlds, if stock exchanges were effectively spaces where society was "made up" around transactions, then change implied so much more than merely a shift in their technologies of production. The illusion of the rational manager, conscientiously selecting one among a variety of competing technologies to best operate in a global financial marketplace, simply fails to capture the weight of these everyday social and organizational ties. What led to this transformation? What motivated exchanges in general, and the London Stock Exchange in particular, to unravel and reknit their kin through the technologies of digital finance?

In this chapter, I explore the roots of financial automation by looking at how digital technologies were introduced to the London Stock Exchange. The history of market automation that I tell in the following pages is necessarily organizational: it deals with how struggles around technology, expertise, and market imaginaries shaped the trajectories of financial automation in Britain – processes that, to some degree, were echoed elsewhere. If technologies are not socially neutral, they are certainly not neutral within organizations where they participate in and shape contests over knowledge, competencies, control, legitimacy, jurisdictions, and procedures. The type of technologies I examine here are peculiar, though. For a broker or jobber standing on the trading floor in the 1970s, these devices operated silently and in the background, constituting part of the taken-for-granted expectancies that embedded the routines of the marketplace. As infrastructures of market action, these technologies were organizationally "invisible." Such invisibility carried over to their makers and maintainers: much like the unnamed people who lived "in service" keeping class and customs in the country houses of Edwardian England, the market technologists that designed, tweaked, tinkered with, and expanded the exchange's infrastructures were largely invisible within the house for most of their organization's history. The account that I now provide examines how these unsuspecting actors, these unseen market engineers, grew in the stock exchange to eventually *capture* British finance. This chapter is, in this very concrete sense, a tale about the power of being invisible.

3.1   OF MARKETS AS FIRMS

The story of capture that I explore in this chapter rests upon an important if neglected feature of markets. In our prevailing imaginary and theoretical sensibilities, markets are often distinguished from hierarchies: following a tradition that ostensibly traces back to Max Weber's seminal work on the development of capitalist economies and the rise of modern bureaucracies, markets are conceived as calculative, transactional, and egalitarian systems of exchange while hierarchies are considered administrative, asymmetric parcels of authority and direct control (Coase, 1937; Williamson, 1981, 1983). Markets and hierarchies are like water and oil; they seemingly do not mix. The previous chapter suggests a different way of thinking in which modern markets do not need to be placed in opposition to charismatic, traditional, or bureaucratic structures but as results of specific infrastructures that make exchange possible. Markets are surfaces to the deeper ecologies of their underlying institutions.

organization's formal structures, can also transform the meaningful frames that shape the broader field. From these positions, they can redefine the organization's market strategy or its developmental road-map. But they can also create systems that, for all practical and formal purposes, transform the socially knotty deals experienced on the trading floor into discrete technical processes that reside in a machine.

Because it involves ongoing contests over practices and mean-ing, capture also entails patently moral struggles about the organization and its embedding field. Captured market organizations, in particular, can be tense and unstable: if a divergence in values existed between the incumbent organizational core and the emerging cadres of infrastruc-tural agents (if, for instance, incoming technologists held different views than extant administrators on how best to manage an exchange), frictions may lead to institutional challenges about what is worthy and meaningful for the market organization (such notions may reflect, for example, diverging versions of what Neil Fligstein, 1996, calls concep-tions of control, or of the type of repertoires of justification identified by Luc Boltanski and Laurent Thévenot, 2006). The morality of market infrastructures and their importance in organizational change are exposed in these organizational challenges. Actors do not simply assemble rational arguments in capturing the organizational field but also engage in concrete and meaningful forms of what Mustafa Emir-bayer (1997) calls "position taking" that are meant to signal the moral qualities of other possible institutional alternatives. So while the moral order of the trading floor may be palatable for the market organization's transactional core, the exchange's infrastructural workers may hold a very different view (or they may not, as happened with the New York Stock Exchange, explored in Chapter 7). Change inevitably confronts the moral dissonance underlying the organization's tense constitution.

3.2   PRICES ON A SCREEN

How did the London Stock Exchange move from the floor to the screen? How did it unravel its kin? How did market engineers capture its organizational hierarchy?

The previous chapter closed with a brief note on the stock exchange's "household" and its initial phase of automation. At the exchange, automation began in the basement where the organization installed the first generation of tabulating machines initially, and computers subsequently, to aid the settlement of growing volumes of trades going through the floor. Although requiring skilled labor, settlement was ripe for mechanization: it involved tallying transactions, elaborating lists, and adding up accounts – the type of tasks that machines could carry out with relative ease.

Buying into the era of office mechanization required an expansion of the household, hiring specialists who installed, repaired, and adapted the new electronic systems at the exchange. These were not part of the gentlemanly crowd of the membership. They were, rather, organizationally and culturally distant from the trading floor and its community. They resembled, perhaps in more than a metaphorical sense, the staff "in service" within the Edwardian country house. As Richard Atkins, a veteran worker of the exchange recalled, "[in] those days if a committee told you to do something, you did it, because employees of the Exchange had no powers at all. Really, it was a master–servant relationship." The exchange clearly reminded its staff of their relative position through both formal structures and occasional rituals. Talking about an annual Christmas party organized by the exchange for its staff sometime in the 1970s, one of the firm's key technologists, John Scannell, evoked a particularly representative episode:

> [For these Christmas parties, the exchange] would get caterers, and they would lay out all the tables with … your gin and tonic and your beers … and it always ended up in a complete mess because [people] went in at six, [and] had to be off at seven, [so] everyone just drank as much as he possibly could in an hour, so by 7 o'clock, people were crawling out … At the time … back in the very early days … the Chairman at the time, he was a very nice guy, actually … very nice guy, actually very down to earth. [But] he was

obviously in a different class, but he had a flat on whatever it was, the 25th floor [of the exchange's building] or whatever, and in that flat he had a stainless steel … cooker that would fit into a unit. Right? And as a gift to the staff, we were all given a sort of raffle ticket, and the raffle was this stainless steel [cooker, because] he had a new one fitted in recently. So somebody … had sort of got the unfortunate luck of getting the ticket. "Oh its someone from the Property Management [department]! So-and-so from the property management has won the Chairman's old stainless steel cooker from his flat." They wheeled it out on a trolley this … old beaten up stainless steel cooker, and the Chairman came up and said "Thank you very much, its very nice of you to donate that." Next day, down in the basement, [there] was the bloody old cooker [in the skips]. It was, you know, the concept that those people have probably never seen a stainless steel cooker before. What a wonderful thing … it was a big social divide.

These recruits, however, were also unlike the established armies of workers in the house – settlement clerks and administrators possessed tacit, experiential knowledge of the bureaucracies of the marketplace, but the recently in-house market engineers had esoteric knowledge about the newfangled technologies of the exchange. There was, indeed, a distinct impression among some of the stock exchange's early technical recruits that they had joined a technologically underdeveloped, hierarchically steep organization. This is perhaps best represented by the recollections of Peter Bennett, an electronic and electrical engineer trained at City University, London, hired by the stock exchange in 1971 and who eventually became one of its most prominent managers. For Bennett, the organization

knew nothing about computers, and to cut a long story short, they spent a lot of money on this machine [the ICT], and conveyor belts and stuff like that. [It was as if it were designed] by someone who'd worked at Ford Dagenham because their idea of automation was to shift the paper from one end of the building to the other one on a

FIGURE 3.1 London Stock Exchange, Throgmorton Street – The Trading Floor, c. 1960, Mary Evans/Grenville Collins Postcard Collection.

conveyor belt. [All] this mainframe ... did was ... sort of very basic process control.[1]

Bennett's memories are clearly tinted by poetic license.[2] The stock exchange was most certainly not like Ford Motors' assembly line in Dagenham (Figure 3.1). The computers bought to mechanize the back-office might have been underemployed, but not as dramatically as Bennett suggests. Evidence from both the stock exchange's internal documents and reports in the *Stock Exchange Journal* show awareness of computing as an important asset for the organization. Admittedly, the focus was primarily on settlement rather than trading. What mattered for the organization was its middleware, that is, the devices, people, and standards that connected the front and

---

[1] Bennett interview

[2] For example, when I first presented my findings to the former exchange technologists, a small discussion ensued through email. For some, Bennett's recollections were slightly skewed. One of his former colleagues, in particular, noted that Bennett had "done a good job of self promotion."

back offices, trading and settlement, and that were deemed cumber-some, laborious, and inefficient. There is no evidence that the exchange ever considered mechanizing trading prior to the 1980s. That activity was simply too culturally charged, too politically sensi-tive. As Geraldine Keen reported in the *Stock Exchange Journal*, the ICT was a valuable yet limited addition. Initially slated for improve-ments in settlement, the system could be extended, in a piecemeal fashion, to interfirm accounting. To use the ICT 1903 in any larger application would certainly be "wasteful and inefficient" (Keen, 1966).

One project at the exchange was unique and became the surprising outlier that Bennett would colonize to build an empire. When Bennett and his cohort arrived in the early 1970s, the stock exchange was already busy developing what became a critical device for the organization and its marketplace: an online price visualization system designed to allow market participants in the vicinities of the exchange to get a better sense of the prevailing prices on the trading floor without leaving their offices.[3] Developed by Ferranti's Informa-tion Equipment Group in 1968, the Market Price Display Service (MPDS) was a response by the stock exchange to the proliferation of ad hoc technologies set up by brokers and jobbers to remotely access the floor. In addition to the telephones that had populated the fringes of the trading floor since the late nineteenth century, the *Stock Exchange Journal* reported that as early as 1957 some broking firms deployed basic video networks to relay quote and price information from the pitches of jobbers to their offices a few buildings away from Throgmorton Street. Figure 3.2 shows the nature of these thoroughly unsophisticated setups: clerks would collect quotes from jobbers in the house to write them down on whiteboards; a video camera would then transmit images of the board to neighboring buildings. Video

---

[3] The system operated as, what Karin Knorr Cetina (2003) calls, a "scope," that is, a mechanism that allows actors to visualize an otherwise difficult to observe market. At the time, the only way of observing the market in its entirety was the daily list of prices reported in the *Financial Times*. The system was supposed to provide a slightly more updated, real-time version of this list.

FIGURE 3.2 Early price dissemination system at the London Stock Exchange, c. 1955. From the Stock Exchange Journal.

technology at the time was grainy and unreliable so the images received in the offices of member firms were often illegible and of an inconsistent quality. More importantly, these makeshift services competed with the stock exchange's official price collection protocols and their associated income streams (the exchange charged newspapers and data providers like the Exchange Telegraph Company, Extel, for the right to report market prices over which they held intellectual property rights; in English law, printed prices were protected by copyright since at least 1896 [TLH, 1917]).

Ferranti provided an elegant solution by combining televisions, computers, and coaxial distribution networks within the City of London through a technology known as Digi-TV that, as the *Financial Times*'s Ted Schoeters explained in 1970, "translates digital information [submitted through] price keyboards on the floor of the Exchange into television signals corresponding to the shapes of the figures and letters being typed out on these keyboards." Based on a Ferranti *Argus 400* originally built in 1958 to operate the Bloodhound Missile MkII, MPDS was designed to display the "current middle prices of approximately 650 [standard] stocks on ... 16 main channels" (Schoeters, 1970). Following the custom on the trading floor, the system also showed the closing price from the previous trading session and up to five changes in the mid-price for the most active stocks. MPDS had an additional six channels that displayed prices for feature stocks (2), news (2), and spare transmissions (2). Rather than walking to or calling the trading floor, brokers could simply turn the dial on their customized television sets to switch between these channels and get a better sense of the market. Even the spare channels proved useful: when conditions were calm, brokers could tune into cricket matches during the trading day – a feature of the system that seems to have garnered appeal among the City of London's gentlemanly brokers.[4] Above all, MPDS was a device of convenience. The system was not meant to change the mechanics of trading or expand the membership of the organization.

The development of the MPDS was associated with a profound, though relatively imperceptible, organizational transformation: it standardized price reporting mechanisms in the exchange, the first step in making the practices on the trading floor compatible with the logical structure of computers and telecommunication networks.[5] The system required, for instance, creating the role of green-buttoned price collectors who were responsible for obtaining quotes from jobbers (Anonymous, 1969). Like jobbers, green buttons specialized in particular industrial sectors to make their paths through the normally bustling and noisy trading floor more efficient. Collecting prices required concrete physical and interpersonal abilities: in addition to walking several miles throughout the day, they had to

---

[4] Bennett interview

[5] We can think of this organizational innovation as the invention of an algorithm that determined how prices were to be collected and disseminated away from the trading floor. As a recipe or procedure, this algorithm was distributed in the roles and attributions of jobbers, price collectors, and the architecture of MPDS itself. This is important to remember: all algorithms are distributed organizational devices and, for the London Stock Exchange, MPDS required an algorithmic transformation that made the marketplace a little bit more rationalized, a bit more computational, a little bit more like a machine.

FIGURE 3.3 Alan Bussey and project manager Sylvia Briggs, testing the MPDS. Photo from the Stock Exchange Journal (1971). Courtesy of London Stock Exchange.

get along with the jobbers – and as one of my informants, Ian McLelland recalled, this happened rapidly following the introduction of MPDS in 1970 when jobbers on the floor developed "pretty good" relationships with price collectors to the extent that "they'd walk to them and almost as they were walking up they would quote them a price."[6] In each round of data collection, green buttons registered the quotes from jobbers on slips of paper containing the names of 18 to 24 shares. These slips were then taken to the edge of the trading floor where they were manually entered into one of the eight terminals consisting of a keyboard attached to a 12-inch monochrome Prowest monitor (see Figure 3.3). These terminals linked to the Argus 400, which compiled and processed the data to store it on a magnetic drum.

[6] McLelland interview.

The data on this drum was converted into a multichannel television signal that was distributed to the screens of the MPDS. Normally taking between ten to fifteen minutes, this cycle was repeated throughout the day making the prices on the MPDS "as fresh as possible."[7] A series of safeguards guaranteed the accuracy of the information. When a collector entered data into the system, the terminals displayed the new price underneath the old one. When he was sure that the new quote was correct, the collector pressed a switch that updated the information in the Argus 400, broadcasting the price throughout the MPDS. But if the change with respect to the previous price was too small or too great, the system required the collector to provide an additional confirmation (Anonymous, 1970a).

The MPDS was quite probably "one of the first stock exchange display systems anywhere in the world"[8] and one of the "first cable networks" in Britain.[9] It was also a great commercial success. Upon its introduction in 1970, nearly 1,000 MPDS television receivers were operating in 220 offices of member firms, the result of 70,000 hours of work by 250 external engineers (Anonymous, 1970b). In October of the same year, the service reached 145 member firms and 22 institutions, including press agencies, insurance companies, an arbitrage house, and merchant banks, who were reportedly "very satisfied" with its operation (Anonymous, 1970c). For the firms, the system provided important administrative advantages. By relieving their blue buttons from the work of getting prices, the MPDS left them "free to gather more specialized information (see Figure 3.4). The new system has not rendered the old one obsolete but it has enabled it to be put to better use" (Anonymous, 1970a). In little more than a year, wrote Margaret Hughes in the *Stock Exchange Journal*, "the City's brokers [had become] a group of push button devotees" (Hughes, 1971). And while the MPDS did not alter how trading occurred on the floor, it was

---

[7] McLelland interview.   [8] Bennett interview.
[9] McLelland, personal communication.

OIL							
BP	82/6	1/3, 6, 2/-	BP	P	$412\frac{1}{2}$	$6^1, 7\frac{1}{2}, 10$	
BMAH	61/6	3, 6,	BMAH	P	$307\frac{1}{2}$	$5, 6^1, 7\frac{1}{2}$	
ROYD	23.E7	E4, S7	ROYD		23.S14	S8, S7	
SHEL	79/-	8/9, 9/-, 3.	SHEL	P	395	$3^3, 5, 6^1$	

SHIPPING							
BCOM	43/-		BCOM	P	215		
CLDN	39/-		CLDN	P	195		
CNRD	29/-	4,	CNRD	P	145		
CORT	34/-	3/9	CORT	P	170	68^3	
FRNW	65/3		FRNW	P	326^1		
P.O.	45/-		P.O.	P	$145\frac{1}{2}$	$6^1, 5, 6^1$	
RDNS	17/9	18/3, --,	RDNS	P	88^3	$91^1, 90$	

RUBBER							
AIP	$5/7\frac{1}{2}$	9	AIP	P	28	3	
GHOP	$6/1\frac{1}{2}$		GHOP	P	30^1		
GUTH	$29/7\frac{1}{2}$	$6, 4\frac{1}{2}, 3,$	GUTH	P	148	$7\frac{1}{2}, 7, 6^1$	
HIGH	$4/6^3$		HIGH	P	22^3		
LAS	5/93		LAS	P	29		

FIGURE 3.4 A typical screen of the MPDS, displaying the best quotes for oil, shipping, and rubber companies.

a financial bounty for the exchange. The system became an important and sustainable source of revenue for the organization (every subscription to the service represented an annual income of £500 from members and £1,000 from nonmembers; at a setup cost of £85,000, the system was amortized within a couple of years).

The success of the MPDS raised a critical strategic issue for the exchange: owing to its financial and practical significance, noted the former market engineer Tony Carey, "maintenance and development [of MPDS] was handled by in-house engineers" (Figure 3.5).[10] At the time of the MPDS's introduction, the exchange already had a small group of technical specialists in its ranks. The project leader in charge of the installation of the Ferranti computer system, for instance, was Sylvia Briggs (whom the *Financial Times* initially misidentified as an

[10] Carey, Personal Communication.

FIGURE 3.5 Tony Carey in front of an MPDS maintenance van. Photo courtesy of John Scannell.

operator, only to then correct itself with a perfunctory note a few weeks later).[11] And in addition to Briggs, there were at least a dozen other technologists working in the organization.[12] These numbers, however, were soon to grow. The MPDS was a turning point in the

---

[11] There is something deeply symbolic about the *Financial Times*'s misattribution of Sylvia Briggs (who I was unable to reach for an interview): while market engineers were relatively invisible, women were particularly ignored. When I asked some of my respondents about Briggs, none remembered her. Similarly, although women worked in developing systems within the exchange, their identities are largely forgotten in both the oral histories that I have collected and the published stories and narratives of the exchange. As this "double invisibility" shows, hierarchies also mattered in the world of infrastructural work.

[12] In his note, Carey recalled other members of his group, including Ray Holliday, John Lloyd, Roger Thompson Terry Casey, and Douglas Sellars. Unfortunately, I was unable to locate these former stock exchange workers.

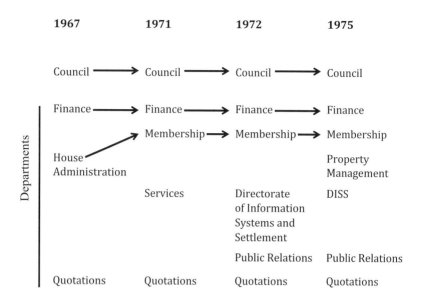

FIGURE 3.6 Changes in the organizational structure of the London Stock Exchange, 1967–1975. Compiled from The Stock Exchange Yearbook, 1967, 1971, 1972, 1975.

exchange's administrative structure (Figure 3.6). Prior to 1971, the exchange was managed through three departments ("Finance," "House Administration," and "Quotations"); but as systems expanded and diversified, the exchange's evolving structure was rationalized to reflect the spaces created by the adoption of new technologies. By the end of the decade, the organization was managed through at least ten distinct administrative units. What technologists from Peter Bennett's generation encountered at the stock exchange in the early 1970s was a distinct space of opportunities within an expanding bureaucracy. The organizational middleware was growing, breaking, and multiplying into multiple subunits and subprojects, slowly but surely colonizing the exchange's traditional hierarchies. The stock exchange itself provided kindling for such expansion: although a culturally conservative and somewhat obdurate organization, the exchange invested in expensive computer technology that provided it members with further conveniences and its coffers with cash, creating niches where innovative projects could develop outside of any rigid institutional roadmap. As long as the numbers made sense, there was plenty of room for growth.

3.3   WEAVING TRANSACTIONS

The MPDS was not the only computer-based project at the exchange at the time, but formed part of a longer although disjointed trajectory of systems that traced their origins to the 1950s when the marketplace took the first concrete steps to automate the costly process of settling and clearing trades. Peter Bennett did not join the exchange to automate trading or price dissemination (areas where, a decade later, he played a central role) – rather, he joined to work on the invisible yet critical gears of the back-office.

The project that Bennett was recruited into in 1971 was the relatively ambitious automation of so-called bargain accounting across member firms through the stock exchange's centralized computer systems. A part of settlement and clearing, bargain accounting involved the laborious work of checking whether both sides of the deals struck on the floor matched across brokers and jobbers. Within a settlement period, the number of stocks bought and sold should be the same (certainly, one can only expect all sold shares to have been bought by someone), and within the market it should be possible to trace, at least in theory, which dealer dealt with whom. This was not a straightforward process. At the time, there was no centralized depository of share certificates, so a single transaction on one end (e.g., sell 1,000 shares of British Petroleum) could have multiple transactions at the other, all conducted at different prices and through different combinations of brokers and jobbers. The process of tallying and matching bargains required a meticulous reconstruction of the deals on the floor that, while largely mechanized by the late 1960s, still required much manual intervention and was ridden with errors. Recalling these systems, Richard Atkins described this so-called bargain accounting as "a bunch of women [clerks]" who collected the tickets of the trading day from metal cages on the floor to then enter the information into a computer in the settlement department; a picture that is far from the sterile imaginary of full automation.

As happened with the MPDS, the production of an automated system for bargain accounting and settlement required an organizational expansion of the exchange, attracting specialists who possessed both proven technical expertise and established managerial experience. Sir Michael Jenkins was a prominent example on both counts. Trained at the University of Oxford, Jenkins started his professional life in the marketing arm of Shell/British Petroleum, where he worked for five years to then realize that he wanted a different career. Not knowing what to do, Jenkins sought advice and was told to get into computing. "Go to IBM," he heard from an acquaintance, "because they train you best. And IBM was looking for anyone with two feet at that point, because they were expanding so fast."[13] There, Jenkins worked on airlines, soon progressing to project manager for the development of the British Overseas Airways Corporation's first electronic seat reservations system. After leaving IBM, he joined a management consultancy set up by a former IBM colleague, where he had numerous clients in London, doing "lots of work for Lloyds and then for the Stock Exchange." The exchange asked Jenkins to evaluate one of their first computer projects in settlement. The project was a mess, recalled Jenkins, and he advised the exchange to write off the very costly investment. He also recommended to the stock exchange to recruit a technical director, which they did dutifully "in a typical City solution" by offering Jenkins the job in 1971.

Jenkins's arrival was revolutionary and epitomized the cultural rift and organizational struggles between the exchange's (invisible) technologists and the incumbent brokers and jobbers of the marketplace. Supported by Michael Bennett, a member of the jobbing firm Wedd Dunlechye seconded to the exchange to oversee its computer operations, Jenkins "created an administrative structure that was

---

[13] Jenkins interview.

partly outside the Stock Exchange" to manage the organization's expanding technological infrastructures.

> We [and one or two others] basically said, "This is the structure you've got to have," and we virtually put a pistol at their heads, and said, "If you want us to do this job, this is the structure you've got to have," which put a lot of noses out of joint, because the Stock Exchange wasn't used to that sort of thing. But it made sense, at least I think it did, but anyway, they, they bought the idea. So we created the thing, we had a very awful title, called "The Director of Information Systems for Settlement" [DISS]. Michael Bennett was Managing Director, and I was Technical Director. And we ... recruited ... a very sort of competent, high-powered team, which caused quite a lot of problems in the Stock Exchange, because we basically said, "Well, we're going to do things this way. Never mind how you've done it in the past."[14]

DISS "operated rather abnormally for the Stock Exchange," noted Jenkins in an interview. Although superior in its technical composition, it was clearly foreign to the organization's established identity. The rift between DISS and the membership was not only predicated on expertise; it was also heavily classed. "We used to have a [work] lunch every two weeks which was held on the sacred 17th floor of the Stock Exchange [tower] which is normally only allowed for members," said Jenkins. Working during lunch was in itself a cultural oddity for most brokers and jobbers. But what shocked was the very presence of staff in such a "special" place: during one of these lunches, and as he used the lavatories on the 17th floor, a member standing next to him said "I'm not sure I appreciate the staff sharing the members' loo." "There was a big ... difference between the organization we created," said Jenkins, "and the existing organization of the Stock Exchange, which was very much master/servant."

---

[14] Sir Michael Jenkins, interview with Peter Spira, British Library, City Lives Oral Histories Collection C409/046/F2844-A/

This social and cultural detachment provided autonomy for market technologists. Under Jenkins's command, DISS designed a vastly ambitious new settlement system for the marketplace.[15] The Transfer Accounting and Lodgement for Investors, Stock MANagement for jobbers, (TALISMAN) "immobilized" shares making the use of tickets to settle bargains unnecessary, hence reducing the paperwork associated to matching deals, clearing securities, and updating company registers. The complete elimination of paper tickets was too ambitious. It required, for instance, passing new legislation that facilitated the transfer of shares without the physical exchange of their paper certificates (this did happen, but only some years later when the exchange introduced a fuller version of TALISMAN). To deal with the increased strain on settlement services, DISS developed an intermediate system based on the existing methods of bargain accounting from the settlement department: introduced in 1975 after much work, CHARM, or CHecking, Accounting and Reporting for Member Firms, was the first of a series of systems that transformed how deals were settled at the exchange, and how, as argued in the previous chapter, the transactional relations created in the market were tied together through the administrative logic of mechanized matching. As former jobber Les Turtle recalled, the system

> didn't do away with tickets but it centralized the calculation of what we called the "trace," in other words who the buyer's ticket went to and he knew who it went to and records were sent and passed to the buyer, and it also produced the ledger accounts and the ledger differences which were settled with the center. So it was

---

[15] As both Jenkins and the documentary sources suggest, the basic design of the system was inspired by a report published in 1970 by a City Working Party on Securities Handling. Essentially, the report advocated centralizing settlement and clearing by pooling shares to then "dematerialize" trading – substituting paper certificates with digital entries on a computer. This process was carried out quite successfully in the United States with the creation of the National Securities Clearing Corporation.

really the first big and significant step in the context of centralized accounting systems.[16]

And while not a radical technical innovation, CHARM's development was a crucial moment for the exchange: unlike the MPDS, which had important input from Ferranti, CHARM was built internally by a relatively autonomous, creative, and increasingly cohesive organizational unit that mirrored the distinct expertise, interests, and struggles of the marketplace.

CHARM was also unique because it introduced a new paradigm of data communications to British finance. CHARM consisted of two main elements. The trade magazine *DataSystems* described the first, a checking system, as superseding "the traditional method of checking bargains whereby Brokers and Jobbers, having dealt on the Floor of The Stock Exchange, prepared lists of bargains to be checked manually the next day at Blossoms Inn"

> [E]very day about 300 staff went down to the Checking Room and called over the bargains dealt the previous day. In many ways the Checking room was like a second trading floor – on average 20% of the bargains did not match exactly and staff had to agree changes on the spot ... Many alterations ... are made in the Checking Room but there is a small residue of bargains that cannot be agreed on the spot. These have more serious errors and must be referred back to the dealers and then checked over the phone ... A checked bargain is the starting point for the settlement process and to ensure accuracy the Council decided that this matching of bargains should be done by computer.
>
> *(Anonymous, 1974)*

Rather than centralizing data entry in a checking room, CHARM allowed each firm to report details of trades directly into a central computer. Larger firms that operated computerized management systems of their own could enter the information by sending

---

[16] Les Turtle, interview by Bernard Attard.

their magnetic tapes and punch cards directly to the Stock Exchange Computer Center on Wilson Street. With this, demand for expensive and laborious central services was much reduced with notable improvements in accuracy.

In small firms where investments in computers were prohibitive, CHARM's networked architecture made it a particularly attractive solution. For these firms, Peter Bennett developed the equivalent of a remote banking terminal that, installed in their offices and connected directly to the stock exchange's dedicated IBM 370/145, allowed submitting details of bargains to the processing architecture of CHARM. The selection of this design and of the makeup of the terminals became an unsuspecting point of entry for other prominent market engineers to the organization. At the time of CHARM's production, the well-known manufacturer of typewriters Olivetti was expanding into the market for terminals and minicomputers, both of which were being adopted within banking and finance. Olivetti, for instance, was involved in the installation of an electronic check clearing mechanism at Barclay's bank where, like settlement at the exchange, dealing with customers' checks proved a laborious activity.

> If you wrote a check, it would go to the banking office and a girl would key in the details into a machine which would punch a card and that would be loaded on the IBM system, because that's all they had in those days.[17]

The introduction of magnetic ink character recognition in United States banking during the mid-1960s made possible automating most of these processes. For example, in the United Kingdom, the Inter-Bank Computer Bureau that represented the interests of several commercial banks implemented the E13B character recognition standard in 1970.[18]

---

[17] Scannell interview.
[18] Inter-Bank Computer Bureau, Bank of England Archives, C156/1.

Like bargain accounting, automated check clearing was not entirely fault-proof. There would always be checks on which the E13B number was damaged to the point of making it illegible to the machines, thus requiring "about 40 girls who were in an office with these punching machines taking the checks that wouldn't go into the scanner, keying it all in into the punch card, [and] loading the punch card into the IBM. Horrendous process."[19] To reduce errors, Olivetti's engineers implemented an error-checking system that used minicomputers. Developed in 1971 for Barclay's Clearing Department, the system connected banking terminals to minicomputers that verified the quality of the data entered into the system, corrected common input mistakes, and formatted the information into its correct electronic form.

Olivetti's solution eventually reached the London Stock Exchange, which saw the Olivetti TE 339 terminal as a particularly attractive solution for the remote data input architecture of CHARM. John Scannell (b. 1944), who joined Olivetti in 1964 as a field engineer and was a section manager by 1970,

> ended up doing a presentation to Peter [Bennett] and a few people of the Stock Exchange when I was working [for] Olivetti to [explain] how we would support [the terminals], because I was running the support operation for it, and I immediately got on quite well with Peter.[20]

The presentation was quite effective: the exchange bought 150 terminals from Olivetti. And when Olivetti closed its branch in the City of London, Scannell sought refuge at the stock exchange. "Within a couple of weeks I ended up working for Peter ... because they'd bought the Olivetti banking terminals."[21]

3.4 REAL-TIME COMMUNICATIONS

CHARM worked reasonably well, though as Jenkins recalled, the project might have not "justified the cost except that from the Stock Exchange point of view you had to get the members thinking about

---

[19] Scannell interview.   [20] Scannell interview.   [21] Scannell interview.

technology, which most of them didn't."[22] It was an opportunity to reorganize the marketplace by foregrounding technology as integral to the work of the organization. Indeed, the success of the system fostered confidence in the work of the emerging corps of stock exchange technologists. As Bennett recalled with some delight, in the eyes of the membership, technologists could "do no wrong. I mean, they gave [our group] more or less a carte blanche to automate everything inside."[23]

In addition to signaling the generic importance of technology in finance, CHARM was a normative opportunity for defining the contours of the market devices that *ought* to be built in the not-too-distant future. As an internal exercise that required the focus and discipline of stock exchange technologists, the project catalyzed an important feature of the engineering cultures of organization that came to shape future encounters with market-facing technologies. Specifically, in designing the architecture of remote data entry mechanisms for CHARM, Bennett and his colleagues stressed with increasing frequency the principles of real-time data processing and systems programming, where design involved creating devices and networks from scratch, in opposition to the existing culture of applications programming that involved developing software for ready-made solutions installed by third-party vendors. As Ian McLelland, one of Bennett's colleagues noted,

> We had to write our own drivers, so you had a programmer who was basically writing a device driver, so he had to know how a device worked, [and would have to] work more closely with engineers. It wasn't like doing a client's requirement [and] saying "well, you know, this is the function that I want," [and] writing it. It was actually getting that in and making that work with, say, our database. So to call [us] application programmers wasn't quite right.

The origins of this cultural divide are visible in the approach taken by Bennett's team to the problem of validating bargains in

---

[22] Jenkins interview.   [23] Bennett interview.

CHARM. Before passing information to the IBM 370/145 for processing, bargains had to be filtered and checked to detect human input
errors. To expedite the process, Bennett's team decided to use an
implementation of minicomputers, and although Olivetti offered a
version of these, they chose "a [PDP-11/40 from Digital Equipment
Corporation] minicomputer instead because . . . they wanted to write
the application on that themselves."[24] This preference for systems
that could be hacked into specific shapes and functions configured the
organization's trajectories and technological affinities: for Bennett's
team, for instance, IBM's computers were "too hierarchical" in comparison to the more "flexible" alternatives of Digital Equipment
Corporation.[25] This division was, of course, not unquestioned. "Why
not go for a real-time settlement?," wondered Bennett about this
feature of the exchange at the time.

> You know, why go through this stupid batch processing [systems].
> They did it because they had an ICL mainframe, which was going to
> spare. And, you know, at the time, there weren't that many
> computers that could not only check, but that could actually [offer]
> real time checking and real time reporting. But that was too far for
> these guys at this stage. So I just basically stayed back and did my
> bit on the telecom front.[26]

Reflecting about these distinct engineering cultures, Peter
Buck, who joined the exchange in 1979 after completing a degree in
computer science at Imperial College, London, also noted:

> In those days there was this big sort of distinction between systems
> programmers and application programmers. And it was like the
> distinction between us and [the settlement] guys. The [settlement]
> guys were applications programmers. Application programmers
> wrote COBOL programs and didn't really understand computers.

---

[24] Scannell interview.   [25] Newman, personal communication.
[26] Bennett interview.

They just strung a few instructions together, put some numbers in at the front and they came out at the end and that was it. And the fact that it was running on a computer was largely irrelevant. Whereas systems programmers had to actually understand how the computer worked because you were working at the level where you were fundamentally using the structure of the computer to do things ... That was very much a sort of system programming sort of approach to things ... Although obviously we were writing applications it was very much more bound into the system.[27]

As Buck's recollections suggest, this cultural divide was constituted as much by how people thought about computers as by the distinct requirements confronted by developers. Systems programmers developed applications that spanned different units of the market and therefore had to create mechanisms that communicated, translated, and coordinated action across a number of dissimilar tasks and operations; they were more prone to engaging in bricolage and tinkering with the makeup of hardware in their problem-solving strategies. Conversely, being devoted mostly to the number-crunching demands of settlement, applications programmers were more concerned with the integrity of calculations and data structures than with the design of the machine. What mattered for them was efficiently mirroring the relations produced on the floor in the electronic tickets and bargains represented by the machine rather than guaranteeing the efficiency in the flow of information across heterogeneous elements of the system.[28] These two cultures were also partly grounded in the concrete technological choices made by the different teams at the exchange, choices that created dependencies and relations with hardware providers outside the marketplace. Consequently, whereas in

---

[27] Buck interview.

[28] An interesting, if quite historical, description of the difference is given by the US Department of Labor's *Here Today, Jobs for Tomorrow: Opportunities in Information Technology* (Veneri, 1998), where application programmers are presented as writing "software for jobs within an organization," whereas systems programmers are presented as those who produce new systems.

settlement, computers from IBM and ICL dominated the architecture of data processing, time-critical systems closer to the market floor were built using the flexible technologies of Digital Equipment Corporation with whom Bennett and colleagues "worked very closely ... particularly on the technology changes."[29]

It was through this cultural division of technological labor, engrained in the organizational bureaucracies of the exchange as much as in the practices and technological preferences of its expanding groups of engineers, that the logic of real-time computing and communications made headway into the marketplace. Propelled by its financial success, the exchange expanded MPDS into a national service (called Country MPDS) in 1974 taking real-time price dissemination to the British Isles. Reaching broking firms throughout the United Kingdom using coaxial cable networks was prohibitively expensive, though. The expansion of the existing system from a local service to a national infrastructure posed a difficult technical and political challenge.[30] In addition to the potentially large installation costs of a dedicated national communications network, the quality of service provided to the regional trading centers (located in Birmingham, Glasgow, Liverpool, Dublin, and Belfast, among others) had to be as good as the one provided to brokers in London. The system had to guarantee parity of representation (foretelling, perhaps, today's debates about fairness and equality with respect to the access that market participants have to the digital feeds of modern electronic exchanges). Rather than building a closed and costly system, the exchange's technologists chose to broadcast data using a combination of tried and tested real-time technologies. In cMPDS, dedicated telephone lines linking London to other regional trading centers carried the digital signals generated by the Ferranti Argus 400 at the heart of

---

[29] McLelland interview.

[30] By 1974, the London Stock Exchange had merged with the "provincial" exchanges. A condition of the merger was sharing technology between London and other financial centers, a matter that was nevertheless technically difficult using the coaxial architecture of MPDS. Newman interview.

MPDS; and in each of these cities, a PDP 11/40 received the data feeds to then recreate a timely simulation of the screens that were shown to the users in London. It was "a sort of hybrid," argued Michael Newman, an engineer who joined the exchange at the time.

> In the centers, [you had] the television cable [network] we'd done [in London], but people weren't actually all living in the centers, so they got the slower version which [was] purely digital. [We] made … it look back to being analog television whereas it wasn't. This was in order to create a so-called fairness with everybody seeing the same thing.[31]

A project of such scale presented notable organizational challenges. In addition to making the systems work, technologists had to enroll diverse users, negotiate access to regional trading centers, coordinate with third parties including hardware vendors and the General Post Office (responsible for the country's telecommunications networks at the time), and maintain costs under control. The clout of the exchange helped, but it did not suffice. "When I joined," recalled Newman in conversation,

> [the cMPDS project] was in a mess. [The] number of errors and faults had risen faster than our ability to solve them. So every time we thought we'd solved three problems and put a new release out, another seven would appear. So one of my first projects was to get control of … Country MPDS and bring some discipline to solving the problems.[32]

Much like developers elsewhere, the technologists at the stock exchange were confronting the operational problems of engineering large-scale systems. The logic of real-time computing was simple and elegant, but its translation into concrete devices required much more than the technical knowledge necessary for hacking together disparate pieces of equipment. Rather, it required what sociologist John Law calls "heterogeneous engineering," a capacity to assemble skills,

---

[31] Newman interview.   [32] Newman interview.

knowledge, expertise, and resources across different spheres of activity to produce systems, users, and practices within a single coordinated space (Law, 1987). Real time implied a distinct form of organizational discipline that combined careful production management with a good measure of interpersonal skills, technical vision, political awareness, and organizational drive.

The close relations forged among the engineers that joined the stock exchange in the early 1970s helped to reinforce this disciplined culture of real-time systems programming. This was particularly relevant given the rapid expansion of the exchange's personnel. By mid-1975, the handful of technologists hired a few years earlier had trebled many times over. Reminiscing over dinner in 2015, Gary Wright, a project manager who worked with the jobbing firm CT Pulley from 1969 to 1986 and is a recognized expert in settlement and clearing, recalled his first interaction with these growing technical and managerial teams. When the stock exchange started work on its TALISMAN settlement system, it did so by amassing an army of specialists that met with their counterparties from industry – from technology vendors to the technical specialists that worked in banks and member firms. The meetings were so large that they were held in hotel conference rooms rather than the cozier offices of the stock exchange in London. There, hundreds of experts discussed the plans and implementation of this ambitious project, refining technical details – from standards of data communication to operational procedures about systems failure and recovery – and coordinating activities within and between financial organizations.

The growth of the exchange's largely invisible technical bureaucracies could have diluted the bonds formed between the original cohorts of market engineers. But expansion was taken as an opportunity rather than a threat: as the exchange developed new technologies and services, Bennett and his colleagues John Scannell, Michael Newman, and Ian McLelland remained close collaborators, gaining recognition across the marketplace. They were the increasingly recognizable makers of the market's devices, having garnered trust (though perhaps not too much visibility) from the exchange's gentlemanly members.

3.5   DIGITAL MARKETS

The organizational influence of the technologists was tested in replacing the Ferranti Argus 400 that operated at the core of MPDS. By 1975 it was clear to both them and the leadership of the exchange that service was becoming inadequate despite its great commercial success. There were two problems. The first was technical. For Michael Newman, MPDS was "absolutely at its limits; [the 22 channels] squeezed every available bandwidth ... so much so that the gap between [them] started to get almost blurred." The problem was obviously material, as Scannell recalled:

> one of the amusing things that used to happen [with the] digital to video computer [was that] it relied on a crystal for the frequency to be set, whatever it was, 220KHz, and this crystal used to sort of run out depending on the temperature, so if it was a warm day and it was a bit warm in the computer room, it would run out, which would make the characters on the screen [of MPDS] to start to tear, because it wasn't in synch, and what we had to do we had to open the door of the Ferranti Argus about 2 inches to cool it down and that would allow the frequency of the crystal to go back to where it was originally set.

This was only one of the problems. More important, perhaps, were the limits on capacity of the original setup. MPDS could handle, at most, 40 channels, and each addition came at the cost of image quality. What was needed, noted stockbroker Patrick Mitford-Slade, then head of the exchange's Information and Communications Committee, was a system that could handle "an unlimited amount of information,"[33] and the Argus 400 was simply not it.

A second source of pressure came from the increased demand for data from users of the stock exchange. At the time, the exchange

---

[33] Mitford-Slade interview.

worked through fixed stockbroking commissions – meaning that all members charged the same to clients to execute trades. To compete, brokers offered additional services to attract and retain customers.[34] Research was one such service, and by the 1970s brokers were heavily reliant on computers, analytics, and data processing. When brokers first invested in computers in the mid-1960s, they did so despite restricting their use to "investment administration and bookkeeping, or else … the production of lists of securities and current prices in sectors of the market where fairly simple analysis based on current prices would be useful" (Grant, 1983: 84). As in the exchange, the first generation of computers in most broking firms inhabited the periphery, the general office departments of contracts, settlement, registration, and dividends (J.D. Hamilton, 1968). Some firms, however, used computers to aid the work of their research and statistical offices. The technically savvy Phillips & Drew illustrates this well.

Phillips & Drew was an early adopter of information technologies, having hired shared computer time as early as 1958 for calculating yields (Reader and Kynaston, 1998). When IBM launched their 1440 series in 1962, senior partner Henry Cottrell hailed the system as "specially designed for stockbrokers" since it could be used in the calculation-intensive work of portfolio valuations, commission analysis, and gilt price ratio statistics. By 1966, Phillips & Drew's IBM 1440 was "running 80 hours a week," and although it did not handle clients' accounts or dividends, it conducted "an enormous range of work, some not even mentioned by IBM (sold transfers) and some much more complex than we then knew" (Reader and Kynaston, 1998: 140). The complexity of applications was impressive. By 1970 their firm offered a commercial advisory service based on a computational ranking model that ran in tandem with established forms of "subjective" valuation. Computers were not reducing costs but expanding business. Writing in 1968, Dundas Hamilton noted that

---

[34] Cheine interview; some established firms retained their customers through connections, as was the case of the blue-blooded brokers Cazenove & Co.

"none of the firms who have [moved from machine accounting to computers] has seen any savings in overheads, and many have been faced with higher costs" (J.D. Hamilton, 1968). A memo by Cottrell echoed these views: "We shall never make a computer into a great success by savings in filing girls or contract clerks. The real profit should come from the help it gives in getting business" (Weaver and Hall, 1967; Hobbs, 1974).[35]

MPDS was an "extremely crude" bottleneck, as Scott Dobbie from the Scottish stockbrokers Wood Mackenzie noted in an interview. But rather than overhauling the system, the technologists at the exchange chose to replace its computational core with a PDP 11/70. (In developing multiple systems that meshed into the everyday experience of the exchange's membership, market engineers made data dissemination infrastructural, with change coming as a result of piecewise adjustments and additions on the installed system, rather than unique radical transformations.) The seemingly innocuous decision of replacing one computer for another, however, produced a critical innovation: the creation of a relational electronic database that contained all, rather than just some, of the market's prices.

Initially labeled Exchange Price Input Computer (EPIC), the project of digitizing the stock exchange's prices was a joint financial venture between the stock exchange and Exchange Telegraph (Extel). As Michael Newman told me, the use of the word "exchange" "was deliberate, because [Extel was] Exchange Telegraph and we were the Stock Exchange, so the common word was 'Exchange,' so that [EPIC] could mean [both] Exchange Telegraph Price [Input Computer] and the Stock Exchange [Price Input Computer]."[36] Excel supported the venture financially in order to retain the distribution rights for the information produced in the marketplace – sold at a premium to newspapers in Britain and overseas. EPIC, however, was built entirely by the exchange's teams and as such reflected their preference for real-time data processing and communication. Following the original

---

[35] Hobbs interview.   [36] Newman interview.

architecture of MPDS, prices for EPIC were entered from the market-place via price input terminals located on the edge of the floor; data was then fed into an electronic database that "held information about every stock traded on the floor [identified by its four-character EPIC code] [and that included additional information] such as yesterday's closing price, today's opening price, the last few prices, etc."[37] Unlike the ad hoc data structures of the Ferranti Argus 400, the PDP 11/40s allowed the exchange to organize the market's information as a relational database that extended well beyond the mid-prices on MPDS. In addition to the prices for most if not all the shares traded on the floor, the system included corporate news items and regulatory announcements as well as a suite of applications that mined and presented the information in specific formats. EPIC, for example, included an application that kept the exchange's official publications up to date. Of these, the Stock Exchange Daily Official List (SEDOL) was perhaps the most important. Produced daily by the stock exchange, SEDOL was the modern equivalent of the *Course of the Exchange* and contained the official prices for all the securities listed in the market.[38] Before the introduction of EPIC, maintaining SEDOL was a laborious task. While there were only about 2,500 stocks that traded regularly in the market and had, by virtue of this, a specific EPIC code, securities in London numbered more than 10,000 listed stocks, each of which were listed in SEDOL.[39]

Few users in the market noticed when EPIC went live in 1977. For brokers and jobbers, the mechanics of trading remained unaltered, as did the visualization of market prices on the screens of MPDS. Orders to buy and sell shares were still carried from the boxes of brokers on the edge of the floor to the pitches of jobbers scattered throughout the stock exchange building. Gaining data on the market

[37] Buck, personal communication.
[38] SEDOL was not merely an element of routine documentation. All tax, probate, and portfolio valuations carried out in the United Kingdom referred to the prices in the official list.
[39] Buck, personal communication.

was more efficient, yet trading happened much in the same way as it did before. But behind the scenes, EPIC embodied a profound transformation in the role of information technologies in finance; it demonstrated that an infrastructure linking computers, telecommunications, and organizational routines could contain an accurate representation of the marketplace. EPIC also reinforced the real-time culture of systems programming as a means for restructuring the marketplace in its many and varied activities. And there was, at least among a growing segment of the exchange's membership, increased demand for these digital transformations. "It was clear," recalled Peter Buck, "that people started to want real time feeds."[40] Soon after its introduction, EPIC incorporated a computer application that intimated the not-too-distant future of finance: the Computer Readable Service, a standardized mechanism that allowed member firms, newspapers, and information vendors to connect directly to the exchange's expanding electronic datasets.

Like most large projects at the stock exchange, EPIC was associated with a change in the organization's management and implied a further step in the professionalization of the marketplace's engineering corps. As the exchange expanded in reach and scope, the ruling council hired a chief executive, Robert Fell, who did not see eye to eye with Michael Jenkins. Jenkins was asked to leave, which he did to then invest considerable efforts setting up the institutional infrastructure for the emerging derivatives markets in Europe.[41] To replace Jenkins, the exchange hired another notable technology manager, George Hayter, who heralded the organization into a critical moment of reinvention. But this is the story of chapter four.

3.6   FROM MIDDLEWARE TO PLATFORMS

Hayter's arrival marked a shift in the exchange's infrastructural logics. As the organization moved into more uncertain and competitive times, its multiple information systems became challenging

---

[40] Buck interview.   [41] Jenkins interview.

terrain. Like forms of middleware that transparently glued together distributed computer applications, the mechanisms of TALISMAN, EPIC, and MPDS linked multiple domains of the marketplace and its community. But these systems were largely incommensurable. They were written in differing languages; they were made of heterogeneous machines. MPDS was built for a world of coaxial analog signals; TALISMAN crystalized the bureaucratic mechanics of batch processing, accounting, and settlement; and EPIC represented the world digitally and in real time. The multiple elements complicated the relationships and hierarchies at the exchange, fracturing the house into multiple alcoves. With Hayter at the helm, things would be different. Middlewares would coalesce into something more unified, more ambitious. They would seek to become a platform, a single system connecting the market from end to end. But as they reconfigured from multiple disjointed services into a single platform, they revealed the invisible technologists working in the house. A platform is not built by one individual, but by an organized army. Technology was becoming visible; it was becoming the heart of the exchange.

4   The Hubris of Platforms

Hiring George Hayter as head of the Directorate of Information Systems and Settlement came with the realization that "this technology thing was something that was eventually going to take over in a big way," recalled John Scannell.[1] Originally trained in natural sciences at Queen's College, Cambridge, George Hayter was a bit of a polymath: he read numerous subjects – including empirical psychology, philosophy, and logic – before becoming an electronics engineer designing aircraft control systems for the military. It was "a lot of fun" noted Hayter fondly, "sort of grown-up Meccano, really, and actually making things that work ... was great." Hayter's knowledge of computers also stemmed from his experience in industry. After developing aircraft control systems, Hayter worked for Elliot Automation, a British computing company eventually taken over by International Computers and Tabulators (ICT), in 1968. There, Hayter was involved in a project validating analog computing results through digital calculations – similar in architecture and logic to the systems developed at the exchange for CHARM and TALISMAN. It was "very slow and cumbersome, but thought to be very reliable and more sort of kosher, in some way or other." While the experience at Elliot Automation got Hayter "interested in what computers could do," it was during his subsequent time at LEO Computers where he uncovered "all sorts of new interesting applications" in commerce. With a strong understanding of computers, Hayter joined the British Overseas Airways Corporation (BOAC), where he pioneered the development of its computerized reservation system. Named BOADICEA, the system was the first such development outside of the United

---

[1] Scannell interview.

States, where IBM launched SABRE in 1964. BOADICEA was a feat for BOAC in particular and the British computing community in general (Littlewood, 1998). For Hayter, working on BOADICEA nurtured a specific – and, as time would prove, quite critical – set of organizational skills. Building the reservations system required managing a complex administrative bureaucracy and coordinating tasks across several technically distinct groups.

> There was passenger checking, passenger ticketing, passenger fare construction, weight and balance calculations, route optimization, all this sort of stuff was being done online. And that was thrilling because it was really leading edge, real-time computing, you know, for the first time for me. That was in 1968, and I was there until 1976. I was in charge of real-time system development. A team of about 120 system designers and programmers, documenters, testers and so forth. And we also sold that package of software, which amounted to about 500 man-years of work, to other airlines around the world. So I had little teams of people dotted about the place. I got to work on a sort of global canvas, which turned out to be important later on.[2]

Hayter found an exciting space of opportunities at the stock exchange. For him, it was clear that digital technology "needed to be introduced in order to broaden the scope of the information systems"

> Because I could see that trading securities, is pretty much a hundred per cent information flow. There isn't much else, really. I mean, there's paper, but the paper represents information and there were ways in which I could see that the paper could be immobilized so that the whole process could be represented as information flow. Starting with market information to the broker and his client, generating an order. It doesn't have to be written on a piece of paper as it was then. It can flow straight into the market, it can be executed against a jobber or market-maker's quotation, the

---

[2] Hayter interview.

resulting trade can then be generated and recorded and then passed on to settlement and generate the necessary trade contractual exchange of ownership, and exchange for money. And money is information as well, with the depositary which [electronically] keeps track of the ownership of shares in the United Kingdom and the banking system for transferring money. The whole blazing thing is actually information flow, from start to finish.

Within the exchange, this vision found allies in both the engineers as within the adapting membership. Bennett and his colleagues ended up reporting to Hayter, "the pair of them made a good combination," noted Scannell. Hayter "had kind of a political mind, [knowing] the right way to go about things," while Bennett was the technological entrepreneur guiding "a sort of forward-looking outfit, crazy techies, who were fantastic, some of them were real cutting edge," recalled Peter Cox.[3]

More importantly, perhaps, the idea that markets are reducible to the management of information indexed a key change in the character of British (and global) finance. As Marieke de Goede (2005) notes in *Virtue, Fortune, and Faith*, the understanding of markets as systems built around information reflects the specific networks of authority that emerged within finance in the second half of the twentieth century. Making and consuming information is necessarily an ambiguous and political process that facilitates the existence of a financial sphere. This extends as much to the discursive labor of economists, financial analysts, regulators, and investors as to the conceptions of the managers, workers, and technologists of stock and commodities exchanges. Hayter's arrival signaled the emergence of a different understanding of the nature and operation of marketplaces – it was not merely about managing the exchange's expanding technological investments as if they were appendages of the core functions of the marketplace; it was evidence of the future couplings between markets, technology, and the distinct politics of information

---

[3] Cox interview.

of the digital age. Forging these connections was challenging, particularly given the classed and hierarchical structure of the exchange. Transforming finance, as we shall see below, would require much organizational work and the opportunities offered by political surprises.

Hayter, Bennett, and the growing corps of market engineers were driving the exchange into new technological and organizational frontiers. The early adoption of computer equipment for settlement and the modest though significant addition of technologists to the organization's hierarchy were slowly but surely "layering" the exchange into a novel institutional path (Streeck and Thelen, 2005; Mahoney and Thelen, 2009). Still, the stock exchange had not changed fundamentally in either structure or cultural logic: it remained a member-owned organization, controlled by a powerful council, and somewhat anachronistic in many of its rituals and performances. Similarly, despite the growing presence of technology and technologists within the organization, the marketplace's operations remained mostly the same: jobbers stood at the center of exchange, though increasingly aided by a growing suite of taken-for-granted devices that lowered trading costs and made price dissemination faster, more reliable, and more convenient.

But while not changing normative structures directly and keeping the dense social relations of the floor relatively intact, the growing bureaucracies of technology altered the marketplace by amending, revising, and adding to the expectations and practices of the organization and its users (Mahoney and Thelen, 2009: 15–31): as early as 1971, a telling note in the *Stock Exchange Journal* stressed the satisfaction of the membership with the Market Price Display Service (Hughes, 1971); in 1973, the stock exchange council recognized that "world-wide provision and reception of market information through visual display screens will in future become a vital aspect of the business of the stock exchange and its member firms" (quoted in Michie, 1999); and in 1979, a review of broking services commissioned by the exchange observed that

It used to be taken for granted that a computer system would be put in charge of its own special priesthood who would make sure that its perfect functioning was not contaminated by the presence of the ungodly. The real problem was to teach the priesthood about Stockbroking, and some organizations never succeeded. Now the control is moving back into the hands of people whose expertise lies in the Stockmarket and its workings ... The atmosphere has changed, and office staff who used to be afraid of the "electronic brains" now take it for granted that they will operate keyboards and terminals as part of their work. The "punch girl" who hammered holes into cards all day long without knowing what they meant is a vanishing species.

(Josephs, 1979)

Plenty was changing surreptitiously at the exchange; and most was not through the visible hand of coercive authority, but through slow encroachment of the bureaucracies of market technologies upon their embedding organizational field.

One important and notable change was that, while still far from the highest symbolic and organizational echelons of the exchange, technologists were no longer like the back-office workers that populated the basements and interstices of the House in the past. They were "in service," but in a very different way to the clerks of a few generations earlier. Through multiple innovations and constant growth, market engineers gained visibility and autonomy, as made evident in their increased capacity to develop new suites of expensive and relatively experimental systems for the marketplace and its multiple users. One in particular – the Teletext Output of Price Information by Computer (TOPIC) – was notable for its practical importance and commercial success. But it also mattered because, as an interactive information system, it constituted the first common platform for collective markets in London.

TOPIC was developed as an upgrade to the data visualization systems of MPDS – as another innovation of convenience. By 1978, exchange technologists noted that MPDS reached its operational limits and required an overhaul – one offering a more robust means for seeing the market from afar. An initial candidate for the type of technologies that could be used to represent the market in more detail was a system known commercially as Prestel that formed part of a broader family of data-dissemination technologies called Viewdata. Developed by the British Post Office, Prestel was a "marriage of industries, technologies, processes and skills" in "telecommunications, the telephone, the computer, and publishing" (Fedida and Malik, 1979: 2). Designed initially as an information publishing service, Prestel consisted of a central computer that sent messages to remotely located color televisions sets using conventional telephone lines as channels for data transmission. Users of Prestel had either a dial-up modem or an acoustic coupler for communicating with the server as well as a keypad to control their television sets and navigate through the numerous pages of the service. Each page consisted of a standard static display of 80 columns by 40 lines of characters. By pressing commands on the keypad, users could request particular pages from the central computer. And unlike predecessors such as Ceefax (offered by the BBC to transmit information via Teletext), Prestel was interactive, allowing for the asymmetric bidirectional flow of data between users and the remote computer (the initial upload/download speeds were in the order of 75/1200 bytes per second; compare this with the current bandwidths in finance, measured in the order of 100 Gigabytes per second). With this, the computer could take into account user inputs as part of its calculations and allowed for near-real-time communication between participants of the platform.

For stock exchange engineers like Bennett and Scannell, Prestel "looked quite good" as a replacement for MPDS.[4] The system preserved the established economies of conventional television sets ("people had got very used to TVs and the cheapness of them blended in well with the concept of having a TV terminal," said Bennett), and

[4] Scannell interview.

it could use the existing network of telephone lines for communicating data between EPIC and the market's users. As a practical system for visualizing the market, however, TOPIC implied some important technical departures from the standard architecture of Prestel. While the relational databases of EPIC could remain the repository for price and company data displayed by TOPIC, the mechanism for updating the pages on the commercial version of Prestel was impractical. As a visualization system, TOPIC could not be slower than MPDS, whose users had become accustomed to the system's quasi-instantaneous price updates: there was, noted Scannell, "a requirement to have something on [the] screen pretty rapid[ly]";[5] changing information on MPDS was fast – it simply required switching between channels on an analog TV. In a standard Prestel system, though, users had to request the central computer to update the information shown on their screens, a process that could take a few seconds depending on network traffic (Figure 4.1). Because Prestel was no longer a simple broadcast service like MPDS, its implementation implied higher message loads between users and the central database: each time a user requested information, a signal would travel from their terminals to EPIC, to then return a message containing fresh market information to render in their screens. The system had to be stronger, faster, and more robust than anything commercially available.

To deal with these real-time requirements, Bennett and his team designed a so-called "super Prestel"[6] that took the original interactive Viewdata technology and made it "formal and reliable."[7] In TOPIC, the television sets were given "some extra logic," allowing them to render the teletext signals coming from the terminal more efficiently. The terminals, in turn, were designed for the toughness of face-to-face finance: in addition to being custom made for a faster response, they were boxed in a metal casing to withstand the many physical misfortunes of the floor and the office. Between these tough

---

[5] Scannell interview.   [6] Newman interview.   [7] Bennett interview.

FIGURE 4.1 John Scannell testing the Exchange Price Information Computer, courtesy of John Scannell. © John Scannell

terminals and EPIC's fast electronic database stood a little bit of rocket science: the terminals linked through multiplexers to high performance process control machines (MODCOMPS from Modular Computer Systems Inc) that allowed signals to travel quickly and efficiently between users and the database. As Bennett remembered fondly, NASA used these for testing rocket engines and launching spacecrafts, applications where real-time sensitive data collection, transmission, and processing were critical. The system also implied some other hardware updates. EPIC, for instance, was redesigned and moved onto relatively fast, but highly reliable Westinghouse hard drives. Similarly, the exchange's engineers set up a rapid access cache of the most frequently requested pages to make the system as responsive as possible.

Launched in 1979, TOPIC opened the floodgates of market information. From the original 22 channels of MPDS, TOPIC soon grew to contain several hundreds of individual pages for each of the companies traded in the market. Bennett said that the system was "ahead of anything that Reuters was running at the time." In addition to its sheer capacity, TOPIC also gained credibility by visualizing data through color, text, and graphics that could be shared both publicly and through private closed user groups.[8] TOPIC was not simply a scoping device, a way of seeing the market: it was, rather, a common platform, a standardized mechanism for displaying market information – from prices and company announcements, to charts and tailored analytics – and reacting to it from afar. It was an almost entirely self-contained informational object. As a platform for communications and interactions, TOPIC was successful: the number of pages in closed user groups quickly surpassed that of public pages for prices and corporate announcements, demonstrating the rapid internalization of the system by member firms. Two years after its introduction, the number of TOPIC terminals rose from the 400 initially authorized by the council to several thousand. For the technologists, purchasing expensive real-time hardware to extend the system became much easier. As Scannell mentioned,

> [when] you've got 2000 orders outstanding, you could not spend enough money. It was virtually impossible. And you had people screaming at you because the place is absolutely booming, you know? There's people ringing up, "can you install one of these next week, I'll give you, personally, I'll give you X to sort of install it."

TOPIC was also a working demonstration of organizational trust. As numerous nonengineers noted, the driving force behind the development and subsequent introduction of TOPIC came from the expanding armies of technologists working around the market floor. For Patrick Mitford-Slade, a seasoned Cazenove broker who served on the council, the process was "definitely bottom up," with ideas coming from people who "knew what technology was available," particularly, the "Peter Bennett's and George Hayter's of the world."

---

[8] Newman interview.

The road to EPIC was not frictionless, however, and required constant symbolic investments in the capacity of the "technocrats" and their inventions. As Mitford-Slade noted in interview, technologists had to pass numerous hurdles; in addition to the technical difficulties of building systems that were not available off the shelf, they "had to sell [their ideas] to me and I had to sell them to a lot of people who didn't understand technology whatsoever." Indeed, for the council, the project "was quite an investment to launch into [requiring] quite a lot of persuasion."[9] The council's support was well founded, though. "In fairness to them," recalled John Scannell about the council, "we'd got the proper documentation. They were quite confident we knew what we were doing. Their own firms were suffering because they'd really needed this equipment for their business, so it was very interesting times."[10]

TOPIC was also a demonstration that infrastructures were shifting in nature within the organization. Prior to TOPIC, the systems operated by the exchange reflected not one but several logics (the analog screens of MPDS, the digital databases of EPIC, and the quasi-mechanical architectures of TALISMAN). Even though they operated in the same marketplace, the trajectories of each system were relatively independent. TOPIC changed this, creating a technological and organizational tie between core functions of data management and the development of visualization and data communication systems. The first generations of infrastructures at the exchange were coalescing into slightly more expansive platforms, systems that while linking multiple functions of the marketplace allowed users and developers to create, disseminate, and consume content under a common set of standards of data production and manipulation. This was a revolution: technologists in London were not simply producing objects for the market, like the original devices of convenience that made the lives of jobbers and brokers less cumbersome. They were,

---

[9] Mitford-Slade interview.   [10] Scannell interview.

above all, building the marketplace itself by creating the spaces where interactions were to take place.

4.1 YOU SAY YOU WANT A REVOLUTION

As technologists continued to develop multiple systems, their layering of the organization captured the hierarchies of the exchange. Let's fast-forward a few years to 1986. By then, perhaps the height of technology development at the London Stock Exchange, the dozen technologists and engineers hired in the 1960s had grown to between 3,300 and 3,500 people working in technical services. According to some participants and observers, the exchange became one of the largest sites for the development of information technology in corporate Europe.[11] The core group of a dozen or so technical experts that joined the organization in the early 1970s grew "to a couple of hundred [engineers], three hundred probably" working in dedicated research and development groups.[12] The number of these groups and divisions grew rapidly: after the exchange created the Directorate of Information Systems and Settlement in the early 1970s, for instance, it also established the Technical Services division (of which George Hayter was initially in charge) to manage the production of new market-facing technologies. Similarly, recognizing the importance of blue-skies innovations, the exchange created the Special Systems Group in the late 1970s that, headed by Peter Bennett, operated "sort of like [a] research department in a university. Everyone was a graduate, smart people" recalled former colleague Peter Buck, who joined in 1979. The exchange was growing, and it was growing fast. By 1986, Hayter alone oversaw between 2,000 and 2,200 employees whose responsibility was to "run the market and [make innovations] operational."[13] Peter Bennett, conversely, held the reins of the newly created Advanced Systems Group, a forward-looking "directorate [with] a very small team of [hand-picked] people"[14] that designed

---

[11] Sheridan interview; Bennett interview. [12] Buck interview.
[13] Bennett interview; Hayter interview. [14] Buck interview.

FIGURE 4.2 Hexagonal pitches on the trading floor of the new building of the London Stock Exchange, c. 1974. In 1972, and after a costly and logistically complicated effort, the Council of the Stock Exchange inaugurated the new home of the marketplace: a modern, 27-story building designed by Lord Llewelyn-Davies, built on the same site as the original stock exchange in Threadneedle Street. Unattributed photograph for Barnaby's Studios Ltd. Mary Evans Picture Library.

and piloted some of the most futuristic projects of global finance at the time. The old house, long substituted by the tower in Throgmorton Street, could not contain these gargantuan efforts. By the mid-1980s, the exchange occupied up to 14 buildings scattered across the City of London housing everything from restaurants and offices, to development laboratories and back-up computer systems[15] (Figure 4.2).

The technologists' capture of their organization – that technology had "taken over," as Scannell recalled – was not a foregone

[15] Scannell interview.

conclusion. The same expertise that helped them solve the technical challenges of the exchange was a double-edged sword that had made them invisible for matters of organizational strategy and market governance: engineers were neither brokers not jobbers, having no apparent stake on the culture and practices of the exchange; they did technology, not markets. As Roger Nightingale (1985: 60), Director of Economics and Strategy for Hoare Govett Ltd., wrote with hindsight in 1985, "computers and advanced forms of communication were employed enthusiastically ... but these new technologies left fundamental City relationships unchanged." After all, as the notorious stockbroker Paul Bazalgette warned those tempted to feeding their business into a computer, "dealing done that way will never be fun. Dealing certainly ought to be, and I think that between humans it usually is" (quoted in Kynaston, 2001: 422). Although prominent and constitutive of the vast bureaucracies of the marketplace, exchange technologists had remained for many years peripheral to making markets.

Nightingale's observation must be read with a grain of salt, though. The construction of the technocratic bureaucracies of the London Stock Exchange did not immediately and radically transform the organization, but it certainly created sets of relations within and without the market that were the sources of changes to come. "City relationships" were expanding rapidly to include multiple interactions, connections, and associations to the growing armies of technologists in finance. The kin were growing, even if at the apparent symbolic fringes of the market. But closer to the core of transactions, market engineers were busy coordinated how relationships developed, setting the standards, rules, and expectations of use for the market's platforms. Stock exchange engineers were a band of brothers – a fellowship of sorts – that found in their infrastructural work a source of power, resilience, recognition, and a capacity to subtly shape the machinery of exchange. And it was precisely through their positions, halfway between the shadows of the basements and the visible light of the exchange's floor and its council that they were refashioning what transactions meant to the worlds of finance.

As they captured resources and visibility within the organization, the collective imagination that coordinated the work of these stock exchange technologists emerged as a continued resource for market reform. Much like the British architects that crystalized class relations in the bricks and mortars of country houses in general and the stock exchange building in particular, market engineers held clearly moralized views of markets that they sought to bring into being. Through technology and purposeful design, trading could be made "better" – perhaps even more socially virtuous – than as conducted through the long-standing practices of the organization. These were not necessarily neoliberal thinkers, exalting the perfection of markets or the superiority of rational finance. The oddly moralized views of market engineers were pragmatic: they were about tinkering with devices, about technical efficiencies. Technologists were after what they considered better machines and more clout within their world. And in this they found an uncanny ally for reform in Margaret Thatcher who, as the former *Financial Times* reporter Barry Riley noted, convened a "very radical conservative government" that "didn't like clubs and . . . didn't like monopolies."[16] This was a perfect *mise en scène* for change.

As early as 1976, the London Stock Exchange was facing greater regulatory scrutiny. At the time, finance in Britain remained highly self-regulated and self-monitored. Most of the rules that governed activity on the trading floor, for instance, were those promulgated by the members of the exchange. Disputed trades were very often resolved over a friendly conversation in the council's chambers and the few external organizations that were created after the 1960s (such as the Panel on Takeovers and Mergers, convened by the Bank of England in 1967 after a series of public scandals surrounding a bout of corporate mergers and acquisitions) were mostly considered to perform a sort of ceremonial oversight. The 1970s were different, though: the politics of regulation in Britain focused increasingly on

---

[16] Riley interview.

competition in the economy. This may well be the result of a shift toward so-called neoliberal politics in the country, or it may well be a response to the greater economic uncertainty of the world economy at the time. Be it as it may, "competition" in industry was now more than ever before at the forefront of the government's concerns. This also extended to the secluded bastions of gentlemanly finance. For the UK's Office of Fair Trading, in particular, the exchange's practices and regulations were anticompetitive obstacles, as envisioned in the Restrictive Practices Act of 1976. Having analyzed its rules and regulations in 1978, the Office of Fair Trading found the exchange in breach of existing legislation. The "future operation of a national undertaking," wrote stockbroker and former exchange chairman Dundas Hamilton, "was to be decided in a court of law" (J.D. Hamilton, 1986: 11). And while the election of a Conservative government in 1979 seemed to have provided some respite for the elite members of the exchange, it did little in practice to thwart the legal case against their organization. At most, a Conservative government created a small, though important window for negotiating a settlement. The exchange took the opportunity (it really had no other choice) and in 1983 agreed to eliminate "by stages and with no unreasonable delay, all the rules which at present prescribe minimum scales of Commissions, and to complete this dismantling by 31 December 1986" (Goodison quoted in Michie, 1999).

The exchange was also facing challenges from the broader adoption of technology in British and international finance. There was *actual* competition that made change necessary. A notable example was the attempt in 1972 by the Issuing Houses Association (formed primarily by merchant banks that could not be members of the exchange) to create a computerized dealing system, the Automated Real-time Investments Exchange (ARIEL), that would provide "an inexpensive efficient trading market which will transcend National boundaries" (Kynaston, 2001). ARIEL's design followed the block-trading system pioneered by Instinet in 1968/1969 (Littlewood, 1998) and thus departed from the methods of dealing long held in the

London stock market. ARIEL guaranteed complete anonymity, was open to all institutions, and eliminated the division between jobbers and brokers by allowing the direct interaction of orders from customers through its digital system – it preceded in many ways the more flexible systems of the Electronic Communication Networks that revolutionized finance in the 1990s. Even in terms of technological cultures, ARIEL was markedly different from the infrastructural cultures at the exchange: whereas patents did not protect the systems developed at the stock exchange (as Peter Buck mentioned in his interview "people just didn't think like that. You just got on and did things," perhaps reflecting both the imprudence and hubris of the exchange as the prime trading site in Britain), they did protect ARIEL's design.[17] Although an established incumbent, the exchange was seeing an uncertain, unsettled future.

Despite the exchange's status as a national institution – supported through networks of power and the organization's technologies of honor and community – its stability should not be overstressed: from the 1930s onward, the existence of the exchange as an independent body was frequently a matter of discussion in Whitehall. During the Second World War, for example, there was an argument for nationalizing the exchange, following the same steps as the Bank of England. The exchange's case for independence rested on its ability to generate trustworthy prices outside of policy, a point where they found sufficient support. This worked well for some time, but was invariably challenged by a changed political understanding of monopoly within the UK government leading up to the 1980s.

Under the pressures of regulation and technology, change was bound to happen, one way or another, making the 1980s a historical period where the organization, its members, users, and bureaucratic corps had to fundamentally rethink their collective future. What

---

[17] In fact, some of the most important historical sources about ARIEL come from a protracted legal battle about the ownership of the system that was only settled recently.

many realized soon after the 1983 agreement between Sir Nicholas Goodison, the stock exchange's chairman, and Cecil Parkinson, the government's Minister for Trade, was that even the apparently trivial elimination of fixed commissions – an arrangement that had been in place since the early twentieth century – would have great consequences for the institutional stability of the City of London's stock markets. For instance, increased competition over trading along with the relatively low levels of capital held by member firms simply made untenable the division between brokers and jobbers, bringing the bicentenary tradition of single capacity to an end. Competition also entailed expanding the membership. In addition to eliminating single capacity and fixed commissions, the exchange agreed to accept foreign firms as members and to allow increased capital stakes from banks in member firms. Rather than introducing each change gradually, the exchange opted to implement all at once on a single date, October 26, 1986.

Known as London's Big Bang, this date rendered uncertain the future of the market. While members of the exchange had practical experience with, and understood the mechanics of, other possible marketplaces owing to their exposure to trading in Continental Europe and the United Stares, questions remained about which trading system best suited London's specific institutional history. As the council noted, "Market participants of the type found in other financial centers cannot be conjured into being at the stroke of one pen ... Different types of Firm may evolve, but the market framework itself cannot immediately create them" (Council of the Stock Exchange, 1984). The problem was not simply organizational: in transforming the participants and mechanics of its trading floor and community, the exchange understood that the systems it had developed over the previous decade required modernization. Exploiting the uncertainty of forced change, Big Bang became a pivotal opportunity for technologists to reengineer the marketplace and its organization.

Big Bang was an occasion for cashing out the confidence and trust deposited in the stock exchange technologists. Reconfiguring the organization was an opportunity not only to install and tinker with technologies around the market, but, critically, it was a chance for building the market anew, atop a single and elegant infrastructure serving the interests of all possible members of the community. Developed by George Hayter's department in early 1983, this market platform became the flagship project of the engineers. The project was vastly impressive, almost utopic: it envisioned a complete sociotechnical integration of the exchange, reassembling the numerous heterogeneous networks of market information and settlement systems (TOPIC, EPIC, CRS, TALISMAN, and other legacy applications installed over the previous decade) under a single technological umbrella, a general-purpose infrastructure to replace those in existence. As George Hayter (1983) noted at the time, this integrated data network (IDN) was set to have "a widespread impact on the working of the Securities Industry over many years." Based on the design principles of packet switching and real-time computing, IDN tackled the "proliferation of networks" within the organization that, for London Stock Exchange (LSE) technologists, were culprits for the "high cost, inflexibility and inconvenience to service users" of the existing systems. Offering a single, standardized communication platform, IDN would facilitate the interoperability of the systems at the exchange, providing "faster, easier and cheaper communications" for the UK securities industry "by setting up a common data network operating to a set of recognized international standards" – a system for London with a view to the world (Hayter, 1983).

A critical and prophetic feature of IDN was how it transformed the interactional logics of trading from crowds on the floor to data queues in electronic digital networks. For Peter Bennett, IDN offered a more democratic mode of market exchange, hitherto absent within London, and upon which stock markets of the future could be built modularly and efficiently. The platform allowed, in particular, "high volume data collection, transaction processing and teleprocessing applications which require two-way communications," wrote Bennett in 1984. The existing systems at the exchange reproduced the historical power of jobbers by stressing in cables and protocols their role in creating quotes and prices; this was visible in the fact that most systems at the time were optimized for the unidirectional "outflow of rapidly changing market information," rather than the direct interaction of quotes and orders between brokers and jobbers (P. Bennett, 1984). IDN was an altogether different and revolutionary construct: by enabling real-time communication and message processing between a multitude of exchange counterparties, it made possible a "globally accessible order book" for London and the world. Part of this was based on the type of technical standards behind IDN. This was not a broadcast system or a network skewed toward the needs of jobbers. Quite the contrary, it was a real-time communication *platform* – a totalizing and contained system – where interactions were queued in discrete data packages and processed through the mechanics of computing rather than conversations on the floor.

IDN revealed the distinct moral and organizational visions of exchange technologists. Big Bang and the opportunity to rebuild the market from scratch gave engineers visibility but also fed a certain sense of empowerment, perhaps even hubris. In addition to challenging the position of jobbers at the center of exchange, IDN embodied a novel conception of the organization. Whereas the exchange's membership traditionally understood their mission as providing "the market where stocks and shares are bought and sold" (Council of the Stock Exchange, 1951; activating the tropes of honor and class that were so central to the early history of the exchange), technologists saw the organization as a producer of the platforms and infrastructures required for the electronic marketplaces of the future. For them, the exchange was in the business of technology, not relationships. This distinct worldview is clear in how British technologists evaluated their foreign peers. Commenting on the difficulties faced by American stock exchanges at the time, Bennett hinted at the existence of very different "conceptions of control" across the Atlantic, to use the term developed in Neil Fligstein's (2001) theory of markets and competition. For Bennett, stock exchanges in the United States had not taken a lead in the development of networked markets, but have instead largely abrogated the responsibility for networking and have handed the business to third party operators. In contrast, the U.K. Stock Exchange has invested, and continues to invest, heavily in information and communications systems and it has built up a considerable systems development and operations skills in these areas.

(P. Bennett, 1984)

With these words, written for an internal memorandum, Bennett justified the growing body of technologists in the organization and stressed the primacy of technology in finance. He was certainly not alone. As Stanley Young, LSE's former Director for New Strategy Development, tellingly noted in his interview, "[we] recognized that the old world had changed and that we were at the forefront of something that was incredible, because technology just freed us from this physical box that we were in called a floor."[18]

Like most visionary utopias, though, IDN was never to be. Perhaps it was simply too ambitious a project: infrastructures seldom respond to a single vision or a master plan, as Paul Edwards (2010) writes, and conjuring up a platform that would serve the entire marketplace was an almost Quixotic task. Infrastructures emerge not through planning and calculated foresight, but through the meandering paths of history, in the mangle of making, tinkering, and wrestling with the obduracy of organizations, practices, and their installed base (Star and Ruhleder, 1996). The system eventually introduced for Big Bang reflected this fragility and contingency of infrastructures: it was the creative result of reshaping legacy devices into a system that did the job for the time being. A band-aid. A product of creative, recombinant bricolage.

By late 1984 and with only two years to spare for Big Bang, IDN proved clearly unfeasible. With pressures mounting and time running

---

[18] Young interview.

out, exchange technologists shifted to the more pragmatic, rather less glamorous, and less far-sighted task of building an operational trading service for the current time, not the future. Confronting great uncertainty (no one really knew what the regulatory changes would imply for trading on the floor), technologists and exchange management sought templates abroad. Key to this was a fact-finding mission to North America where the council identified two broad possibilities for London's markets: one was the principle of broker-to-broker auctions with specialists serving to assist the market process; a second option was based on competing market makers that were required to provide liquidity to the market by creating continuous two-way prices. For the council, one of these options shined with particular strength: "In London," recalled Hayter over a cup of coffee, "we intuitively felt that New York and London were of similar importance, and therefore that we ought to look quite closely at what they'd done. [If you look] at the domination of the New York Stock Exchange, it was self evidently true that this was the way to go." The council agreed and contemplated as early as 1984 "adopting different trading systems for different categories of securities," giving specialist market makers control over the most active shares in the market. Alas, by July of the same year, stock exchange management recognized the fading importance of New York specialists: "[to] introduce a specialist system with all its faults, on a largely unwilling membership would be to impose the second best at a time when the opportunity to make the right choice existed" (Council of the Stock Exchange, quoted in Michie, 1999).

The second, initially less appealing possibility inspired the more sensible organizational roadmap taken in the lead up to Big Bang: NASDAQ, the automated quotation service of the National Association of Securities Dealers, based on the principle of competing market makers, provided a trading mechanism to which the exchange could relate. "NASDAQ was intriguing," recalled Hayter, "because [their] market makers looked a bit like [our] jobbers, except that they were dual capacity, they were able to trade on the one side with their clients and on the other side for themselves."[19]

Building a NASDAQ-like system from the bottom up was simply impossible – NASDAQ itself was a product of plenty regulatory and technical tinkering throughout more than a decade of automation of over-the-counter markets in the United States. As Hayter wrote to the membership at the time, there was "a wide river to be crossed and time only to build a Bailey bridge initially."[20] In a demonstration of the power of bricolage, the blocks of Hayter's bridge were not the elegant standards and queue-oriented architectures of IDN but the locked-in legacy systems that enveloped the exchange and its member firms (David, 1985). Initially code-named SEMANTIC (for Stock Exchange Market ANd Trade Information Computer) and later known as SEAQ (Stock Exchange Automated Quotations), Hayter's solution used the designs of TOPIC and EPIC to enable the bidirectional distribution of quotations and prices from the trading floor and the offices of member firms to the screens in TOPIC, where they were read by a large audience of brokers and market users. As Hayter explained in December 1984, in arriving at this solution his Technical Services department

> had to face up to a number of practical problems. Firstly, we have a short time scale in computer developments [which] will not allow us to build radically new services from scratch with any degree of confidence that they will work effectively and reliably under high volumes of loading from the first day of the new market. Secondly we have a fundamental uncertainty about the real requirements of

[19] Hayter interview.

[20] Developed during the Second World War by Sir Donald Bailey, a "Bailey" bridge is a portable, ready-made, standardized, and interchangeable structure that a few "unskilled" soldiers can erect rapidly across a river or depression during a military operation. Bailey bridges were instrumental innovations during the war and remain widely used in both civilian and military applications. Yet an important characteristic of these structures is that they are temporary tools for getting things done.

the system ... Finally we have little idea about the absolute level of trading which is likely to take place and the consequent level of system activity.

(Hayter, 1984)

The system was "not exactly rocket science," recalled Buck. All SEAQ was, said Bennett in his interview, "was TOPIC, really. It was just TOPIC and EPIC brought together. [The system was] two legacy systems [put] together essentially, which was actually quite a safe route." For technologists, beyond the narratives of deadlines and great transformations, Big Bang was becoming a series of "scarcely discernible pops," caught in the echoes of the organization's history (Pagano, 1985).

4.2   MARKET CHOREOGRAPHIES

Although a "temporal solution," SEAQ's development required great institutional efforts and was part of a complex ballet of tinkering, testing, and developing systems and procedures for the new marketplace. SEAQ was but one of seven interlinked projects, all aimed at providing the electronic systems required in time for Big Bang (from trading and settlement, to reporting and information dissemination). To coordinate efforts across these projects, the exchange created an ad hoc Projects Committee chaired by Patrick Mitford-Slade that drove developments "all with that final deadline" in mind.[21]

> [We] started off by having weekly meetings, getting all the leaders of each project [together], the Peter Bennett's, the George Hayter's ... running it all ... People from all sides of the market were developing their own systems, [and we got] them together once a week to make sure they were not conflicting with each other and were driving at the right sort of speed.[22]

---

[21] Mitford-Slade interview.   [22] Mitford-Slade interview.

The pace of preparations was fast and soon frequent meetings dissipated, delegating much of the managerial decisions to the technologists and the growing army of consultants hired to audit the activities of the exchange. As Peter Cox noted in his interview about the added support to the decisions of the technical teams: "there was some skepticism about the exchange's ability to bring on the plan," he said, "and so we said 'Look, what we'll have is a respected consultancy firm who will have monitors.' They weren't actually project managers, but they'll have monitors sitting on the shoulders of the project managers."

Like the hodgepodge building of the exchange's house a few decades earlier, the version of SEAQ released for Big Bang was a compromise between the obdurate investments of the past and the practical needs of the membership's present. And just like the old house embodied the social logic of the classed stock exchange membership, SEAQ embodied some of the networked, pragmatic logic of its market engineers. With a remarkable record of 35 minutes downtime per month (Anonymous, 1986), EPIC provided a reliable system for processing, formatting, and storing market data; the robust and cost-efficient TOPIC disseminated information to market users; and the exchange's private telephone system was the communication tool for market makers and brokers in their trades. Linking these technologies, a crucial organizational innovation induced by regulatory change: in SEAQ, dealing operated under dual (rather than single) capacity, meaning that market makers could trade on their accounts and those of their investing clients. Rather than being uttered on the floor, market makers' quotes were entered into SEAQ through custom-built terminals to then be displayed to brokers and other market makers through TOPIC. Upon seeing a satisfactory quote on their screens, brokers would phone market makers to agree on a deal – and, preserving the logic of the floor, once their phones rang, market makers could not modify their quotes. This was certainly the case for the most active stocks (the so-called alpha and beta stocks that represented more than two thirds of the shares listed in the

```
SEAQ EXAMPLE                                                    PAGE
7210
INT COMP LTD          ICL  A    S  1000                     CLOSE 81
CHG + 3  VOL  156    LT 82  3  9X  2  3  4                      11:22
           AKD    LMB    CTY   83 5   WED   SMI   GRN
AKD        83-7   1X2    GRV   81-6   2X1   SMI   82-5   2X1
BUC        82-6   2XL    HGV   82-7   3X2   SKG   82-7   1X2
CTY        83-6   3XL    LMB   83-7   1X3   WED   81-5   3X1
GRN        82-5   1X1    P&D   82-7   1X1
```

GEC	GLXO	BP	BTOL	RCAL	SHEL	TSCO	MEPC
212	965	491	243	244	643	191	*318#

FIGURE 4.3 A typical SEAQ screen.

market).[23] On SEAQ, each alpha and beta share had a page of its own that displayed the live quotes from all the market makers as well as the sizes they were willing to deal in (see Figure 4.3). The best prices in the market were highlighted in the so-called yellow strip – a simple innovation that allowed brokers to see supply and demand in the market for that stock. With the yellow strip, walking between pitches

---

[23] The newly formed Quality of Markets Unit of the Stock Exchange had identified four categories, and to each corresponded a specific behavior that market makers were to follow. Alpha shares, for instance, represented the most actively traded equities, accounting for an estimated 56% of the UK equity market. For a share to be considered alpha, ten or more market makers had to deal in it, turnover had to be in excess of GB£195 million in the first half of 1986, and capitalization had to be above £740 million as of June 30, 1986. For these shares, market makers were obliged to provide continuous, two-way prices during the mandatory trading hours between 8:30 and 16:30, and (initially) details of all trades were immediately published on SEAQ. Beta shares were somewhat less actively traded, and although market makers in these were also required to display continuous, firm quotes, details of trades were published the following business day in the Stock Exchange Daily Official List. Gamma shares required market makers to produce only indicative two-way prices, and due to their low turnover, delta equities only entailed displaying mid-prices.

on the floor in pursuit of the best price was unnecessary: these were readily available on the screen, constituting a system of observation and projection that, as Karin Knorr Cetina and Alex Preda (2007: 126) write, "assembles on one surface dispersed and diverse activities, interpretations and representations which in turn orient and constrain the response of an audience." Linking communications through phones and representations through real-time price reporting and visualization systems, SEAQ made an electronic market actionable with technological means.

Some of SEAQ's representational capacities were the product of other innovations introduced by the exchange's technologists. The pages on SEAQ, for instance, were quite poor at capturing the experience of the market floor: embodied and sensory cues were not originally replicated or simulated on the system. SEAQ initially displayed supply and demand, but not levels of market activity. To overcome this, Michael Newman devised a novel representation of the floor onto the screen. As he explained in interview,

> I conceived ... a proxy view of the market on a screen. How do we do this? I came up with the idea that if we got the top 100 stocks ... and jammed them on to one page, then that would be a proxy. If you're not on the floor, and you can see what's going on in the main stocks, that page would be a proxy for you. Now, how do you do that? A static view would not tell you the dynamics of the floor behavior. So it's no good just seeing the prices. What we came up with was a scheme we inherited from Teletext in which you could pulse signals, so that if a stock price had gone down, the price was shown on a red background, and it stayed like that for ten seconds and then went back to "steady." So as it changed, it lit up in red or blue, a bit like red and blue lights going on. And it stayed like this, so that if you kept seeing flashes, red or blue, you knew that the thing was damn active, and the more you saw changing, the more active it was. So if you saw the whole wretched hundred in changing color you knew that there was mayhem, absolutely chaos.

The other thing you could see by eye was that if you saw nearly everything red, you knew the floor was bombing out. If you saw everything blue, you knew it was all going up. [So] you got this feeling of what it was like. I designed [this page and] called it the trigger page, because the idea was that it would trigger you to go and look up [the shares] in [TOPIC]. The trigger page ... became the most popular we'd ever had.

The trigger page (Figure 4.4) is something we know well today: turn on the financial news on any day of market turbulence and some form of higher-level representation of the market is conveyed through shifting images of different sorts. As a means for representing the system-as-a-whole, Newman's trigger page was original and unique. Unlike the systems that existed at the time at the exchange and elsewhere, it presented users with global informational surprises, allowing them to evaluate and compare the "events of interest" as they swam into their views (Knorr Cetina and Preda, 2007). In addition to

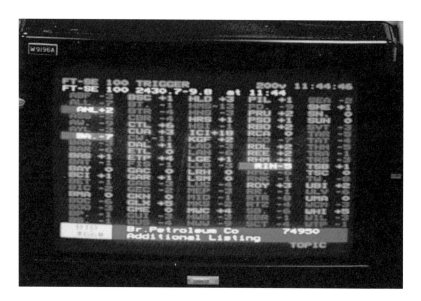

FIGURE 4.4 Trigger page, courtesy of John Scannell; © John Scannell.

being a substantively new way of seeing markets, the trigger page was based on another revolutionary innovation: it accounted for the 100 most active shares in the market – those forming the *Financial Times* Stock Exchange Index 100 that has come to represent London in global finance. FTSE 100 was partly developed by exchange technologists who, working with economists and member firms, sought to create an information mechanism for selling index derivatives for the emerging British options market.[24]

The move to SEAQ implied some other more subtle changes. Whereas trading on the floor occurred between familiar faces, dealing counterparties on SEAQ were firms – represented online by three or four characters next to their quotations. In Figure 4.3 for instance, the letters "WED" stand for Wedd Durlacher, the well-known British market maker (absorbed by Barclays Investment Bank in 1985). Traders on the system did not know whom they were trading with personally. Members took some time to adjust to this new mode of relatively anonymous, impersonal interaction as demonstrated by the dress rehearsal on October 18, 1986, a week before Big Bang. The simulation was "designed to resemble a normal trading day as closely as possible," noted Richard Lander (1986) of *The Times* in London. Institutional investors and brokers "will be in their offices to telephone their orders to market-makers, each of whom was given an equity 'book' averaging £14 million to begin with." The participating firms "were working to a script," recalled Patrick Mitford-Slade. In practice, however, their script proved difficult to follow: brokers and market makers had yet to learn how to navigate through the system under their new identities. John Scannell recalled some of the difficulties.

---

[24] Dimson interview; Newman interview. The links between the stock and derivatives markets in London were not strong. As a former derivatives trader suggested, the cultures across these two domains were vastly different – despite innovations and change, stock markets were still associated to a more gentlemanly crowd, while derivatives were seen as spaces for less privileged debutants to the world of finance. Within the exchange, David Steen was the key proponent of options trading, but recognized being a "bit of a maverick." Interview with former LIFFE trader; interview with David Steen.

[Some firms had] changed their name, and on the dress rehearsal day I had about 21 computer operators working for me and about 15 or 20 people on the helpdesk. [On that Saturday,] people were ringing up saying "I don't know who I am." So, you'd say, "Right, ok, that's your problem." [And they would answer] "Yeah, I don't have any idea of who I am." So I would say, "Right, who were you, before?" "Well, I was Wedd Durlacher but I don't know who I am now, so do you know who I am now?" Bizarre conversation! So I just sort of [asked around], "Does anyone know what Wedd Durlacher is called now?" And so, "they're called KAS or something like that." "Right, you're KAS now." "No, I can't be KAS." "Why not?" "Because he's KAS." "Who's he?" "The guy who's [on the other side]." And it was just so funny. I'll never forget that. Absolute mayhem, it really was.

Dealing on phones was also quite new to some members and required inventing new conversational conventions on how best to carry out transactions (these were not calls to inquire about the weather or recommendations on where to eat; they were distant from the more leisurely chats jobbers and brokers had on the old stock exchange floor). Telephone dialogs had to be "concise and to the point," said Ian McLelland in an email, and so necessitated a new culture of interaction. There was a learning curve, steeper for some than for others: some of the firms failed to get their computers to log on to SEAQ; some traders claimed they could not contact counterparties over the telephone; and others said that, in a breach of the exchange's rules, some market makers were making false prices by not answering calls (Truell, 1986). "There were some problems, but nothing really serious," said Mitford-Slade at a news conference following the dress rehearsal. "The system has performed exactly as expected," he added.

As Big Bang loomed, uncertainty remained. *Computer Weekly* noted cautiously that most of the firms would "go live with partial and patched systems" (Anonymous, 1986b). Michael Newman,

SEAQ's development director, was nevertheless confident that the exchange's system would manage 80,000 trades a day, well beyond the marketplace's record; SEAQ, Newman reportedly said, was "rock solid" (Anonymous, 1986c). Hedging their bets, the two (largely identical) operations rooms of the stock exchange – one in the Tower and one in an unmarked building on Christopher Street – were turned into "emergency rooms should the City go berserk" (Brown, 1986). And as the eyes of London City focused on SEAQ on the eve of Big Bang, the exchange's chairman, Sir Nicholas Goodison (1986), confidently assured that one thing was certain, "screen-based dealing is here to stay."

Despite expectations, it was not SEAQ's quote reporting function but TOPIC's visualization interface that crashed when the exchange's new systems went live on October 27, 1986. Just as business was about to start on the morning of Big Bang, trading on SEAQ was suspended for 50 minutes. When the systems were down, dealers reverted to face-to-face trading on the floor. The event became the news of the day. "Instead of high technology taking over completely," reported Nicholas Owen of ITN News (aired October 27, 1986), "books and pencils were still required, the computer age having not arrived quite on schedule."

TOPIC's failure was not entirely unexpected. Peter Bennett remembers raising the issue well before Big Bang. "I'd written any number of memos on this and given them the actual calculations, and I knew [it] was going to work out a problem on day one. They had about half the capacity they needed." Buck concurred: many technologists "weren't convinced that [TOPIC's MODCOMPs] were going to handle [the levels of] traffic, because we knew exactly what would happen."[25] Tested for up to 4.5 million-page requests, TOPIC was overloaded by a "tidal wave" of users on the morning of Big Bang. John Scannell, who was then standing in one of the operations rooms, recalled:

[25] Buck interview.

Eight o'clock comes and the systems all come up. And we're looking at the page response request and it goes up to 1.7 million almost immediately, which is a little bit bloody worrying. Then it crept up to sort of two million, three million, and four million. What's going on? This is quarter past eight. Then it got to five million, then everything is going berserk. Bells, and whistling, and ringing, and popping and banging.

It took some clever on-site programming, a restart of the system, and bringing the government bond market offline to reestablish order. Dealers in the government bonds market were not impressed. "It's the government's market, you can't take it off the system," they said. "But we said 'You've been dealing perfectly satisfactorily without the system for god knows how many years, you can continue without it for a little bit longer' and of course they did, to satisfaction."[26] Despite the glitches, Goodison reflected on the day as it came to a close: "The fact that the system worked at all this morning was a triumph" (quoted in Clark and Thompson, 1986). Normality soon kicked in. Minor problems continued to surface occasionally, but SEAQ became the undisputed platform for market transactions. "So much for being a Bailey bridge," said Peter Buck. "It was still there some years later."[27]

4.3   THE LIMITS OF CAPTURE

It would take the stock exchange another decade to move away from SEAQ and the trading systems introduced by market engineers at the time of Big Bang. Order-driven trading, where investors and traders submit their orders to buy and sell securities directly to an order book without the need for market makers, was only introduced in 1997 with the (forced) development of the Stock Exchange Trading System (SETS), a story that I explore in the next chapter. SEAQ's persistence may well demonstrate its success at maintaining rather than

---

[26] Mitford-Slade interview.   [27] Buck interview.

challenging the social structures of London's markets, the forms of relation making that had maintained the local communities of finance for decades. Exchange technologists might have captured the marketplace and its bureaucracies, but in producing systems for the government's mandated target, a core conception of how markets should operate remained unchallenged. In SEAQ, market makers (or jobbers, in the previous terminology) remained in their privileged positions, tightly controlling price formation and, with it, much of the institutional dynamics of the exchange.

There are two vignettes that show some of these limits of organizational capture and the false sense of promissory change that technologists carried with their visionary projects of unified data platforms. The first concerns the durability of social relations in the electronic marketplaces introduced after Big Bang. Recall that relations were everything on the floor, not only because they moderated transactions but also because they allowed agents to extricate themselves from awkward deals (if I traded with a trusted counterparty in a deal that harmed my position, for instance, it would be possible to renegotiate the deal struck on the floor *ex post* to guarantee minimum losses to all those concerned; opportunism in dealing was moderated by the cultures and practices of the exchange). The SEAQ Automated Execution Facility, an automated trading system introduced in 1989 on the back of SEAQ, made these relations impossible: the system executed orders electronically and automatically according to the best prices available in the market, independently of the identities of their originators. It introduced a logic of queues to the marketplace by specifying a first come first serve, price-time priority principle to the processing of small lots. Some firms simply did not agree with this procedural logic, preferring interpersonal judgments to mediate their transactions. The technologists at the exchange complied with the members' view and introduced a feature that distinguished SAEF from other competing small-lot services offered to the investment public in London: SAEF allowed brokers to route their orders to a preferred market maker to guarantee that, if a deal went awry, a friendly phone call would unwind the situation. Nic Stuchfield, formerly a jobber for the prestigious investment bank Barclays de Zoete Wedd, recalled

> once SEAQ was introduced, we knew immediately what the best price was because it was up there on the screen. And we may not make [it]. But there were an awful lot of retail brokers that would rather deal with Wedd Durlacher or BZW as it was now called, or Smith Brothers, or one or two other firms, rather than all these brand new 25 market making firms they had no relationship with whatsoever, and didn't even know how to get a hold of them.

But SAEF wasn't only a mechanism that automated established structures of "trust." More importantly, it manifested the importance of relations in the production of a legitimate market. Recall the metaphor introduced in Chapter 2, contrasting markets and kinship as distinct yet similar forms of relation making. By routing transactions to certain market participants, SAEF reproduced particular relations of identity and equivalence in the market. Maintaining some degree of best execution, it allowed its users to channel business to "friends, [people and firms] they knew. And very often you could get a better price on the telephone than you saw on the yellow strip," as Hayter noted.[28] Much in the same way as Daniel Schneider famously posited notions of "blood" as generating a form of identity in American societies, transactions are generated, too, as forms of relatedness evaluated through the language of legitimacy. SAEF maintained the purity of transactions, the sense of a bounded and legitimate community, while simultaneously introducing automation to order execution.

The resilience of relations was also made visible in a second episode: what seems, with hindsight, an almost irrational commitment of the membership to the trading floor. For the technologists, the introduction of SEAQ clearly signaled the end of face-to-face

---

[28] Hayter interview.

trading: by making all quote information available on the screens of the members in their offices, SEAQ voided the floor's informational primacy. In early 1984, for instance, Hayter's teams advised firms to think of a 3-year horizon for the trading floor, hinting at the fact that deals would soon move into their offices where trades would take place primarily over the phone and on screens; firms could then optimize their investments, placing greater emphasis on the design and compatibility of their systems with SEAQ than on their reliance on the information obtained from the floor. Mitford-Slade concurred, identifying the floor as a temporary element that "might become obsolete, although many Market Makers would still want to make use of it at first, at least until information systems were bedded down" (quoted in Kynaston, 2001: 646). Many members, however, considered the floor a critical technology, with or without SEAQ. Some of their concerns were clearly practical and pecuniary. Hayter recalled that interpersonal knowledge of the organization's membership meant that the floor allowed jobbers to "measure up" brokers to differentiate prices.

> The crunch [of SEAQ] was that jobbers had to commit a price to the screen. And they didn't like that, because they said "well, my price depends on who I am asked to deal with. If I deal with the spivvy, if I'm asked by the spivvy broker what the price is, I'll give him a wider one than if I'm dealing with XYZ over here."

Not all brokers deserved the same price – and some profits could be made by carefully tailoring quotes to the specific counterparty of an exchange. But the members' concerns also reflected a sense of collective stability linked to individual moral duties. Talking about his experience at the exchange, the former broker and council member Graham Ross-Russell noted that

> [an advantage] of the open outcry floor in those days was that one of the roles [the jobbers] did exceedingly effectively [was that] they had a very good ideas as to who was honest and who was dishonest, and

they would tell you to mind your eye if they thought that there was anything unusual going on. So it was a self-policing mechanism ... It was an absolute eye opener to me when I first went on the council as to what some firms got up to. As the English proverb [says], birds of a feather flock together. In other words, there were half a dozen firms which if there were going to be problems the chances were they were there, as it were. If there was going to be something approaching dishonesty that's where you'd find it.[29]

For the membership, then, the floor was an ethical device: it made markets legitimate by guaranteeing transparency – and, in the case of London, a form of transparency heavily mediated by relations of status and class.

Members exerted great control over the organization and in the lead up to Big Bang lobbied heavily for a refurbishment of the floor. Under their pressure (particularly from jobbing firms), the stock exchange invested more than £2 million redesigning and refitting the floor with "screens facing two ways so that everyone was being kept informed."[30] By September 1986, twenty-eight market makers had signed up for one of the reinvented hexagonal pitches on the shiny new trading floor (Figure 4.5), with Smith New Court "making particularly trenchant noises about keeping at least four dozen dealers on the floor" (Kynaston, 2001). Big Bang proved technologists right, though. Within days of the introduction of SEAQ,

some [market makers] had gone, and within three or four months even [those who pushed for it] had gone because they'd realized that business wasn't on the floor ... And it moved very fast off the floor.[31]

Recalling a conversation with a member, SEAQ's project manager, Michael Newman observed:

[29] Ross-Russell interview.   [30] Mitford Slade interview.
[31] Mitford-Slade interview.

FIGURE 4.5 The hexagonal pitches of the trading floor, equipped with screens for the new marketplace. Source: "Big Bang Shake Up," PA Images.

I was told this by one of the dealers I knew quite well when I visited him on the floor in the first or second day post Big Bang. He said "Christ all mighty! By the time I wander round the floor and find out the prices, they all know it in the office. They are ahead of me!" When he said to me "they are ahead of me in the office," in living memory, this had never happened before. I knew that the days were up for the floor.

SEAQ did as predicted. By March 1987, only options were traded on the floor of the exchange (and even those soon disappeared). "In terms of physical markets," said Luke Glass, spokesperson of the stock exchange to *The New York Times*, "it's the end of an era in London" (Anonymous, 1987).

While Big Bang did not necessarily transform the culture or social structures of trading in London, it highlighted the power of technologists in the market's organization. Propelled by their relative success at stitching together the systems for Big Bang, market engineers created further spaces for innovation and growth. While Hayter's group developed SAEF (facing competition from member firms that were developing similar commercial systems of their own), Bennett and Peter Giles worked on the ambitious SuperTicker, a project that would harness satellite communication networks to create a global trade and market information routing system to compete with those of Reuters (and the then emerging Bloomberg). Bennett thought of using CNN's satellite network as the basis for this system. "Unfortunately," recalled Hayter in the interview, "Ted Turner didn't see the commercial logic of it".

Technologists had certainly captured the organization and saw its future cast in terms of their expertise: "Now we're off the trading floor," Hayter told *Computer Weekly* in 1988, "we're in competition with anyone who can build a network" (Anonymous, 1988). For Hayter, capture guaranteed the survival of the stock exchange in an era of global competition. "I regarded the whole thing very early on as an information business," he noted in interview, "and if you wanted it to succeed, you had to grow it, and to do it commercially." Bennett agreed: "The IT people," he noted, "were effectively setting policy. And, like it or not, around Big Bang time it was working very well. It was a bull market, everyone was onwards and upwards, the old member firms were cashing out, new member firms were coming in." The bullish years leading up to Big Bang were fertile grounds for transforming the organizational hierarchies of the exchange, fostering the growth of devices and infrastructures created with a clearly commercial and competitive objective in mind.

Technologists did not just command systems design and business strategies, they also dominated the payroll. The trading floor may have disappeared, but within the organization's complex ecology, it was supplanted by armies of technology-oriented divisions that cared for the ever-expanding infrastructures of the marketplace. In the years following Big Bang, analysts, programmers, systems engineers, and other members of the technical services staff represented the largest segment of the stock exchange's employees, hovering above 2,000 workers out of a total of 3,000. Middleware was everywhere. Much had changed since the old days of the house. Finance remained a matter of relations, but these were now shaped through the technologies and esoteric expertise of the exchange's market engineers.

Capture came at great organizational costs, though. A year after Big Bang, on October 19, 1987, global financial markets suffered a sudden, interconnected crisis. In a matter of hours, the Dow Jones Industrial Average fell 22.61%, while London's FTSE collapsed by a similar amount. London may have well contributed to the turbulence: on October 16, a hurricane-like storm that struck the British Isles forced all markets to close (all but one; as one informant told me during our interview with some pride, the London International Financial Futures and Options Exchange, LIFFE, traded through the gales) adding fuel to the fire.

After the event, known as Black Monday, markets remained subdued – the UK's main stock index, FTSE 100, only recovered to its pre-crash levels 23 months after the crash, in September 1989.

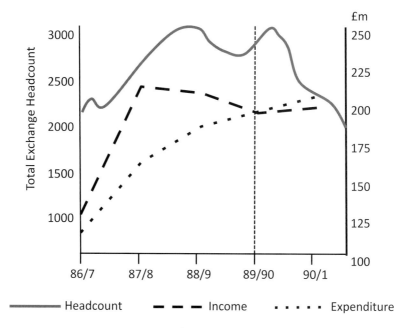

FIGURE 4.6 Composite graph representing number of employees, profits, and losses at the London Stock Exchange between 1986 and 1991. Data provided by John Scannell.

As trading volumes fell, so did the members' and the exchange's income, and in late 1989, on the back of ever-growing expenditures in technology, the organization incurred its first substantial loss (Figure 4.6). Controlled by a peculiar recombined membership – Big Bang allowed foreign firms to join the LSE and to sit on par with their established British counterparts – the exchange's management reconsidered their strategy. For the membership, the crash rendered investments in technology disproportionate to the exchange's key responsibility of providing a market for stocks: for them, and in particular for the new foreign members, Bennett noted, "[this was] not the way to run an Exchange. [They thought we] need to concentrate on other things, like designing a bigger and better market."[32]

[32] Bennett interview.

The first casualty was research and development. Rapid change and a small, though growing, rift between the members and the established bureaucracies of the organization greatly affected the patterns of innovation at the exchange. SEAQ, the Bailey bridge, recalled McLelland, was locked in as the cornerstone of future systems rather than the interim solution it had been intended to be. "New systems would not be developed, we would build on the existing limited capability due to time pressure (e.g., SAEF – a must have because the US has [the Small Order Execution System])."[33] The vast size and clout of the technical staff was also a liability: "Developers were now spending much more time in meetings, project office updating, reporting and all the bureaucracy of big organizations." The type of experts flowing into the marketplace also changed, according to Peter Buck:

> there was suddenly this massive increase in computer people coming into the City, people from all over the country, most of whom hadn't got a clue about real-time information or trading or anything like that. [All] these people who only ever worked on a payroll system before suddenly [came into] the City claiming that they knew everything about trading systems, and [the exchange's management] didn't know any better, so they employed them, at contractor rates, for two years and a lot of them didn't deliver. [We] had so many problems with these systems that were rubbish because the guys who were doing them didn't have a clue what they were doing. [After] two years they just buggered off with large amounts of cash back to Newcastle or whatever, and probably never worked again, they didn't need to. Which really pissed off my team because, we were getting paid quite well you know, City sort of City tech salaries.[34]

In sum, the technological culture of the stock exchange was "lost ... Developers were no longer allowed to develop without

---

[33] McLelland, personal communication.   [34] Buck interview.

a long process of approval. For many, including myself, it was time to move on."[35]

For Peter Rawlins, the recently appointed chief executive of the stock exchange, change was necessary, and so in 1990 he began a two-year process of restructuring the organization's approach to technology. "There is now no doubt," wrote the *Financial Times*'s Richard Waters (1990) at the time, "that Mr Rawlins intends to introduce an entirely new management team to what he has often in the past criticized as a ram shackle and bureaucratic organization." This was a critical moment. As *Computing* reported, the "spills and thrills" of Big Bang had come to an "abrupt halt with the announcement of 110 redundancies in January with more to follow [including] several layers of entrenched middle management as well as the more predictable foot-soldiers" (Anonymous, 1991). The exodus soon followed. Michael Newman, Peter Bennett, and George Hayter left in late 1990 – "[If] you're going to outsource [IT], you don't need a director who's responsible for internal IT services," noted Hayter.[36] By 1992, technology development was altogether transferred to Arthur Andersen, the management consultancy firm, who were contracted to "to rationalize and then run [the exchange's] entire IT operations for the next five years in a deal which observers say could be worth a staggering £50 million a year" (Anonymous, 1992). Hayter reminisced in 2007

> In a funny way, the Big Bang which everybody said was going to rid us of the club mentality and make the whole thing more commercial ended up coming full circle to the point where the members were saying "We don't want the Stock Exchange to do commercial things. We want it to just be the place that coordinates the regulation of the market, and not very much else."[37]

The days of market engineers at the exchange had come to an end.

---

[35] McLelland, personal communication.   [36] Hayter interview.
[37] Hayter interview.

4.4 CONCLUSIONS

The transformation of London's markets from the days of dealing on the floor of the house to trading on the mashed-up electronic networks of SEAQ was a long and sinuous process of piecewise material and organizational innovations. This story of transformation is, however, quite unique within the broader history of finance. The capture of the exchange's hierarchies by technologists did not happen in other markets, at least not with the same quality or intensity. For example, while the New York Stock Exchange was notorious for developing systems for its marketplace, it did so by creating organizationally impermeable walls between its technologists and corporate strategists, reducing the ability of the former to influence the latter (I explore this in more detail in Chapter 7). Similarly, at the Paris Bourse, cultural tensions between the members of the market and the external technologists were nowhere as stark as in London, resulting in a much smoother process of automation that was not followed by the type of organizational expansion that characterized similar efforts at LSE (Muniesa, 2003). London's unique experience resulted from its distinct historical and institutional trajectory, combining the dense ties of class and English kinship that bound the market's membership (and removed them from most things technological) with the entrepreneurial struggles and visionary imaginations of the engineers and self-made technologists that sought to create markets in novel ways.

Above all, however, the history of the automation of the London Stock Exchange was about infrastructures, their creators, and their changing positions within their corresponding market organizations. From being relatively invisible and powerless workers surrounding the stock exchange's floor, engineers developed to transform the market. Their work altered dealing, perhaps not its embedding social structure, but certainly by mutating the leisurely trades once created through conversations in the streets and alleys of London City into short lived transactions made over the phone and mediated primarily by electronic screens. These engineers were not simply creators of devices and standards; they were as much creators of the relations and bureaucracies that made these new forms of transactions possible, producing novel interactions and financial practices at the exchange. Central to this story is a lesson on the coupling of bureaucracy and infrastructure. The empires that market engineers built were as much fueled by their access to technical knowledge as by their emotion and foresight, by their commitment to specific design principles (such as systems programming and real-time computing), and their ethics of technical efficiency and organizational reform that reflected upon their projects a certain gravitas, a certain weight within the market-place and beyond. These were, for their times and in their very par-ticular global field, revolutionary agents that questioned through sweat and silicon what it meant to create markets. Their power was limited, though. Much more than bureaucracy, technologists required charisma to change the field. When they left the exchange in the early 1990s, they were leaving an organization still dominated by powerful jobbers or market makers. For their revolutionary technologies to come to life, something other than capture was required. They needed nothing short of a revelation. And this is precisely what they engineered.

5   The Wizards of King Street

For the scholar of science and technology, Geoffrey Bowker (2015), infrastructures do not inhabit human lifetimes but overflow individual experience. Their origins are fuzzy, they are never complete, and they never entirely come to an end. Their stories are somewhat unexpected, lacking the heroic elements that so often characterize conventional accounts of innovation. Infrastructures simply beckon a different genre, a knitted collection of tales without plotlines, histories without Napoleons or Alexanders, a messy ensemble of vignettes of continual maintenance and tinkering with no clear endpoint in sight.

The systems produced for the London Stock Exchange's marketplace were much like Bowker's infrastructures, transcending both the individuals who built them and the bounded organization where they operated. When Peter Bennett and his colleagues left the exchange in 1990, British stock markets neither stopped nor decelerated. In multiple sites and through numerous devices, they continued in their relentless buzz of trading and exchange. Through standards, screens, cables, codes, and distributed practices that were second nature to market participants, the infrastructures of the stock exchange survived the exodus of the market's engineers. They were now testaments to the vast armies of techies that, through decades of iterations and creative bricolage, erected an invisible empire beneath the meek skyline of the City of London.

But while infrastructures transcend the individual, their fates can become partly entangled with those of their engineers. When Peter Bennett left the exchange, he was not severed from his work but carried with him the expertise fostered over more than two decades in making systems for the marketplace and its community of members. Infrastructures may have no commanding generals, but they occasionally have their influential Haussmanns[1] – architects who carefully organize how devices, standards, and techniques are deployed, shaping the *mise-en-scène* of the market. These architects matter, for while their careers may be relatively ephemeral, their creations certainly endure.

In this chapter, I explore this theme by looking at how a distinct group of market engineers transformed the organizational field of finance in Britain through automation. More specifically, the chapter addresses the process by which electronic order books, devices that are central to the infrastructures of electronic trading in global financial markets today, were adopted in the City of London in the mid- to late 1990s. As with previous chapters, the theme is organizational. Intimately connected to the question of how financial markets were automated is the question of how the cultures, objects, and practices of their embedding organizational fields changed – how, for example, the messy orders of investors that once made their ways through interpersonal interactions in the streets of the City of London and the crowded brethren of the floor mutated into digital signals traveling close to the speed of light in proprietary communication networks. What motivated automation? What triggered, in particular, the adoption of the electronic order book as the standard technology of the marketplace?

For students of markets and organizations, it would be tempting to think of these transformations as triggered by the rationality of cost reduction, the institutional forces of isomorphism, or the authoritative politics of regulation. Surely, order books were adopted because they either made economic sense (for example, by increasing trading efficiencies or reducing operational costs) or because regulators somehow mandated their use. Some of these processes certainly shaped

---

[1] Georges-Eugène Haussmann was the architect responsible for the monumental renovation of the urban layout of Paris during the reign of Napoleon III. Haussmann's designs introduced large open spaces, broad avenues, and the distinctive geometry that characterizes modern Paris.

automation. An electronic order book is clearly cheaper than a human market maker, and more efficient in many ways. There are also network effects that provide incentives for adoption once others have moved onto the system. Similarly, regulators are often quite favorable of organizations that implement these technologies; currently, European and American regulatory agencies are working hard to move trades in so-called over-the-counter instruments (dealt on a discretionary basis in one-to-one transactions) onto order books that ostensibly provide greater transparency, fairness, and surveillance of the marketplace.

Although important, economic and regulatory pressures were just part of a more complex process of cultural and institutional change. Even for an informed observer standing in the early 1990s, the benefits of automated trading were by no means obvious: in addition to challenging the incumbent institutions of the City of London (in particular, the powerful jobbers or market makers), electronic order books posed great uncertainties. Would the markets be more or less liquid? Would they be more or less stable? What type of investors would benefit most from their adoption? Despite increasing economic evidence,[2] these questions simply had no authoritative answers and were filtered, interpreted, and negotiated through the politics of London's financial circles and the work of their bureaucratic corps.

What compelled, then, the automation of financial markets, at least in Britain? In this chapter, I think of automation not as an entirely rational choice confronted by institutions and tackled through a neatly organized process of innovation but rather as the type of myths that structure and coordinate action across

---

[2] Studies about the impacts of automation on market quality were increasingly frequent and visible in the late 1980s and early 1990s. These included, for example, work about British markets carried out by Ailsa Roell and Marco Pagano of the Financial Markets Group of the London School of Economics and Political Science and CEPR respectively, as well as the work on transparency and trade reporting standards developed by Gordon Gemmill of City University, as well as the larger contributions of Ian Domowitz, Benn Steill, Eric Clemons, and Bruce Weber.

organizational fields by depicting what seem to be the legitimate "rational means [for] the attainment of desirable ends." Inspired by the work of John Meyer and Brian Rowan (1977) on educational institutions, this perspective shifts our understanding of infrastructural workers in important ways. Although they are not commanding generals able to bring into being the designs of their minds, the architects of electronic financial markets – the Haussmanns of modern finance – are nevertheless capable of shaping their world by shifting the language of what was possible, desirable, and legitimate through the creation of myths. As Meyer and Rowan (1977) argued, with little entrepreneurial energy, actors can then assemble such myths "into a structure. And because these building blocks are considered proper, adequate, rational, and necessary, organizations must incorporate them to avoid illegitimacy." Infrastructural workers did not simply produce automated market devices – more importantly, they also fabricated the organizational building blocks and cultural vocabularies that rendered them a legitimate, almost necessary route for the future of finance; they crafted technologies of honor and community to justify their novel technology of consociation.

Here, I am inclined to return to Weber to gain a better perspective of how infrastructural workers produced these distinct organizational building blocks. If truly heterogeneous engineers, market technologists did much more than *simply* build devices. As explored in the previous chapter, the Bennetts and Hayters of London were also clever political agents within their organization, capable of articulating vast bureaucracies that redefined what it meant to be in the market and its messy community of exchange. Structurally transforming the field, however, required a different type of prowess. What made automation such a powerful myth was not only the weight of bureaucracy and rational expertise; as, importantly, the attractiveness of automation was also the result of nurturing charisma, prophecy, and spectacle around the technologies of the marketplace.

The mythical/prophetic character of automation is important for two reasons. First, it underscores the role of charisma in developing infrastructures and reorganizing sociotechnical fields. Donald MacKenzie (1996) skillfully showed how Seymour Cray's charismatic personality shaped the breadth of the commercial and technological networks through which his supercomputers traveled. The success of Cray's supercomputers was as much a consequence of their technical affordances as of the personable qualities of their chief engineer. Similarly, Charles Thorpe and Steven Shapin (2000) argued that part of the success of Robert Oppenheimer in regulating the normative uncertainty of the awkward organizational structure of Los Alamos derived from his intensely charismatic persona. The role of charisma in technoscientific institutions simply cannot be discounted since, as Thorpe and Shapin concluded, it is "right at the heart of those forces shaping the late modern world."

Second, understanding automation through prophecy and spectacle brings attention to the moralized character of the electronic infrastructures of modern finance. Market automation was almost a religious-like mantra, embedded in the "personal calling" hailed by some market engineers to create "better" markets of one variety or another. Taking full advantage of the Weberian archetype, in this chapter, I focus on three ways in which market engineers acted as myth-generating prophets to account for the power that they had in order to transform the field of British finance. In particular, I will look at how market engineers embodied three facets of the prophet serving as lawgiver, magician, and revealer of a unified, promised future.

5.1   ORDERING INTERNATIONAL MARKETS

In his sociology of religion, Weber examined prophets and their relation to the emergence and rationalization of religious groups. In two chapters and throughout his larger works, Weber studies how the charisma embodied in prophets becomes an organizing element of religious activity – prophets who, unlike priests, claim a personal revelation and, unlike magicians, exert their power "simply by virtue of [their] personal gifts." For Weber, the prophet was a productive, if traditional, institution-builder (Weber, 1978).

Weber did not shirk taxonomies and accounted for the role of prophets in his sociological writings by classifying them into distinct types. Among these was first the lawgiver who, like Moses, were charismatic individuals "called to … office when social tensions were in evidence." The connections between Moses of fourteenth-century BCE Goshen and the technologists of the twentieth-century City of London might seem slightly farfetched. Yet there are notable parallels in how the narratives of both of these actors represent the type of charismatic lawgivers that Weber saw as key to founding universalistic (religious) organizations. Consider, in particular, what we could call the "technological charisma" of the London Stock Exchange's leading market engineers – people who, like Peter Bennett and George Hayter, commanded the organization into Big Bang with great success. These were certainly well qualified experts, having demonstrated that they could develop systems that worked for the marketplace. Yet they were not the only technologists in London, less so in Europe, far less in the world. By the late 1970s, electronic technologies were advancing relentlessly across banking, finance, and consumer services. Real-time applications were no longer the wonder that they had been a decade earlier. And personal computers, although initially expensive, were now making the paths of innovation wider and more inclusive.

Like other top technologists at the exchange, Peter Bennett and George Hayter possessed something distinctive – a form of symbolic capital legible within their organization and connected to their success at marshaling the exchange through tough and uncertain times. This resource was clearly tied to their personas – even today, mentioning their names among those who were active in the City of London at the time elicits immediate reactions; they possessed, in a very meaningful Weberian sense, a distinct form of charisma. But the charisma of the stock exchange's engineers was not a divine gift – nor would we expect it to be so, given the fact that they inhabited and had built a highly bureaucratized, secular institution. It derived, rather, from accrued investments in symbolic forms, from the slow accumulation of the trust and confidence of the market community by virtue of developing systems that proved stable and useful.

As we have seen in previous chapters, these systems were numerous, from the slow and bureaucratic machineries of settlement to the fast and resilient quote dissemination networks of MPDS, TOPIC, and, eventually, SEAQ. All these systems demonstrated technical prowess, a command of cables and code that certainly contributed to the engineers' credentials. But among the numerous projects, there was one that the technologists whom I had interviewed referenced in particular as signaling their capacities to the marketplace community at large (as opposed to simply *within* their organization). The project, called SEAQ International, involved creating a market from scratch and positioned exchange technologists in the role of lawgivers, experts, and charismatic individuals called upon to bring order to an otherwise confused and rowdy domain.

SEAQ International was built upon a long tradition of trading in overseas securities in the City of London. Although eclipsed by the activity and cultural prominence of Wall Street in the late twentieth century, throughout most of the nineteenth and early twentieth centuries London was the undisputed hub of international finance – the central node of an ever-expanding network of commerce, empire, and entrepreneurialism that achieved one of its concrete expressions on the floor of the stock exchange. Even the government-imposed exchange controls, which restricted the convertibility of the British pound since 1941, did not erase this rich historical memory. As the national economy grew and the financial sector recovered some of its lost institutional grounds, the City of London rekindled its connection to global finance by creating what is now the $4 trillion-a-year market in Eurobonds. Designed in 1963 by Stanley Ross, the son of a London bus driver, Eurobonds were a creative way for overseas companies to raise money in the City of London without paying the high penalties for converting American dollars, French francs, German marks, or Japanese yens into British pounds. As Ross proved with the successful sale of the bonds for Autotrade SpA, instruments in foreign currencies were an attractive investment for the City of London's institutions: from 1963 to 1967, London issued more than $4.8 billion dollars of Eurobonds (K. Burk, 1992).

While the Eurobond market thrived across the City of London, it found no place at the exchange – the organization's restrictive rules and regulations, the absence of foreign firms, and a certain hostility toward innovation among large portions of the membership meant that only 1 percent of the Eurobond market was traded through the LSE. With the end of exchange controls in 1979, though, some within the organization recognized the missed opportunity. For Sir Nicholas Goodison, recent changes in the regulatory environment "[made] it possible for far more attention to be paid to overseas markets by domestic investors. It forced member firms of the stock exchange to think more constructively about overseas markets than they ever had before … change was inevitable from 1979 onwards" (Kandiah, 1999: 104).

Change occurred not by capturing trading in Eurobonds but from the fact that internationally oriented markets were, for obvious practical reasons, populated by computing and telecommunications, areas where the exchange had a growing record of achievements. If an international market prospered in London, it was in part because the infrastructure and expertise needed for laying out global real-time communication networks had had a strong foothold in the City of London for a number of years. Consider Reuters, a firm that is emblematic of trading around the clock and throughout the world and that was rescued from the brink of financial collapse by the introduction of its Stockmaster system in 1964. Like the market it served, the original design of the Stockmaster was also foreign to London: it was developed by the engineer Robert S. Sinn of Ultronic Systems, who intended to produce a device that would allow US investors to see, almost in real time, the most recent prices for stocks traded in the fragmented American marketplace (to which I will return in two chapters). Licensed to Reuters for use outside of North America, the architecture of Stockmaster allowed for relatively seamless expansion. By using Reuter's high speed Atlantic communication network, a "slave" memory drum was installed on the second floor of 85 Fleet Street in London to serve as a reliable point of information for the city's firms on the state of US stock markets (Ransom, 2014). Quote and trade information from American markets traveled from the Stockmaster's central processor in the United States to London, where trade could now occur on the basis of reliable and trustworthy prices and without the costly need of going through a US exchange. Global finance was not only built on trust and institutional power; it also required cables, circuits, and software linking offices, records, and money across space.

Despite commanding a vast trading network, by the late 1970s, Reuters did not dominate trading in foreign stocks in London. Their threat was nevertheless real, as Hayter noted in his interview.

> Reuters sensed there was an opportunity for them to move in and be the market in some major respect. In the same way that they had already become the trading mechanism for foreign exchange, they wanted to do the same thing for equities. And the first area that they started in was in was foreign equities that were not listed in London . . . And so they set up pages that looked a bit like SEAQ, in black and white, on their Reuters monitor screens, company by company, and [in these] you could see all the market-makers' quotations. [They] thought "Well, this is our opportunity to corner, to provide the electronic infrastructure for the foreign securities market in London."

The engineers were mobilized. With its newfound motivation to become a hub of a global trading, the exchange embraced an aggressive strategy. "I put Peter Cox in charge of competing with Reuters on this," said Hayter, "and we succeeded in creating a primitive market that actually beat Reuters at their own game."[3]

---

[3] Hayter interview.

At the time, Peter Cox was closely involved with the development of at least three of the stock exchange's largest projects and therefore possessed enough intra-organizational capital to embark on such an ambitious task. An engineer by training, Cox was seconded to the stock exchange from IBM in 1976 where he had worked on expert systems applications. Based on this experience, Cox was made responsible for designing the settlement system TALISMAN, which relied on a recently acquired IBM 370/145. For Cox, the development environment for TALISMAN was formative. The stock exchange had

> brought in some new people. They had decided that we were going to do it in a different way. And there was sort of a clean broom that swept through the project. That was extremely exciting, because it had really good people on it. There was a determination to do the thing properly. It was a terrific project. For me, at the time, and for everybody working on it.[4]

Launched in 1979, "two weeks later than the plan [because] we were going through some very extensive market testing," TALISMAN became an emblem of the exchange's technological prowess: the system survived for almost two decades and was widely recognized as a feat of the exchange and its technologists.

On the back of TALISMAN's success, Cox moved to a joint project between the Bank of England and the London Stock Exchange to mechanize the settlement of so-called gilt-edged securities (or government debt bonds, equivalent to United States Treasury bonds) within the Central Gilts Office, working under the auspices of the Bank of England. There, he worked alongside Peter Bennett, who was also involved in redesigning settlement for government securities with a view to "dematerializing" record keeping. Toward 1984, and with Big Bang fast approaching, Cox was asked to join "a loose team of

---

[4] Cox interview.

planners" that reported directly to the then deputy chief executive, John Young. As Cox recalled,

> our job was to work out what needed to be done for Big Bang. We came up with a plan, which was to create the SEAQ system ... modeled on NASDAQ but ... based on an information system the Stock Exchange was already running called TOPIC [of which] Bennett was the architect ... I was actually the only permanent member of this planning team.

Formed by Michael Newman, Peter Bennett, Daniel Sheridan, Cox, and others, the planning group was not only focused on technological questions – the work of remaking the market's devices also entailed rebuilding the organization and the relations that it contained. This was particularly true given the fact that technical and organizational roadmaps on how exchanges should automate did not exist within the industry. As Cox stressed, working out the "functionality that would suit the market [was] not a foregone conclusion in those days"; at the time there were not any "models which [had] been proven in the market, when you design[ed] an electronic market."[5]

There were several possibilities among many emerging and somewhat embryonic market designs. One was to build a market using the systems pioneered by Instinet in the United States for trading blocs of securities over the counter. If a UK pilot of this system were successful, it could be expanded for the market at large in time for Big Bang, circumventing the need for developing an entirely novel platform from scratch. The choice of Instinet insinuated a particular market for the trial, as Cox said:

> The idea was that, since we were running Instinet technology and all their expertise were in American securities and [that] there [was a] market in American securities in London, [we should] start a market in [these] running on the Instinet system and then, if

---

[5] Cox interview.

successful, roll it out into other markets, potentially into the UK equity market.[6]

But the trial did not take this shape. When Cox and his colleagues looked into the feasibility of this pilot, traders in American securities in London quickly rejected their plans. "Hardly any of [them] were members of the Stock Exchange," recalled Cox.

> They were almost all big [investment banks], Morgan Stanley, and Shearson Lehman, Merrill Lynch … We [told them] "We have this great idea. We want to launch a European time zone market in American shares. You guys are in the business, you're doing it right now, it'll be great. And just sign up being alongside us with this pilot." And they said "Oh, that's a stupid idea. You're talking about putting a sophisticated system which runs in the most structured and regulated market in the world out here in Europe, where this American shares market runs with no regulation at all, and nobody has oversight of it. [London is] a bit of a Wild West market. And you want to put all this sophisticated transparent technology in there. Well that's a daft idea, and we're not going to do it."

The failure of their original idea did not stop Cox's team. On the contrary, they concocted the "craziest plan B" they could have thought of.

> [Most] of [the foreign dealers] were saying, "Well, you know, an organized market is not such a bad idea." So we said "Why don't we organize a market in these shares. We don't have to put all the sexy technology in place, but just try to organize a market for these players."

If the prevailing view among foreign firms was that the market for American securities was "a bit of a Wild West" then an obvious solution was to tame the chaos by structuring and regulating the market.

---

[6] Cox interview.

The electronic marketplace introduced by the exchange depended not so much on a singular technological innovation but on forms of heterogeneous engineering anchored on knowing the market's history and dynamics, on the careful articulation of relations and devices (both legal and material) to create a space were trading through the exchange's systems made practical sense for all participants. Sitting in a large room near Pall Mall in London, Peter Cox noted that,

> [In thinking about the market,] we went right back to first principles. What are stock exchanges? Why are there stock exchanges? Stock exchanges started because these people were buying and selling shares in rooms like this centuries ago [and] suddenly there were rogues amongst them. And the good guys got together and said "Well we'll form a club of good guys and we'll sign up to a code of conduct that says we're good guys and [when] somebody slips up and doesn't meet the code of conduct, we'll throw him out and that way we'll gain confidence, you know, a market." And that was exactly the situation we were in with these international dealing guys. They were doing the business but not everybody was quite playing by the rules.

While necessarily predicated on the rationalizing force of the stock exchange's ever-expanding bureaucracy, at least some of the market's success depended on the personal qualities of individuals that, like Peter Cox, were called to office to inform the rules that should govern trading. Success derived, at least partly, from impressing upon the market's users some sort of charismatic authority, based as much on the technical competencies of exchange engineers as on their ability to engage in the type of fine-grained relational work required to convince foreign firms to use a novel British trading system. Like pensive lawmakers, the exchange's technologists brought together the different users across the City of London to determine the standards for the market. Note the difference between the engineers and the image of a staff expert in a traditional Weberian bureaucracy, an individual that derives power from the uncertainty of the situation confronting management. Although the creation of an international market was certainly new for the exchange's management (and therefore potentially risky, particularly given the fact that this was occurring in parallel to the preparations for Big Bang), the technologists acted as brokers and arbiters rather than as distant and authoritative experts. In deciding the operation of the market, for example, "[we] allowed [prospective participants] to set the rules for how [their] quotations were to be interpreted," noted George Hayter, who oversaw Peter Cox's project.

> And [we also allowed users to define] things like what the standard size would be for the quotations, what currency they should be quoted in, what settlement house would be used for the clearing process. These were not universally accepted, they were not standardized, until we got these people together in a room.[7]

If there was an area where the exchange technologists possessed uncontested authority, it was certainly in developing visualization technologies for the marketplace. In the view of Cox's team, the market simply lacked a "uniformity of presentation, [instead] working according to how each individual firm interpreted it."[8] For a single market to emerge from the multiple ad hoc platforms and mechanism that existed in London for trading international securities, exchange engineers imposed visual and operational uniformity, embodied in a common electronic price bulletin board where quotes were simultaneously broadcast to all participants. With their accrued recognition as makers of market devices, Cox's group grew into a competent builder of market institutions: "from creating a sort of ... bulletin board," he recalled, "to being a market department which regulated the market, wrote the rules, and also created a membership scheme for foreigners."[9]

---

[7] Hayter interview.   [8] Cox interview.   [9] Cox interview.

Like other developments surrounding Big Bang, SEAQ International was a form of opportunistic bricolage, combining tried and tested innovations across several domains. It cobbled together existing systems, most notably the price dissemination platform provided by EPIC and TOPIC, with a new organizational arrangement that incorporated foreign firms into the exchange. "When you think about it," said Peter Cox,

> it was a bit of a major step. But again, it was it was small-scale stuff when it started. Nobody thought it was really important. The argument we made was "let's try to get these guys inside and collaborate with us and then we'll gradually reel them in."

Although built with existing pieces, the system was nevertheless revolutionary. From having occupied a marginal position in the market for overseas securities, the exchange became, once again, a hub of international (or at the very least European) finance. As SEAQ International matured, it colonized neighboring markets, and by the late 1980s it captured between 26 percent and 60 percent of the trading in shares of the 250 largest European companies. By 1990, trading in French stocks on SEAQ International represented as much as one fourth of the volume of the same type of transactions on the Paris Bourse (Jacquillat and Gresse, 1998). The platform "sucked liquidity from the continental market centers," recalled Peter Bennett with visible pride.

SEAQ International confirmed that, as Cox wrote in 1985, "in the future the business of buying and selling securities is going to be heavily computerized and based upon large scale networks" (Cox, 1985). Yet the experience of building the market also indicated that future developments did not "therefore [lie] entirely in the hands of the technologists." If anything, SEAQ International's success resulted from the careful rearticulation of relations and from the act of weaving the social fabric of an engineered marketplace by creating systems, standards, rules, and organizations that were seen as legitimate by traders and their counterparties in the market. In this, SEAQ International demonstrated that "traditional" stock exchanges were still necessary, even in an increasingly automated world. They created "confidence in the marketplace, [allowing] for it to reach its full potential." The future, wrote Cox, "lies in the successful blending of modern technologies with some of the more customary functions performed by stock exchanges today." If traditional stock exchanges still mattered it was also because of their engineers: through years of work, they nurtured valuable forms of tacit knowledge and heterogeneous skills that were key for producing markets anew.

5.2   PIPE DREAMS

The significance of SEAQ International was twofold. First, it demonstrated practically that the exchange's engineers could build an ordered, functioning market from a bunch of unwieldy transactions. No international market existed within the stock exchange prior to their efforts to establish what became one of Europe's largest platforms for stock trading. Market engineers soldered relations as effectively as wires; they produced rules as efficiently as writing code. Within the organization, they were recompensed for their contributions: Peter Bennett was promoted to executive director and joined the exchange's management board along with George Hayter and Peter Cox (see Figure 5.1).

But SEAQ International was also significant in a second way: it involved working outside the organizational boundaries of the exchange and its membership – expanding the market community, so to speak, by wrangling foreign firms into using the LSE's systems. The platform was a thoroughly interorganizational achievement that projected the competencies and charisma of the engineers well beyond the exchange and the City of London. As SEAQ and SEAQ-I demonstrated their resilience, they became known across the global financial industry as flagship cases of technological innovation in the marketplace (Clemons and Weber, 1990, 1997; Schwartz and Weber, 1997). As Bennett recalled, "The people at the New York Stock Exchange at the sort of technical institutional level were jealous of our systems ... they couldn't believe we had this system, because

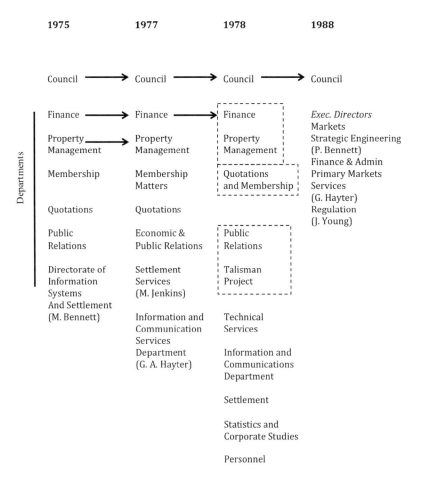

FIGURE 5.1 Changes in the organizational structure of the London Stock Exchange, 1975–1988. Compiled from *The Stock Exchange Yearbook*, 1975, 1977, 1978, and 1988.

they had Quotron … and this was ten times better than Quotron. They couldn't believe we owned and controlled this [and that] we could actually use this as a centerpiece of our market automation program."[10]

---

[10] Bennett interview. There is, again, some poetic license. As Chapter 7 shows, the NYSE developed its systems in an entirely different context and under quite different constraints.

Of course, the visibility gained by the engineers behind SEAQ International and the LSE's other trading infrastructures was not only a result of their technical competencies but also of carefully knitting relations and curating their identities within the burgeoning global field of market technologies. Remember that, by the 1980s, electronic technologies were common in most financial markets – and had been so for at least a decade, creating a field of mutually observing actors involved in developing the newest generations of trading and settlement systems for banks, brokerage houses, and exchanges across the world. As a field rife with both competition and opportunities, then, the exchange's technologists sought to stake their claims. Some, such as George Hayter, actively cultivated networks within the industry by organizing specialist conferences on innovations in banking and finance (notably, Computers in the City, a series of meetings that provide a glimpse of the numerous developments at the time),[11] and participating in international summits on technology, including the International Federation of Stock Exchanges' committee on technology, co-created by Hayter with other European market technologists, and to which they "dragged [in] people like Bill Lupien and Bill Porter from Instinet and E*Trade, respectively ... to sound wake up calls for the sleeping stock exchanges."[12] Peter Bennett similarly nurtured his networks, contributing to international projects such as the US Congress, Office of Technology Assessment's (US Congress, 1990) Electronic Bulls and Bears report, and establishing working relations with important brokers in the industry, including Michael Porter (founder of the Monitor Group), Peter Schwarz (founder of the Global Business Network), IBM's Federal Systems Division, and Boeing's Information Systems group, with whom he discussed the challenges faced by the exchange and financial services in general.[13] And on the back of their relational investments and the prominence of the systems they developed, technologists like Peter Cox and Iain McLelland were

---

[11] Hayter interview.   [12] Hayter interview.   [13] Bennett interview.

invited to join the efforts of automating other marketplaces, including futures and options exchanges in Britain and across the world.[14]

The rise of a field of global market technologies was also coupled to an emerging impetus to automate the work of financial organizations. This was particularly clear in the United States where, since the late 1960s, automation was seen as a way of controlling the spiraling costs of managing larger trading volumes. Consider the example of the computerized dealing system presented by John Herzog of the market-making firm Herzog, Heine, Geduld Inc. in the 1984 edition of Computers in the City. As Herzog (1984: 46) wrote, between 1983 and 1984 trading volumes grew from about 4,500 daily trades to over 9,000, with "increased errors while morale declined. The magic of computers seemed to be the only answer." The description provided by Herzog is striking, but not because of its uniqueness within the industry (similar systems were common in the United States at the time). His statement is striking because of its distinctiveness relative to other contributions in the volume. Automation may have already been an organizational myth in American finance, but it was not the case in the United Kingdom, where discussions tended to focus on settlement and information dissemination rather than automated trade execution.

Fast-forward eight years to 1992 and the culture of the exchange had not changed that much. The engineers may have transformed the marketplace in substantive ways, but some critical elements of the market's structure remained unaltered and immune to automation. Although an entirely electronic market (the vast majority of transactions were conducted through SEAQ and reported on TOPIC), the London Stock Exchange of the early 1990s still respected a mechanism of trading that had existed since its founding almost two centuries earlier: trading was quote-driven, meaning that market makers quoted prices throughout the day, competing with each other to draw the business of interested brokers. Order-driven markets – prime

---

[14] Cox interview; McLelland interview.

candidates for automation through the introduction of electronic order books – had yet to arrive in Britain.

Producing an organizational myth around the possibilities of automation intelligible to London's community required more than simply the authority derived from technological expertise. It implied convincing the market community to engage in a fundamental shift, to move from quotes to orders. Much was at stake in this transformation: most importantly, it eliminated the centrality of the jobber or market maker as the source of legitimate prices, delegating its responsibilities to a device where orders interacted seamlessly and anonymously, a move from the controlled, elite crowds of the virtual trading floor to the inclusiveness of the order book's algorithmic queues. The trick for catalyzing this transformation was a well-orchestrated performance: to signal the power of automation, market engineers demonstrated that they possessed particular gifts and that these were of consequence to the market. What they needed was a form of charismatic authentication that, as Weber (1978: 440) wrote in his discussion of prophets, "in practice meant magic."

Staging a convincing, almost magical demonstration of the power of automation was certainly not the first choice of market technologists. On the contrary, they seemed to have preferred working through and within the bureaucracies of their organization. For instance, before leaving the LSE in 1990, Peter Bennett "earned [his] bread" by convincing "the top exchanges in Europe to agree that there was a need for a European price dissemination system" that could lead to the automation of trading throughout the continent.[15] Initiated in 1990 under the benevolent chairmanship of Andrew Hugh-Smith, the project that Bennett commanded through his new consultanly firm was tied to a long genealogy of technologies at the stock exchange. On the one hand, it had the same ambition as the failed Integrated Data Network, seeking to establish a single, stand-ardized infrastructure for trading and information dissemination

---

[15] Bennett interview.

across Europe. More importantly, perhaps, the project sought to "develop and capitalize on the SEAQ International market place," read a confidential memorandum from March 28, 1990, making it the "basis for [an] iminent [*sic*] decision on European Strategy."[16] This drive was born out of not only an expansionary logic among the exchange's management (using SEAQ International was clearly an attractive route because it would give LSE even more control over the shape and content of the emerging European equities market), but also followed on from accumulated work at the European level to foster communication across the exchanges of the region. As early as 1982, for instance, the Directorate-General of the Commission and the Committee of Stock Exchanges in the European Economic Community (EEC) had studied the options for greater integration, seeing the development of NASDAQ and the Intermarket Trading System in the United States as potential templates for communicating trading floors in the continent, but also noting the great difficulties of building a mandatory trading platform across European borders.[17] But while the details of intermarket communication were never truly hammered out, the European Commission set 1992 as the deadline for implementing the free flow of financial services between the then twelve member states. This confluence was an opportunity for entrepreneurs like Bennett.

In this project of European integration, Bennett was joined by two colleagues from the exchange: Michael Waller-Bridge and Stephen Wilson. Unlike other experienced LSE technologists, Waller-Bridge was a bit of an outsider to the city's culture. After studying theoretical physics, working at CERN, and prior to joining Bennett's Advanced Systems Group at the exchange in early 1986, Waller-Bridge worked in the domain of holographic technology and

[16] Peter Bennett, Memorandum, March 28, 1990.
[17] Michael Hall and Malcolm Duncan (1985), "Proposals for a European equities market through linkage of the community stock exchanges," Report to the Commission of the European Communities and the Committee of Stock Exchanges of the EEC.

aesthetic 3-D imaging, a "mixture of science, creative and entrepreneurial work." Although exciting and consistent with Waller-Bridge's artistic affinities (today, he is also a successful photographic portraitist), a career in holographic technology and art was not sustainable; but it was an unexpected path into the exchange. After a chance introduction to Peter Bennett in 1986, who in turn introduced him to George Hayter, Waller-Bridge was hired to help Bennett's team research the impact of new technologies on the exchange's future operations. "I had established an early UK form of start-up associated with Imperial College ... we had achieved three patents and had been trying with some difficulty to introduce the applications for this intellectual property to aspects of PET scan imaging, and I think this somewhat wild stuff was one of the reasons I was recruited. I was thrilled at the opportunity to work with Peter," recalled Waller-Bridge. This same experience would prove important later on. As he noted in his interview,

> we [Bennett, Waller-Bridge, and Stephen Wilson] generated ... the idea that there should be [a] cost effective infrastructure on a pan-European basis, not in a federalized sense but a set of cooperative arrangements [between the members of the Federation of Stock Exchanges of the European Community]. Peter and I and others in the group were assigned to it. And this became a joint venture. It was a joint venture between the principal stock exchanges of the then 12 member states. Peter was in charge of the strategic vision and the technology. I coordinated the joint venture agreement negotiations and, with London's blessing, was put in charge of the joint venture company established on behalf of the then 12 European Community stock exchanges through the Federation of Stock Exchanges in the European Community.

Much like SEAQ International, the Price and Information Project for Europe (PIPE) involved navigating a complex political landscape, both within and outside their organization. The system, chartered by the Federation of Stock Exchanges of the European

Community and similar to a combination of the United States' Consolidated Tape and the NASDAQ's Small Order Execution System (SOES), required individual national stock exchanges to partly surrender control over their price and quote data feeds. It also required harmonizing practices across exchanges. As Malcolm Duncan from the Milan Stock Exchange and by then a veteran of European market integration noted, for prices on PIPE to be reliable "exchanges must develop similar rules for reporting prices [and should develop] similar trade clearing and settlement procedures" (quoted in Crockett, 1990: 21). As Waller-Bridge recalled, the system was an ambitious attempt to create "a central information capture and delivery point for regulated and strategic securities market information" enabling the "the dissemination of this information in real time throughout Europe." The early documentation for the project demonstrates this well: the network would have been "capable of providing interactive access to market systems operated by [national] Exchanges," thereby creating "a central point for automated trade execution, trade confirmation and settlement message routing," similar in design to the globally accessible order book envisioned for IDN (1990 PIPE business plan by the Federation of Stock Exchanges in Europe Authority).

The initial support for PIPE was mixed. On the one hand, the project presented a formidable solution to the problem of off-exchange trading. A table from the 1990 business case for PIPE stressed this aspect of the project: whereas only some European exchanges possessed effective proprietary information dissemination systems, Reuters, Quotron, and Telerate had more than 250,000 screens across the continent, trading upward of 190,000 instruments. For smaller exchanges, PIPE could become a means for reaching a broader market, taming the competition of non-exchange screen-based trading that increasingly fragmented the continent. On the other hand, PIPE challenged the established monopolies in the region. Incumbents agreed on the importance of integration, but differed on how it should be achieved. Fearing that London would control the market, for instance, Paris proposed a so-called "Euro-list" that would concentrate trading reports on the most active European shares in a single system, securing trading levels on the existing national exchanges while eroding the regulatory standing of SEAQ International. The German Federation of exchanges was, in contrast, quite enthusiastic about a common platform and insisted on developing it even further into a fully operational trading system and settlement linkage. For London, however, integration made sense only insofar as SEAQ International remained the stronghold it had become. Documentary evidence confirms such a position, as made clear by a confidential note written by the LSE's then chairman, Andrew Hugh-Smith in 1990. London, wrote Hugh-Smith, "will find itself in an exposed position and its interests put substantially at risk if it is seen to seek a separate, non-European path." As Hugh-Smith suggested, the centerpiece of the LSE's strategy "should be to propose to the other European exchanges the formation of a wholesale or professional marketplace [necessarily] based initially on SEAQ International and its current membership." With this, he surmised, London would keep its central role in the international market.

But like IDN a few years earlier, PIPE never materialized. Its failure was not catalyzed by the constraints of implementation timelines but by the new politics that reigned within the London Stock Exchange. As Waller-Bridge recalls, planning for PIPE reached quite advanced stages: as early as January 1990, the Federation of Stock Exchanges in the European Community issued an open invitation for tenders to build the Pan-European Market Information Network. By April, the Technical Planning Committee for PIPE had conducted a formal procurement exercise that resulted in a short-list of four potential providers: Citicorp, Andersen Consulting, General Electric Information Services, and Price Waterhouse. In May, the federation signed the joint venture agreement that served as the basis for PIPE, authorizing funds voted by the participant stock exchanges and expenditures for the project. Soon after, the selection committee narrowed down the possible providers to Citicorp/Quotron and GE Information Services. "This caused a wobbly," said Waller-Bridge.

Our office got a call from Peter Rawlins [the LSE's incoming chief executive] who said "can you rethink this choice?" And we said "this is a result of a formal process," and he said "can you show me the papers?" And so we shipped to him a cabinet full of copies of committee meeting records and formal minutes. And then we got a call from Andersen Consulting saying "we're not on the list," "well no, I mean, the due process has come up with these other shortlisted candidates." And that's the point that I believe that Andersen Consulting said "right, if we can't get into this European scale [infrastructure project] we'll just work with the London Stock Exchange as that's the biggest and frankly our 'low fruit.'" Which had not been in the planning before that. Then, when the great outsourcing started, we felt that it was really time to move on.

The resulting powerful opposition from LSE – undoubtedly a hegemonic force within European markets – made the project of an integrated platform untenable; the very idea, noted Waller-Bridge, "became taboo."[18]

On the face of such unexpected adversity, one could easily imagine that the technologists would have abandoned their project of creating an interconnected regional marketplace. Surprisingly, they remained ardently committed to their worldview. The path they chose to realize such vision was bewildering:

[When] Peter and I and [Wilson] had left the London Stock Exchange, we had started a consulting company. And from that consulting company, named Bennett, Waller-Bridge & Wilson or BWW … we had a plan to [show that a] European-wide infrastructure could work. It really was going to work, so now we decided to anchor it in the U.K., i.e., absolutely no try to start it again through international or institutional committee structures nor establish it "offshore." We wanted it to come into being as a venture but within a regulated environment. It could eventually

---

[18] Waller-Bridge interview.

lead to a [regional] system, though built in the UK. [But] we were no longer within [a financial] institution, which of course had both its pluses and minuses.[19]

To build a common infrastructure, Bennett, Waller-Bridge, and Wilson required institutional support beyond their small consultancy – they needed to be in the field, they needed an electronic exchange. But aside from the unsuccessful Automated Real-Time Investment Exchange, ARIEL, there was no electronic trading platform in Britain. And so they set out to design and build one in Thames Wharf.

5.3   FLAT-PACKED MAGIC

Creating an exchange in the early 1990s was mostly a problem of recruiting users and dealing with regulatory constraints, rather than one of developing the technologies necessary for electronic trading. For instance, both the Toronto and Paris Stock Exchanges had operated sophisticated electronic trading systems since 1977 and 1986 respectively. While admittedly far from being automated, the New York Stock Exchange also had its own suite of electronic trading systems that were fully patented and licensed to other users. NASDAQ was, by then, also well experienced with its Small Order Execution System. Elsewhere in the world, electronic trading technologies were also making their way onto the floors of long-established stock and derivative exchanges. As Michael Gorham and Nidhi Singh (2009) show, by 1992 the National Stock Exchange in Chicago, Finland's OMX Nordic Exchange, and the stock exchanges of Chile, Saudi Arabia, Australia, Warsaw, Thailand, and New Zealand were fully electronic. This was certainly not occurring in a vacuum. On the contrary, the growing global field of market technologies was characterized by an expanding ecology of inventors, firms, and consultants that built electronic trading platforms for numerous clients across the world. In many ways, exchanges were becoming off-the-shelf commodities.

[19]   Waller-Bridge interview.

Within this sprawling ecology, there was increasing recognition of a dominant design. In the rare cases where exchanges had fully automated, the process was invariably linked to the adoption of electronic order books that allowed for the direct interaction of instructions from investors without the intervention of humans to coordinate transactions. The same design was used by firms that emerged in the late 1980s and early 1990s to challenge the place of incumbent exchanges: they, too, opted for markets built around electronic order books rather than specialists or competing market makers. Owing to its clear computational behavior, its frugal economies, and impressive efficiencies, the bets were down and in favor of the order book: as the financial economist Lawrence Glosten wrote in 1994, order books were "inevitable," "the only stable institution" given the environment and trading structures of finance at the time (Glosten, 1994). This seeming inevitability was also partly ethical: actors deemed old markets closed and inefficient particularly when contrasted to the open and transparent functionality of the order book. Stephen Wilson recalls:

> all we'd really done with Big Bang is taken the trading process and moved it from the floor to screens, because you still had market makers, jobbers, you still had two way prices, there was still very restrictive access and we thought that there was a different way of doing things. SEAQ International had been quite successful in a sense, in moving liquidity away from the continental European exchanges, so what that did for them was giving them a kick up the bum, if you will, in the sense that they very quickly automated and they all had made around [electronic order books]. [We] felt that there was an inevitability in that, that we would move away from SEAQ but also that … we needed [to] really embrace institutional access to markets and actually make it more attractive for them to actually get direct access to the London marketplace.[20]

---

[20] Wilson interview.

The choice for Bennett, Waller-Bridge, and Wilson was given: their exchange would have an order book at its core.

To create their new marketplace, Bennett, Waller-Bridge, and Wilson set up offices far from the City of London's gentlemanly streets, choosing Thames Wharf in Hammersmith as their home. "That's where all the creative work was done," noted Wilson.[21]

> [That's where we defined] what were the market constructs, what the technology was, what the regulatory structure was, et cetera, et cetera. And that was really the genesis of the whole thing that became Tradepoint. [It] took us the best part of five years [to launch Tradepoint] [You've] got to remember that when we started we were literally three guys, a bunch of packing boxes and an assistant answering the phone, some IKEA tables and chairs, one phone line, trying to think "right, how are we going to do this" with literally a clean sheet of paper.[22]

Waller-Bridge recalled that, at a later press interview, he was asked what was the first asset that the team acquired to build its new exchange. Was it some sophisticated new computer? the journalist asked. "No," replied Waller-Bridge. "It was the electric screwdriver to put the IKEA furniture together."[23]

Hosting the studios of architect Richard Rogers, Thames Wharf could not have been further culturally from the old and established spaces of the city. The building that hosted Bennett, Waller-Bridge, and Wilson's early efforts was also home to the renowned River Café, a culinary magnet that attracted the senior city denizens that they needed to lobby. Meetings, recalled Waller-Bridge, were almost always scheduled "around noon." And even if far from the city, people "tended to accept … meals for visitors at the River Café constituted nearly our entire project marketing budget which was, in this context,

---

[21] As Waller-Bridge noted in a personal communication, the premises at Thames Wharf were rented by architect Richard Rogers, who as a gesture for creativity, offered entrepreneurs spaces on a month-by-month basis with no deposit.
[22] Wilson interview.   [23] Waller-Bridge personal communication.

great value but of course for us somewhat tough to maintain any sort of discipline in holding back on the fabulous fare ourselves in favour of the visitors – we had necessarily financially often to restrict ourselves to the spectacular menu's 'sides' only. But it worked in getting influencers to visit us away from their own offices and so create a chance to put our case to them."[24]

There was something notably symbolic in their choice of office location: for Bennett and his colleagues, their exchange was necessarily different from the incumbent, both in design and in meaning. Tradepoint was clearly an "oppositional" challenger to the London Stock Exchange (Fligstein and McAdam, 2011: 6), offering "[a public] electronic order-driven marketplace with guaranteed performance of trades."[25] Tradepoint was predicated on a moral imperative: by allowing competition beyond the control of the LSE's market makers, their electronic order book would narrow spreads, driving down the costs for end investors. As Wilson recalled, "[our] view was that we needed really to embrace institutional access to [the] London marketplace … we were really clear that we needed to do was to have a marketplace which was open, it wasn't just a sell side classical stock exchange with broker-dealers." Their exchange was, as Waller-Bridge noted, "consumer led at the institutional level." Investors would "have equal access to the price formation mechanism, which would then bring along competition, lower charges, increase service levels, be better for the pension funds, better for the savings community as a whole. We even thought of calling it 'The People's Exchange' … in the sense that it would be working very much at a neutral stance to the institutions."[26] Even at the level of symbolic investments, they were clearly different: rather than projecting an image of trust built on tradition, they cultivated edginess and innovation in public (Figure 5.2).

Tradepoint was not entirely detached from the exchange, of course, benefiting from the expertise built throughout the

---

[24] Waller-Bridge, personal communication.   [25] Waller-Bridge interview.
[26] Waller-Bridge interview.

FIGURE 5.2 Photograph of Tradepoint's founders. Peter Bennett is second from the right, followed by Stephen Wilson and Michael Waller-Bridge.

organization's previous decades of infrastructural growth. In addition to Bennett, Waller-Bridge, and Wilson, Ian McLelland and John Scannell – both veterans of the exchange's technical teams – joined Tradepoint. But unlike their experience at LSE, their challenge was not to create a trading system from scratch but to contrive ways and means of tinkering with commercially available solutions to quickly create an electronic platform compatible with London's institutional environment. Like the IKEA chairs in their offices, the solution was also prepacked: "We bought ... the basic software package from the Vancouver Stock Exchange, [a] basic market package," recalled

Waller-Bridge. "It was excellently built, and while not entirely suitable for our design, it got us to base camp, [and] we could then change it. [McLelland] added to, substracted from, and [modified] the software, and routine parts of it that they weren't doing themselves they would outsource to India. [It] was a huge development. [What] Ian built was absolutely amazing at the time."

Tradepoint's engineers also placed great efforts on creating the clearing and settlement infrastructures that would make the marketplace viable. Recall that a central feature of exchanges (and, arguably, of markets at large) is the understated role played by the bureaucracy and organizational infrastructure that ties and rearranges relations, processing transactions from their point of origin to the moment when buyers and sellers are "quits." A trading platform is useless without its clearing and settlement architecture, a point that the technologists at Tradepoint knew all too well. To build their exchange, they had to articulate much more than devices. They needed to create legitimate relations.

For Stephen Wilson, this was one of the critical elements for Tradepoint's success. If the market were to operate in an efficient yet anonymous fashion, Tradepoint had to guarantee that all orders were logged in records linked to the trading accounts of the relevant market participant. Orders had to index an underlying administrative reality that determined who owned what and when. For the London Stock Exchange, this mechanism was largely given by the way it had organized membership around a common, pooled settlement department: between members, there was an expectation that settlement would occur. With Tradepoint, however, the issue was more complex. Users were not members in the same sense as with LSE but "participants," as Waller-Bridge recalled, and clearly it was simply unrealistic and impractical to ask firms to make deposits in advance of stocks they were willing to trade.

The solution crafted by Wilson challenged the institutional boundaries of the city. Rather than setting up their own clearing mechanism, Tradepoint reached an agreement with the London

Clearing House who provided clearing and settlement services to the London International Financial Futures Exchange, then headed by the indisputably seasoned and experienced City veteran Sir Michael Jenkins. Jenkins, who had been instrumental in setting up the exchange's settlement services in the 1970s, had then moved on to foster futures trading in London and now joined forces with Bennett, Waller-Bridge, and Wilson and their team. Certainly, when Jenkins joined the board of Tradepoint, he joined a group of odd insiders, including Stanley Ross, the banker who set in motion the Eurobond market in 1963. The exchange's past was challenging its uncertain future.[27]

5.4   THE POWER OF SPECTACLE

Heavyweights like Jenkins and Ross were necessary for gaining legitimacy within the still relatively conservative field of British finance. As most of its contemporaries argued, Tradepoint represented a radical departure from the cultural logic of London's markets: "[There] was absolutely no heritage to lean on in this respect, no one in the UK market at the time had any real knowledge or experience of order book trading. It was a completely foreign construct whereby you physically put an order into the market rather than trading on the phone and reporting it using some kind of price discovery," recalled Waller-Bridge in his interview. How best, then, to convince prospective market users of the advantages of their system?

In recruiting support during its initial phase, the makers of Tradepoint engaged in a calculated strategy of what I call a "revelation" through which they made public and visible the infrastructures of the market that they built. In addition to securing a fixed-price deal from Brunswick, an emerging public relations firm that would become one of the most renowned in Britain,[28] the engineers at Tradepoint manifested the superiority of their system by staging

---

[27] Bennett interview; Jenkins interview.   [28] Waller-Bridge interview.

demonstrations of its awesome, almost mystical, materiality. Waller-Bridge recalled:

> [Tradepoint's system] was built [with commercially available] computer technology at the time, [and] I do remember that we had issues with both investors and market players saying: "This must be a huge computer, absolutely vast to deal with an actual real electronic market! Have you got big enough computers?" And I'd say "Oh, we've got very good computers, brilliant development skills and world-class communications tech. Peter Bennett knows his stuff, Ian McLelland knows his stuff, and John Scannell knows his stuff ... That's a world-class constellation of talent. We've got it all spec'ed properly [and] of course it is going be seriously backed up and thoroughly stress-tested." Typically, in those days, enterprise computers were about still the size of [a very small] room, but [we'd recently] moved to [King Street off] Covent Garden.[29] We had this one large room [to securely house the Stratus] computer. Once placed in the room, it looked rather small, because actually, [without] all the peripherals, the actual computer was probably the size of [a large] sofa. So I said "We can't show someone that, because ... they will think it's too small for its purpose. I mean, you can go through this rationally but they just won't [trust] us." And Peter said, "You're right! What are we going to do?" And I said, "Look John [Scannell], please, could you go and buy the biggest, fattest ventilator-cowling [possible], like [the ones] in a James Bond film? And you have the room, and it says "Computer Room" on its door, and you put the computer in there, and then you put its mains-supply wire inside this giant ventilator-cowling, and [this] sort of pipe thing visibly [comes out from the room] through a cabinet on the side of the door and goes down the corridor [as if drawing upon a huge power plant]" [At] least then we [could] say "The computers are

---

[29] As Waller-Bridge noted in a personal communication, "We chose Covent Garden not only because it took us back into central London but symbolically because the 'Piazza' had hosted other 'real' London markets (e.g., in food, flowers) for centuries."

in there, we don't really like to disturb the computer environment or its security, so visitors go in there rarely, but that is the Computer Room, and the machinery has to be kept supported with its own Uninterrupted Power Supply." And people would come on the tour of the general facilities, see the demo of the trading system, be shown the Control Room which we put together in a high-tech design style behind a glass viewing window, and then they'd see there was a special room bearing a large sign on the door which said "Do Not Enter: Computer Room," John Scannell's domain, and they'd see this huge duct going in, and *it somehow gave a sense that there was power and depth to it*, because people found it very difficult to believe that you would actually reliably support a market on the technology of the time – but you could do it, and [we] did do.[30]

Waller-Bridge's recollections clearly allude to what MacKenzie identifies as the "embodiment of the charisma and expertise" of engineers in their machines (MacKenzie, 1996): in creating an artificially elaborate computer room on King Street, Waller-Bridge and Scannell performed a theatrical infrastructural inversion of their marketplace (Bowker and Star, 1999), stressing the "sense of power and depth" of the computerized order book that amplified its materiality through props and expectations. The strategy was vital: although Bennett's involvement in Tradepoint was "critically important; [people] knew [the system] was going to be substantive," market acceptance of expertise was undermined by the novelty and uncertainty of the platform. To be convincing, Tradepoint had to deter hesitation, and for this it utilized Waller-Bridge's idea of threading the normal mainspower cable through a "large ducting thing" that established a "sense of security in the system" (Hargrave and Van de Ven, 2009: 130) by speaking to the user's expectations about technology and the "huge" amount of computing power perceived required for the endeavor. The performance was successful: before going live in

---

[30] Waller-Bridge interview; emphasis added.

September 1995, Tradepoint managed to recruit more than 45 members, including an emerging group of quantitative traders interested in the speed, anonymity, and efficiency of the system.

Tradepoint's creation is a rather peculiar episode not the least because it challenges conventional ideas about the rationality of market organizations. The staged revelation of Tradepoint's infrastructures was not entirely "rational," in a traditional sense: it was not a strategy that sought to gain dominance in the field by imposing a particular cultural worldview; it was not predicated on an underlying reality; and it probably was not even believable for those versed in technology at the time. It was, however, an effective form of spectacle that created an opportunity for the skeptics to commune with Tradepoint's electronic systems. At a basic level, the props were almost a form of magical instrumentality, to use Weber's term, that created a moment where users and engineers could fraternize around the possibilities of digital markets. It was, in other words, a process of fabricating myths that could travel easily and legitimately within the cultural milieu of London's financial community.

5.5   CONVERTING THE FIELD

While invoking trust in their system, the strategies followed by Tradepoint's technologists also questioned the taken-for-granted status quo of London's market institutions: they demonstrated practically that a different marketplace was possible. This was certainly a controversial proposal, as Wilson recalled. "At the time," said Wilson in his interview, "the idea [of competing] with the [London] Stock Exchange was unthought-of. Because, why would you? The [regulations] somehow don't allow it because, of course, there can only be one stock exchange. You have the London Stock Exchange, the Paris Stock Exchange, the Frankfurt Stock Exchange, [and] the Milan Stock Exchange. They are a bit like the village pub or church. You have one. And there is no concept of competition."[31]

[31] Wilson interview.

But it was precisely the divisive power of this controversy that underpinned the conversion of the organizational field toward the electronic order book. Although contentious, the trading structure of Tradepoint and the moralized position taking of its founders aligned (see Emirbayer and Johnson, 2008) with the political and technical frames of three important sets of agents within British finance. On the one hand, Tradepoint's emphasis on reducing costs for end investors found support in Her Majesty's Treasury, from whom they required authorization to operate as a recognized investment exchange. For the Treasury, the question at hand was one of the externalities of innovation. Over the previous decade, and despite tremendous changes in London's markets, the costs of processing small trades for private investors "shot up," as Hayter wrote in 1993, by allowing "market forces to operate freely, [Big Bang] clearly benefited institutions at the expense of small investors" (Hayter, 1993: 159). While certainly preoccupied with the stability of the British financial system, the Treasury was not particularly concerned with potential fragmenting effects of Tradepoint's introduction. As one former Treasury official confided, the regulator's view was that "The City could protect itself"; what mattered was "improving protection for ordinary retail investors." And in this, Tradepoint stoked the Treasury's sensibilities: "The way I looked at [Tradepoint] is that, kind of like in the business of making goods or transporting goods, we had 300 years of industrial revolution, but actually the business of doing deals and the way we did deals never really changed." Technological change transformed finance, thought the Treasury, yet "the actual doing [of] the deals was very much the same." Tradepoint was interesting in this regard: by representing an "industrial revolution ... in the dealing process," it embodied "the benefits of competition ... for investors ... The whole point [of authorizing Tradepoint] really was the belief that competition was a good thing. We wanted more competition in financial services."[32] And so, in September 1995 with Waller-Bridge having

[32] Interview with Treasury official.

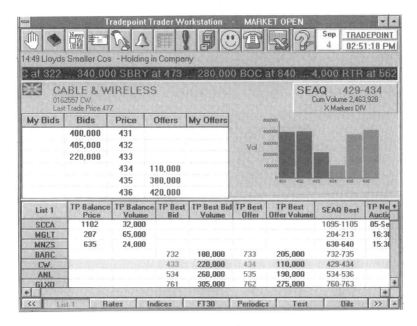

FIGURE 5.3 Image of Tradepoint's trading screen.

led the work to gain ascent from both Her Majesty's Treasury and the Securities Investment Board (the regulator created after Big Bang), Tradepoint could go live, becoming the first official UK Recognized Investment Exchange to challenge the LSE's market position.[33]

Tradepoint's technical specifications also attracted a growingly important set of institutional actors. For the foreign investment banks that joined LSE with Big Bang, the exchange had become an unreactive, "slow-moving" organization.[34] The marketplace needed change, they argued, and the electronic order book developed by Tradepoint served as a tangible template for the future (see Figure 5.3 for an image of Tradepoint's order book). For incumbent market makers, order books were antithetical to the established practices of London's markets. Decrying the modernizing ambitions of the LSE's foreign

[33] Waller-Bridge interview.   [34] Wilson interview.

corporate membership, Mark Potashnick, head of Equities at the British merchant bank Kleinwort Benson, warned of the "cultur[al] change [for institutional investors of having to] be part of a price formation system as opposed to react to prices which are made to them" (Treasury Committee, 1996: 33). In defending its market makers, the stock exchange concurred, noting that "To have … ready made liquidity, you have to pay for it" (LSE Councilman Ian Plenderleith, quoted in Treasury Committee, 1996: 19). But for Gordon Lawson, the managing director of Equities at Salomon Brothers, LSE's market making system was neither natural nor culturally unavoidable: "Having had the experience [of dealing] in other markets [Salomons can] draw [its] conclusions about the efficiencies and inefficiencies [of the LSE's system]" (Treasury Committee, 1996: 34). The privileges afforded to market makers "should be removed" (Treasury Committee, 1996: 44), argued Lawson, for they resulted in an unnecessarily inefficient and expensive marketplace.

Tradepoint was also relevant for an emerging though institutionally heterogeneous set of actors that shared trading practices within the marketplace. In addition to being, perhaps, a "more comfortable [mechanism for] transacting business in London" (Potashnick in Treasury Committee, 1996: 34) for international firms, the lower transaction costs of Tradepoint's electronic order book and the anonymity it conferred on its participants catered to the needs of a new class of market participants, such as derivatives traders, hedge funds, and proprietary quantitative trading firms, that were heavily involved in Europe's expanding stocks and derivatives markets.[35] Hedging

---

[35] As the *Financial Times* noted, by 1995 market makers were facing increased competition from better-capitalized foreign investment banks. Some of them "have already said they would reduce their dealing spreads if necessary in order to compete, simultaneously indicating that electronic market-making solutions were more attractive" (see N. Cohen, 1995b). Much of the pressure to reduce spreads came from firms that engaged in trading and investment strategies that were particularly sensitive to transaction costs. Foreign firms were, again, catalytic as the *Financial Times* noted: "US fund managers, in particular, use 'passive' index-matching strategies that aim to mimic the performance of a stock index [and] don't

market risks by replicating as accurately as possible the underlying portfolios of their traded derivatives, for example, these market participants valued the technical features and economic qualities of Tradepoint's electronic order book. As Waller-Bridge recalled,

> there suddenly were members participants [of Tradepoint] that were represented by installed boxes literally sporting flashing lights. And by this means, there was definitely experimental early algo-trading. [The] speeds of transactions per second and latency and things like that [were] quite inferior to those today. But it was definitely there.

The success of Bennett and his colleagues in producing a legible organizational myth around the electronic order book was consequential. As Tradepoint demonstrated the feasibility of order-driven trading and enrolled market constituencies, pressure mounted on LSE's management. In 1996 and despite strong opposition from market makers (Graham, 1996), LSE proceeded with the development of their own electronic order book, Stock Exchange Trading System (SETS), to attenuate public and regulatory criticisms (SETS would only become operational in October 1997 due to the complaints raised by some market participants about the tight deadlines for implementing the system: "Just because order-driven trading is used in overseas markets doesn't mean it is right for London," said one fund manager to the *Financial Times*). While it is likely that the electronic order book would have arrived at LSE independently of Tradepoint's efforts, the infrastructural investments of its market engineers certainly accelerated its delivery.[36] Tradepoint had changed the language of what was possible and permissible. It manifested, in screens and cables, a potential unified future. Through the power of prophecy, spectacle, and promise, London was converted.

___

need immediacy [and] only care about low transaction costs" (N. Cohen, 1995a). A senior LSE official also acknowledged this point during interview.

[36] Waller-Bridge interview; Smyth-Osborne interview; Barnes interview.

5.6   A POSTSCRIPT

While important historically, Tradepoint failed commercially as an independent entity. The platform may have induced a transformation in the field, but over the next period it did not manage to capture enough trading volumes to sustain operations. With the new exchange established, in late 1997 its incoming venture capital investors decided that to hopefully accelerate trading volumes it would replace the leadership of Bennett and Waller-Bridge with executive management brought in from the traditional banking sector. The culture of the exchange was changed and the gambit did not prove a success. Tradepoint did not disappear entirely, though: its sophisticated clearing and settlement arrangements and its status as a regulated exchange made it an attractive investment. After three years, at the close of the century, Tradepoint was to be sold to the Swiss Stock Exchange, who used its regulatory recognition as a channel for accessing the British stock market.[37] It was the end of an era in British finance. As an old-time exchange insider, Daniel Sheridan, reminisced, the power of the market engineers that faded with time. After Big Bang, he recalled,

> we had more knowledge than many of the players that had been there for many, many years under the previous system. Once a system changes, previous knowledge isn't terribly important. We all like to think that experience is a great thing, you know, but actually if you completely change the system, it's not a great thing. [If] they transplanted me now into the Stock Exchange and they said "run that place" I would be completely lost, because it's changed. In my day I was completely on top of it. I really felt there wasn't a thing I didn't know about how that market ... I wouldn't feel that way now, wouldn't feel at all as comfortable. And I wouldn't have the authority I did have. You know, authority vanishes with changing systems.

[37] Barnes interview.

The entanglement between the lives of the architects and the infrastructures was temporary; as order books triumphed in Britain and throughout the world, the Haussmanns of the first wave of automation withdrew from the scene, making way to a new generation of experts and their devices.

The story of these architects nevertheless illustrates an important characteristic of markets. As explored in previous chapters, making stock markets in London was a dense, relational, organizationally distributed process. In formatting trading, machines, kinship and the imaginaries of honor, community and gentility mattered as much as pecuniary incentives. To say that markets were made only by transactional agents would be to miss too much of their convoluted stories. Brokers, jobbers, market makers, and investors certainly played a fundamental role – both in present times and in the formative period of British finance. In his detailed study of eighteenth-century joint-stock markets in Britain, for instance, Bruce Carruthers (1999) demonstrates the depth of the political and social project deployed by early cadres of investors and intermediaries as they established what became the central institutions of British finance. Until demutualization in 2000, the London Stock Exchange and its marketplace were largely controlled by the LSE's membership, who dictated on the grounds of their interests the course of the organization. Had jobbers and brokers not used the electronic order book, and had regulators aligned with the privileges of market makers rather than with the competitive moralities of Tradepoint's creators, this infrastructure would have likely disappeared. This was, in fact, a distinct possibility faced by Tradepoint in its very early days. Its systems were "too fast" for manual traders, some of who were used to dealing with markets made by jobbers over the phone.[38] Infrastructures of exchange, like those elsewhere, are irrelevant unless meshed with the practices of the organizational fields they inhabit – without the acquiescence of transactional workers, markets would not have changed.

[38] Smyth-Osborne interview.

But it would also be incomplete to think of London's markets as made only by transactional agents, not the least because such account would conceal the long, conflictive, and deeply moralized organizational trajectories that transformed market infrastructures in finance. The details of history matter for understanding these knotty processes: they expose, for example, the distinct moral projects that underscored the design of key financial innovations as mechanisms for generating justice in finance. Moralities may not have determined singularly the success of the electronic order book, but they spoke in concrete ways to the orders of worth (Boltanski and Thevenot, 2006) through which market agents adjudicated the value of competing configurations of exchange. Predicated on the unanticipated consequences of the mechanization of the back-office, the transformation of markets in London was thus framed by tensions and battles between incumbent and challenging conceptions of control over exchanges, technology, and finance itself: should exchanges be marketplaces that, like the 1960s' stock exchange, provide investors with the ability to buy and sell stocks and bonds; or should they be businesses geared toward the production and commercialization of electronic platforms for trade (Lee, 1998)? Recalling a reception for financial services industry invitees that he attended in Downing Street, hosted by the incoming New Labour government following their general election victory in May 1997, Waller-Bridge's interview underscored some of these definitional struggles and their associated forms of moralized and political position taking: as he worked his way through the crowd of regulators, politicians, and financiers, Waller-Bridge crossed paths with a well-known senior British market maker. Their conversation was brief and "tense": "*You* might very well have created an electronic exchange," said the market maker to Waller-Bridge (who recalls the interlocutor's smile conjuring a sense of "rays of wintry sun glancing off a coffin-lid"), "just remember that it's *me* that makes the prices."

A detailed "infrastructural inversion" (Bowker and Star, 1996) of the history of finance also exposes forms of agency and organizational change that are often rendered invisible by the transactional conception of markets. Opening the black boxes of global finance (MacKenzie, 2005) entails much more than understanding the imbrications between exchange counterparties and their material and cognitive appendages. Although the sociology of finance has produced great insights on how markets work, perhaps placing stronger emphasis on how varied forms of market making coalesce in stable institutions would furnish a richer appreciation of markets and their location in modern capitalist societies. The arguments of the economist Alvin Roth may well be a step ahead of the game: as he wrote in his forward-looking essay *The Economist as Engineer*, as "marketplaces proliferate throughout the web," scholars are presented with a unique opportunity of studying the forms of "market design ... done by computer programmers, among others, [who] possess some of the essential expertise" for building today's electronic platforms of exchange (Roth, 2002: 1343). Certainly, the work of these engineers is as much social as it is technical, and their success is not only grounded on their market power or access to specialist knowledge, but also on their practical and multifaceted experience, cultivated heterogeneous connections, and diffuse organizational clout. In the case of London's transformation to introduce what was a patently radical and moralized innovation, infrastructural workers had to capture the exchange to create a voice within their field despite initial organizational invisibility, reveal the bounties of their efforts, and enroll novel market constituencies through moral and technical affinities only to then effect change. Their capacity to act was thus not punctual but distributed through the making of devices, standards, and organizational niches over a long and convoluted trajectory of institutional change.

As the cases explored in this and previous chapters suggest, emphasizing infrastructures and their makers changes the stories of markets we can tell. Much like sociologist Mark Granovetter's (1985) seminal case for taking into account the embeddedness of transactions within social relations, our imaginary of markets can also expand by studying them in the plural (Zelizer, 1988), as historically contingent, realizations built not as collections of transactions but as complex moralized assemblages of organizational tinkering and material intervention. Karl Polanyi (1944) was famously correct in highlighting market societies as political projects. He was also right in showing economies as achievements of social organization. Yet in rethinking markets through their infrastructures, his substantivist approach and the transactional conception that founds our modern sociological imaginary seem limiting. Perhaps market societies do exist, not as stark utopias, but as imperfect and always evolving contested realizations, crystallized in the cables, silicon, standards, and sweat of market engineers. This is the theme of the following chapters.

6   Making Moral Markets

In the *Protestant Ethic and the Spirit of Capitalism*, Max Weber linked the evolution of cultural practices to the production of novel economic forms. For Weber (2013), capitalism was not the unavoidable product of changes in the patterns of accumulation of European societies that generated new ways of organizing labor, production, and society. An important element in the emergence of capitalism, argued Weber, was the development of a specific *Kultur*, an ascetic discipline of Calvinism that allowed justifying and reproducing historically unprecedented modes of economic behavior. For Weber, capitalism was not only a material project – one, for instance, of class domination through the control of markets and the forces of production. Importantly, it was a holistic ethical mission where work and profits were made meaningful through the vocabulary of virtues, rights, discipline, and moral obligations.

Although separated by more than a century from the electronic matching engines and algorithms that power stock markets today, Weber's accounts of the origins of capitalism are relevant for understanding some of the motives for the automation of finance. Like capitalism, finance hinges on the logics of accumulation, profit, arbitrage, and derivation, on self-interest, greed, and the reproduction of money for money's sake. But also like capitalism, the institutions of finance are intricate tapestries of interpersonal relations, technical bricolage, organizational work, and ethical worldviews that make markets arenas of moral action (Zelizer, 2017). Infrastructures are central to this universe. The wooden floorboards of the old stock exchanges rested as much on a search for profits as on moral convictions of community, obligation, and common destiny. The cables, screens, and electronic communication systems of recent finance are no different. These technologies of consociation are "saturated with normativity" (Star and Ruhleder, 1996: 113; Fourcade and Healy, 2007: 299); they crystalize the codes, assumptions, and taken-for-granted expectations (Garfinkel, 1967; Edwards et al., 2009: 366) of their makers, users, and the markets they inhabit.

In this chapter I explore the moral and ethical worldviews associated to the electronic limit order book, one of the key infrastructures of market automation. I do so with two objectives. The first is to present how a sense of moral duty and market ethics informed the initial generation of electronic order books. By studying the first patent for one of these systems, for example, I show that its design was heavily influenced by the weight of concrete ethical considerations. My second objective is to qualify the role of moralities in market infrastructures. Markets are certainly spaces of moralized action, but this does not mean that they accommodate all ethical dispositions as not all worldviews sell equally well in the marketplace for markets. While the plans for the first electronic limit order book were part of a zealous ethical project, the system never came to be. The order books that eventually populated finance were couched in the slightly less ardent, slightly more pragmatic language of "efficiency." Studying the first successful commercial electronic trading platforms, I show how these embodied a compromise between promises of fairness, "good" design, and financial success.

6.1   INFRASTRUCTURES AND THEIR EXPLICIT MORALITIES

To understand how infrastructures embody moral claims within finance, I often think of Caitlin Zaloom's *Out of the Pits*, a magnificent study of futures traders in Chicago and London. Zaloom's work is not focused on infrastructures or the intertwined biographies of technological objects in finance, yet one of the chapters of her fine book discusses the history of how the Chicago Board of Trade (CBOT) redesigned a key market device – the trading floor – in the tumultuous years surrounding the Great Depression. At the time, futures con-tracts[1] were traded face to face, so changes to the structure of the trading floor had effects on the quality of market transactions, altering "the daily paths of the traders and [configuring] whom they can see and hear, their access to information, and what communication tech-nologies they can use instantly and which they must stretch to pro-cure" (Zaloom, 2006: 39). The trading floor manifested what Bruno Latour (1992) calls the "strongly social and highly moral" substance of technology: in addition to being a platform for interactions, the design of the floor could "bring the marketplace more closely in line with the ideals of commerce, shaping the [trading] pits to reflect market prin-ciples of individual competition and smooth circulation" (Zaloom, 2006: 40). The categories motivating the floor's redesign were moral, reflecting not only ideals of what markets are in the abstract, but also notions of how interpersonal exchange should occur. In Zaloom's study, morality was certainly situated in the relations enacted by dealers and traders, but it was also encoded within the physical makeup of the marketplace.

It is perhaps an interesting historical coincidence that the elec-tronic order book that took over from boisterous trading floors of stock and commodities exchanges has roots in New Holland, Illinois, not far from the pits of the Chicago Board of Trade (CBOT) and their midwestern agricultural heritage. Much like the project to redesign the CBOT's trading floor in the 1930s, the making of the first elec-tronic order book in the 1960s was also an attempt to reform trading in American stock markets through infrastructural change. In study-ing the ethical and normative considerations that went into the patent of this first electronic order book, this section presents some of the explicit moralities that surrounded discussions about finance and automation in mid-twentieth-century America. The story that follows is decidedly enticing: it presents plausible connections

---

[1] A futures contract is an instrument that obligates buyers to purchase an asset at a predetermined future date and price.

between the inventor of the first electronic order book, Calvinist religious doctrines, and a series of public scholars conventionally associated with the birth of key socioeconomic ideologies of the late twentieth century. But this section is cautionary. The story of this early Illinoisan order book is a fascinating historical dead end; this order book was never used, other than as a perfunctory citation for patent claims down the road. Like the failure of other inventions, this dead end is revealing, hinting at how some moral worldviews might simply be too explicit to sell in the marketplace.

What is an order book? Like double-entry bookkeeping, order books are mundane yet prominent technologies of the capitalist enterprise (Sombart, 1924; Weber, 1978; Carruthers and Espeland, 1991). At a very basic level, order books work as organizational devices that allow managing the intermittent flows of transactions within uncertain market settings. They are systems of accounting crystalized in a list: supply and demand are often unpredictable, and in dealing with variations in the orders placed by consumers throughout time, market actors developed lists that indicate the schedules of delivery from sellers and the requests submitted by buyers that, through a given rule, establish how items were to be distributed. The lists can be quite simple – and are indeed common to contemporary commercial practices: an order book can consist of a simple notepad, a preformatted off-the-shelf paper device, or an electronic system governed by algorithms running on a computer.

The history of order books is rather imprecise – they are, after all, so widespread a technology and so simple a design that identifying an accurate origin is probably a futile task. We know, however, that order books are an old solution to the problems of managing the erratic supply and demand. As the British economist William A. Shaw (1906) wrote in *The Economic Journal,* one of these solutions was already central to the financial organization of Restoration England in the mid-seventeenth century when the King's Treasury installed a paper and ink order book to control the supply of government credit. The problem faced by the Treasury of King Charles II was the discontinuity of cash flows coming into and out of the Crown's coffers. Previous ways of tallying credit and debt were riddled with bureaucratic complexities, and whereas revenue trickled into the Treasury gradually, expenditure was abrupt and usually clustered at the beginning of the fiscal year. By recording the supply and demand of money through the Treasury's order book, the Crown was able to administer credit over time. This innovation certainly had important long-term consequences: as England expanded its overseas territories and created new trade routes to the Far East and New World, devices such as the order book allowed for a better administration of the growing national debt, a fact that may have well contributed to the emergence of London as a key international financial center.

In different guises, order books were reinvented across several sites of economic activity as mundane yet critical devices for the management of transactions. In financial markets they acquired particular salience among the type of market actors whose role was to "make markets" by receiving orders from brokers, setting the prices of traded instruments, and matching trades accordingly (Abolafia, 1996). Sitting at the core of each transaction, market makers occupy a critically important (and eminently powerful) position in financial markets. By bearing the risk of short-term price fluctuations, they provide liquidity to brokers and investors at the expense of a spread in prices: they buy at lower rates than they sell, profiting from the difference. This difference is the cost of the immediacy of exchange that market makers provide to the marketplace. For this, they must manage with great care and sophistication the flow of orders; much like the demand for government credit in seventeenth-century England, orders to buy and sell stocks arrive asymmetrically and unpredictably, creating an incentive for the use of an inventory of sorts. This explains, perhaps, why order books became so central to the operation of Western stock markets, for they provided market makers control over their inventories and the power to adjust the prices of their stocks according to changes in supply and demand.

Like many of the early recording technologies of finance, the first order books were analog devices of paper, pencil, and ink. As the stock market moved, a designated person – whether the partner of a market-making firm or one of its employed clerks – would update the information on the order book with the interests submitted by investors through their brokers on the trading floor along with any relevant changes to the firm's inventory. The importance of these devices to the practices of the stock exchange's operations was such that it eventually became reflected in language. By the early twentieth century, "making" or "keeping" the book was synonymous to making a market in a particular security, be it among the New York Stock Exchange's specialists or the London Stock Exchange's jobbers. In these early years, the politics and morality of this market technology were strongly associated with their concrete physicality. Because their material reach was limited to the pitches of market makers on the floor, the valuable information contained in order books was easily controlled; the contents of the book, like knowledge on the state of the market, were available only to select groups of market makers who, in exchange for this privileged access to the ebb and flow of market transactions, guaranteed liquidity to brokers and their end users, that is, private investors.

Market makers undoubtedly performed a valuable role. But not everyone sanctioned their privileged access to the order book. Opposition was particularly prevalent in the United States, where stock markets were percolated by an earlier rise of public discussions about financial democracy and investor protection. Even before the stock market crash of 1929, the financial marketplace was seen as a reflection of American society, one that ought to have transpired the spirit of democratic entrepreneurialism that was so central to the nation's imagination (the early financialization of American culture and finance is explored in detail by Ott, 2011; see also J. Burk, 1988; Krippner, 2011). And so, in mid-twentieth-century American stock markets, hitherto dominated in volume and organizational clout by the New York Stock Exchange and its market markets – the specialists – critiques against privilege gained prominence. And by the early 1960s, these critiques had captured the attention of the Securities and Exchange Commission (SEC), the nation's prime stock market regulator.[2]

For the Securities and Exchange Commission, American stock markets required a transformation. Part of the problem was strictly operational: as trading volumes grew in postwar America, the established mechanisms of trade had to accommodate changes in market participation and, in particular, the needs of an emerging (and increasingly important) class of actors – namely, large and well capitalized institutional investors such as pension and mutual funds that pooled investments across the nation's industry and its workforce. For the SEC, the pursuit of operational efficiencies would both increase investor protection and lower trading costs, including the notorious spreads made by New York Stock Exchange specialists that were partly anchored on their monopolistic control over the order books of individual shares. For the SEC, the paper and pencil order books of specialists were far surpassed by the novel suite of computer technologies increasingly used in business (Cortada, 2003). Market makers, argued the commission in its 1963 "Special Study of Securities Markets," needed to change their ways by automating much of their routine activities and perhaps even how they captured and executed trades (the commission was a great promoter of automation, but their work was mostly directed toward the creation of a national stock trading system, a story that I explore in more detail in Chapter 7).

---

[2] It is possible to speculate that market structure also had a thing to do with the opposition to the order book in America. In London, multiple market makers or jobbers on the floor traded the stocks of corporations. This gave them comparatively less control over the market than NYSE specialists who had a de facto monopoly on single corporations. Automating a competitive market-making system was, perhaps, less interesting than automating a central auctioneer. See also Muniesa (2003).

The SEC was not alone in advocating automation. Writing some years later in the *Financial Analysts Journal*, Fischer Black – a renowned economist who developed modern option pricing theory along with Myron Scholes and Robert Merton – reflected on the possibilities of automating stock exchanges and their market-making specialists. Although Black acknowledged the importance of the specialists' judgment in determining prices, he was also keenly aware of the conflicts of interest that emerged from having unfettered access to the order book. "Any participation by a specialist for his own account [in the market] is unfair if there are potential buyers or sellers who would have taken the same position the specialist took if they had been standing at the post," wrote Black. Such unfairness was, furthermore, unavoidable given the existing institutions of finance: aside from the sheer constraints of space, all investors could not stand on the floor simultaneously "because the cost of doing so is prohibitive. The cost is high because the system is outdated … it is possible to give potential buyers and sellers access to the market at a cost that is smaller to the present cost," greatly reducing the need for a stock specialist (Black, 1971). Practitioners also objected. "Just as monopolies in public utilities have been subjected to regulation not bestowed upon other businesses," wrote the investor and financial entrepreneur Donald Weeden to the SEC in 1971, "so the specialist must accept special regulation along with his privileged position" (Weeden, 1971).

An automated system such as the one envisioned by the Securities and Exchange Commission in 1963 ultimately emerged, but only in the relatively untamed over-the-counter stock market. There, computer-based quote dissemination and bookkeeping became the template of the National Association of Securities Dealers Automated Quotation system (NASDAQ), rolled out in 1971 as the first nation-wide trading network within the continental United States (Ingebretsen, 2002). Based on a public electronic bulletin board, the creation of NASDAQ and its demonstration of the possibilities of partial automation failed to erode the established position of NYSE market makers who remained firmly in control of their order books. On the contrary, many at the NYSE read the introduction of NASDAQ as a pernicious form of competition that unnecessarily fragmented the marketplace at the expense of liquidity (Muniesa, 2003). When NYSE specialists eventually automated, they did so only to lower their organization's operational costs, keeping their privileged access to price formation and information flows from the market.

For other more acerbic critics, market makers did not need retooling but extinction. Automation should replace rather than simply discipline the specialist (Black, 1971). This radical opposition to stock exchange intermediaries was certainly part of the rationale for the invention of the electronic order book: issued by the United States Patent and Trademark Office to the Illinoisan industrialist, entrepreneur, and amateur economic philosopher Frederick Nymeyer in 1971, the patent presented a "new and improved computation system for commodity exchanges, stock exchanges, and similar auction markets [for] establishing exchange prices for any form of fungible goods … without requiring the exercise of human judgment as a substantial factor in price determination" (Nymeyer, 1971). What seems an instrumental response to the practical problem of organizing exchange and determining prices was, nevertheless, a profoundly moral project. After all, making prices was the remit of specialists, and in implementing a computational system that eliminated their judgment in the marketplace, Nymeyer sought to do what Fisher Black could only dream of: create a system of exchange that, without direct human intervention, was fair, economically efficient, and morally virtuous.

The dense morality of the electronic order book is best reflected in the zeal of one of its early creators to reform stock markets, economic theory, and American society at large. Born in Hull, Iowa, in 1897 to the owners of a small hardware store, Frederick Nymeyer graduated from the University of Chicago in 1920 to then become a successful consultant and businessman throughout the remainder of his adult life. In addition to serving on the boards of several corporations including the Parker Pen Company and J. I. Case, a firm specializing in farm machinery, Nymeyer was prolific in creating intellectual connections within the ideological mélange of postwar United States. Although relatively understudied as a historical figure, Nymeyer was important within American conservative business networks from the late 1940s to the 1970s, having been close to such figures as Robert W. Baird, John T. Brown, and J. Howard Pew, and acquainted with James Kilpatrick and William F. Buckley, among others.[3] But more importantly for the matter of this chapter, Nymeyer was a consummate essayist, and it is in his published works where the connections between morality, markets, and automation underlying his patent are evinced.

With both his writings and proselytism, Nymeyer was perhaps the prime apostle of Austrian economics in mid-twentieth-century United States. After reading *Theory of Money and Credit* and *Omnipotent Government* in 1946, Nymeyer wrote to Ludwig von Mises, a central political and intellectual reference of Austrian economic thought, asking for clarification of a particular passage in the text (Greaves, 2006; Hülsmann, 2007). Mises replied, thanking Nymeyer for his "thoroughness and critical acumen," and starting what would "turn into a long-term" friendship (Hülsmann, 2007: 853). Through multiple epistolary exchanges, Mises introduced Nymeyer to the broader works of Austrian theorists (including the seminal writings of Eugen Böhm-Bawerk – whose *Capital and Interest* was referenced in the 1971 order book patent) and of which he became "a dedicated admirer" (Hülsmann, 2007: 854). After meeting in person in 1948, Nymeyer reciprocated Mises's attention, providing ample support for him and his colleagues. For instance, noting that "Austrian works were not sufficiently well known" in the United

---

[3] References to Nymeyer are sparse within the literature but they point to clear connections with America's burgeoning conservative political elites. See, for instance, Jörg Guido Hülsmann's (2007: 855) biography of Mises and Doherty's (2009: 298) *Radicals for Capitalism*.

States (Hülsmann, 2007: 855), Nymeyer attempted to create a "Liberal Institute" under the direction of Mises at the University of Chicago (the plan failed due to Chicago's unease with the model of funding and staffing preferred by the institute's benefactors). Similarly, observing the lack of English translations of Austrian economics texts, Nymeyer founded the Libertarian Press in 1955, a "'specialist' publisher, with a limited objective dedicated to making known in the English-speaking world the *revolutionary* ideas of the Austrian Neo-Classical economists" (Nymeyer in Mises, 1974; emphasis in the original). Nymeyer's Libertarian Press soon grew into an important publishing house devoted to communicate Mises's writings, serving as the undisputed point of translation, publication, and dissemination of Austrian economics to American audiences (Hülsmann, 2007: 574; Sennholz, 2007). Also tellingly, Nymeyer contributed to building networks and relationships that had enduring effects in American politics, having "probably had some influence in bringing Hayek to Chicago, and in the early 1950s played a significant role in raising funds for Mont Pèlerin Society meetings" (Hülsmann, 2007: 856).

Nymeyer's numerous activities were quite likely motivated by a strong elective affinity between his religious convictions and Mises's economic worldviews. For Nymeyer, "the economics of Dr. von Mises" constituted "by far the most satisfactory means to modernize the ethics of the Hebrew-Christian religion." "When that kind of synthesis is made," wrote Nymeyer to industrialist Howard Pew in 1959, "one turns out to be an extraordinary conservative adherent of the Christian religion. But also some of the absurdities are removed" (Nymeyer in Hülsmann, 2007: 915–916). Indeed, for Nymeyer, Calvinism and Austrian economics were part and parcel of a single project: to achieve moral perfection in a society marked by change and structured by markets. The most succinct evidence of this ethical and philosophical position was *Progressive Calvinism*, a periodical pamphlet published between 1955 and 1960 funded by Nymeyer that served as the official voice of the Progressive Calvinism League, a

group formed with his son, Martin B. Nymeyer, and John Van Mou-
werik, a businessmen associated to International Harvester Co. of
Peoria, Illinois.

Progressive Calvinism was a peculiar intellectual project, the
nature of which was perhaps best reflected when it changed its title to
First Principles in Morality and Economics in late 1959. As Nymeyer
wrote, the pamphlet presented a "hybrid" social philosophy, "a cross
between Hebrew-Christian ethics and neoclassical economics" (*First
Principles in Morality and Economics*, 1960a).[4] Through this combination, Nymeyer sought to generate "awareness of the limitations
of the human mind [to] promote true humility; [resisting] the arro-
gance of all attempts at universal planning, that is, all attempts at
pretending we are as God, and all Comtian Positivism" (*Progressive
Calvinism*, 1955). Nymeyer was a reformist, advocating a novel yet
conservative way of thinking about the social world: he wrote not as
a theologian but as a "*practical* social science [man]" who saw in
business an activity that "solves correctly and naturally many
important matters about which professional social scientists
have impractical and even dangerous ideas" (*Progressive Calvinism*,
1955: 2–3).

Within this moralizing intellectual project, and through a
number of reflections on topics ranging from the consequences of
automation on profits (*First Principles* in Morality and Economics,
1960b) to the implications of Weber's work for modern progressive
Calvinists (*Progressive Calvinism*, 1956a), Nymeyer's pamphlets
sought to explore human action through a praxeological perspective,
studying "the relations of men to men ... and the relations of men to
things" (Progressive Calvinism, 1956b; *First Principles* in Morality
and Economics, 1960c; Mises, 1998 [1949]). Through this conceptual
division, Nymeyer reflected the singularities of his moral and religious philosophy. Specifically, for Nymeyer, the precepts of Calvinist

---

[4] Note that for Nymeyer 'neoclassical' economics denoted 'Austrian' economics.

and Christian theology only accounted for two sets of relations in the world: first, the "relation of men to God," which he identified as belonging purely to the realm of religion; second, the "relation of men to men," which he understood as constituting the domain of practical ethics (*Progressive Calvinism*, 1956c). But as Nymeyer wrote, something was amiss in this theological conception; "a very important relationship is … practically lost sight of by our two-fold division," he wrote. "This important relationship is the relationship of men to things, the relationship of men to the natural world around us" (*Progressive Calvinism*, 1956c: 196). For Nymeyer, the significance of economic theory resided in its ability to "aid the interpreting of scripture" by offering insights on, first, on the relations of men to men as discerned through the study of "prices"; and second, the relations of men to things, as captured under economic discussions of "value."

Nymeyer explored this projection of Austrian economic theory onto Calvinist theology in a brief though revealing discussion published in *First Principles in Morality and Economics* in 1960. For Nymeyer, relations between men and things are structured by how individualistic values are attributed to discrete economic goods. The way that we relate to commodities, just as in the way that we relate to the world, is driven by how each of us determines the relevant value of the things with which we interact. Here, Nymeyer followed the subjectivist philosophy of Austrian economic thought. For Austrian thinkers such as Mises (1998 [1949]), Hayek (1948), and Kirzner (1996), the value of commodities is neither a reflection of some essential use nor a specific crystallization of labor but rather a subjective evaluation that hinges on the interests of individual economic agents. Building on this, Nymeyer considered that the determination of values was as much influenced by practical utility and the "objective" psychology of scarcity as by the "the significance which a good or a quantity of goods possesses for the well-being of a certain subject," as Böhm-Bawerk (1891: 91) wrote in his discussion in *Capital and Interest*.

While the determination of *value* was central to men's relation to things insofar as it created an ordering of objects and their relative worth, it was *prices* that, in Nymeyer's thinking, arbitrated the relations of men to men. As he wrote,

> Primary economic relations between men pertain to questions connected with the exchange of goods or services. One man produces shoes; another produces food. In how "just" or in how "brotherly" a manner they treat each other depends on how they agree or come to accept the prices used in the exchange. If the price of the shoes is too high, the shoemaker has misdealt the farmer; if the price of food is too high, the farmer has misdealt the shoemaker. To appraise the justness (or brotherliness), of how men treat each other when exchanging, it will be necessary to describe accurately how prices are determined in a free market. In the usual discussions about brotherly love (in the field of economic problems) by moralists and theologians, a description is seldom presented of what takes place in the price determining process. Moralists and theologians rather freely pass judgment on a process concerning which there is evidence that they do not understand it. Factual and scientific description ought to precede appraisal and condemnation.
>
> (First Principles *in Morality and Economics, 1960c*)

The reference to brotherliness matters by indicating the moral order that Nymeyer defended within society. Unlike the caritative and renunciative versions of brotherly love that featured in universalistic Calvinist traditions (Symonds and Pudsey, 2006; Weber, 2013), Nymeyer anchored his economic and theological propositions on a radically individualistic understanding of this concept. Rather than being circumscribed to a particular group and defined on the basis of religious virtuosity, Nymeyer's conception of brotherly love was a universal dimension of transactions, made apparent in the ethical status of the relations established between agents negotiating over a price. As Nymeyer wrote,

The "backbone" of brotherly love CANNOT be charity, instead it
MUST be mutual exchange, or trade, or buying and selling . . .
Charity can only supplement exchange.

(First Principles *in Morality and Economics, 1960d: 101*)

Nymeyer's philosophy diverged from the forms of puritanism
that Max Weber analyzed in his *Protestant Ethic* in important ways.
Specifically, it pointed to a different type of moral inclinations than
those that, according to Weber, gave rise to the forms of ascetic
Protestant capitalism in northern Europe. Whereas Weber saw "personal" or "human" relations between people as key sites for ethics
and thus for the production of the dispositions that led to organized
forms of economic activity (Symonds and Pudsey, 2006: 138), he also
insisted that morality was removed from "the realm of economically
rationalized relationships, where personal control is exercised in
inverse ratio to the degree of rational differentiation of the economic
structure" (Weber, 1978: 585). Morality was not to be found, argued
Weber, in the rationalized mechanisms of market activity. Nymeyer
reversed Weber's logic, rendering markets as *the* generative sites of
ethics. Formed by free associations between men, the legitimacy of
markets and their effects on the allocation of resources – that is, the
relations of men to things, and of men to men – dovetailed "the [free]
individual wills of the [trade] participants" that engaged in commerce
and exchange (Weber, 1978: 585). The free market was virtuous precisely because it created the conditions for a just evaluation of goods
and counterparties making it, in Nymeyer's worldview, the paragon of
true brotherly love.

Nymeyer's economized reading of brotherly love was laid bare
in his analysis of the morality of prices. Noting that "the free action of
competition in the marketplace is often decried and criticized as
unbrotherly, unchristian, as a violation of the ideal of brotherly love"
(*First Principles* in Morality and Economics, 1960d: 102), Nymeyer
referred again to Weber's work to criticize the preponderance of these
"medieval economic ethics . . . based on the principle of just price and

the assurance to everyone of a chance to live" (Weber, 2013: 357–358). But, Nymeyer asked,

> What is a "just price"? Nobody knows. The ideas of a "just price" and a "fair price" independent of free market activity are utterly meaningless ... We would declare that God himself does not know and cannot know what a "just price" is, were it not that we feared offense would be taken at such a statement.

"[B]rotherly love and price determination are related," contended Nymeyer, making it necessary to understand "accurately how prices are determined in a free market" (*Progressive Calvinism*, 1956d: 286). This is where Nymeyer reveals the moral orientation of the electronic order book he would invent: it was not an apolitical utilitarian device for ordering transactions and attaining operational efficiencies but an arrangement that created the conditions for producing "fair" or "just prices," a machine that fabricated brotherly love.

In Nymeyer's Austrian-inspired philosophy, "fair prices" resulted from how the struggles between market participants aimed to determine a "single price for all. Probably most people would agree that that is 'justice'" (*First Principles* in Morality and Economics, 1960e: 330). In a market with a single price for all,

> no buyer coerces a seller beyond the limits that the seller is willing to go; and vice versa, that no seller coerces any buyer beyond the limits that the buyer is willing to go... Every buyer and seller, by this definition, himself wishes to be a buyer or seller at the price that prevails. Every actual buyer and seller prefers to pay the price he is paying or receiving, versus not trading at all. Every buyer and seller, according to his own estimation, gains by the transaction. He trades willingly. The market he creates or helps create is, in that sense, a free market.
>
> *(First Principles in Morality and Economics, 1960f)*

Nymeyer was keenly aware that single "fair" market-clearing prices are rare achievements in real economies, a critique that was

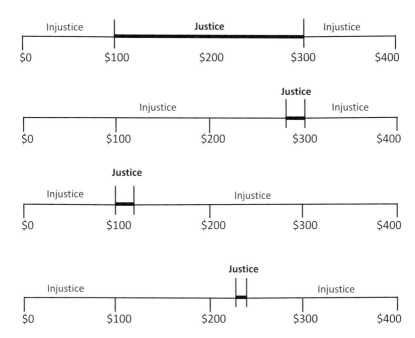

FIGURE 6.1 Nymeyer's representation of justice as overlapping preferences in the sale of a horse. According to Nymeyer, competition fosters narrower prices that reflect less asymmetries in power between buyers and sellers.

often presented against standard neoclassical models of price formation by neo-Austrians. Rather, as suggested by economists like Mises and Böhm-Bawerk, Nymeyer understood exchanges in the marketplace as occurring along a range of multiple prices that reflect the overlapping preferences at which agents are willing to engage in a trade (see Figure 6.1). For Nymeyer, all transactions occurring within this range must be considered "just" insofar as buyer and seller are not coerced into exchange. The ultimate price paid for a good, however, can vary substantially and particularly so in thinly populated markets, ultimately making market prices "arbitrary" outcomes of the asymmetry of bargaining skills between buyers and sellers (Böhm-Bawerk, 1891). She who holds more sway in the transaction will be able to pull prices in her benefit, an asymmetry that affronted Nymeyer's vision of justice.

There was a remedy for these arbitrary prices that, according to Nymeyer, impeded attaining brotherly love in the marketplace: as Böhm-Bawerk argued, increased competition *narrowed* the range of values at which agents are willing to trade by exerting pressure on market agents to create better offers. Nymeyer observed,

> When there are many buyers and many sellers, the range in which the buyers and sellers can be "tough" toward each other is narrow... Skilful and ruthless traders have no real range in which to "extort" from another what their intelligence, wealth or strength might induce them to attempt to "extort." The "market" restricts them ... [Competition,] which is no respecter of persons, is the most influential factor in the world for promoting justice.
>
> (First Principles *in Morality and Economics, 1960f: 359; see also* First Principles *in Morality and Economics, 1960g: 317)*

When Nymeyer wrote these words, American stock markets were spaces of restrained competition – in the New York Stock Exchange, "probably the *greatest market* that has ever existed in this world" (*First Principles* in Morality and Economics, 1960h), opportunism was controlled and so were its competitive dimensions (J. Burk, 1988; Abolafia, 1996). The mechanics of trading maintained by NYSE specialists, who generated prices through the manual matching of orders in their pen-and-pencil order books as the instructions to trade arrived from far-away clients and local floor brokers, implied that competition could only be partially reflected in the marketplace: prices on the NYSE would always encode the market maker's profit and his unique (and private) knowledge of information flows.[5] Nymeyer addressed this structural feature of the NYSE in the patent for the electronic order book, where he wrote that,

---

[5] This theme is often explored in the literature on market microstructure. See O'Hara (1995).

> The maintenance of a fair and orderly market becomes difficult in
> direct relation to the increasing complexity of business structure
> upon which the markets are based ... the increase in the number of
> individuals participating in the markets but not directly present
> increases the possibility of manipulation of market prices by those
> persons, such as the stock specialists actually present at the
> exchange and actively engaged in making market price
> determinations.
>
> *(Nymeyer, 1971)*

Through the "possibility of manipulation," NYSE specialists
imposed barriers on brotherly love; complete automation of their
activity provided moral resolution. By transforming the order books
of specialists into an open, yet anonymous, electronic trading mechanism, Nymeyer sought to create conditions for fair prices as determined by the competitive struggles of a "free market" (*First Principles
in Morality and Economics*, 1960c: 103). Nymeyer was not primarily
eliminating the "exercise of human judgment" in price determination; rather, he was contesting what he considered as the arbitrary,
unbrotherly prices of the NYSE.

To read Nymeyer's patent as either a "deliberate effort to
cheapen the costs of production" or a device designed with the pri-
mary justification of increasing efficiency, as some students of
markets and technology might argue, would miss a critical point
(Collins, 1986: 25; Fourcade and Healy, 2007: 301–302). Insofar as
Nymeyer considered stock markets "sensitive barometer[s] of the
expectations of business men" (*First Principles in Morality and Economics*, 1960h: 8), the prices they reflected had an exacting obligation:
"*cause and effect* are intermingled in the New York Stock Exchange,"
wrote Nymeyer, but just as "opinions 'outside of the market' ... influence the trend of the market ... in a reverse sense, the trend of the
market" influences the opinions of businessmen and investors alike
(*First Principles in Morality and Economics*, 1960h). In proposing a
radical transformation of the structure of American stock exchanges,

Nymeyer also advocated reconfiguring the moral spaces of finance to guarantee the legitimacy of the market's prices and of the transactions that led to their determination – echoing, in important ways, the debates that saturated the reconstruction of trading floors in Chicago forty years earlier (Zaloom, 2006). Nymeyer's patent is historically interesting precisely because of *how* it sought to redeem markets. The form of moralization that he professed was not based on eliminating the vices of trading agents. Nymeyer followed an altogether different path: in responding to the ethical problems apparent in price determinations, Nymeyer's solution was to change *designs*. Nymeyer was the architect of a transactional order predicated upon specific conceptions of justice, fairness, competition, and brotherly love. His patent was market morality crystalized in a machine.

6.2   EFFICIENT MORALITIES

It is tempting to read Nymeyer's story as emblematic of the hidden politics of automated markets. The personal and intellectual connections that Nymeyer fostered throughout his life and that were condensed in the patent for his electronic auction system are the type of historical nuggets that are too enticing to ignore – his friendship with Ludwig von Mises, support for Frederick von Hayek, allegiance to Calvinism, and intellectual engagement with Max Weber easily captivate our imaginations. Nymeyer seems to be the missing apostle of financial neoliberalism, the one that managed to conjure the ghost of free markets into the making of one of their most important machines. But this nugget is fools' gold. Frederick Nymeyer's invention never saw the light of day, remaining as a peculiar and, for quite some time, forgotten curiosity in the annals of innovation. History is rarely seamless. But it is saturated with important lessons. Nymeyer's failure is one, demonstrating the difficulty of evangelizing markets from the outside. His order book had all the trappings of a modern system and was revolutionary in and of itself – as legal scholar Philip Leith (2007: 11–16) argues, Nymeyer's was the first successful patent for a business method that relied not on a new device but on existing, off-the-shelf computing technologies. Although revolutionary, how-ever, the patent did not sell. Distinctly moralized trading systems eventually emerged in finance, although driven by altogether different ethics. The order books that made it in the market for marketplaces, the ones that colonized the peripheries of the field to then transform the world they inhabited, were framed in the rather more humble, pragmatic, though equally politically charged, language of efficiency.

Efficiency has a long and intricate lineage. The concept, for example, transects several strands of the history of science and tech-nology. In the development of thermodynamics, it was bound to the metaphors of engines that inspired the economization of nature in terms of outputs and inputs of energy and heat (Mirowski, 1991). In mechanical engineering, efficiency became shorthand – a percentage – for the effectiveness of system in transforming energy into force. For financial economists, efficiency serves as a proxy of how well markets reflect the information of their environments in prices (MacKenzie and Millo, 2003). In logistics, it informs the organizing principles for managing and operating distribution chains. And taken to the individ-ual level, personal efficiency has long stood as a signal of integrity, economy, and prudence. Several scholars have written in greater detail about the polyvalence of efficiency. What matters greatly from their studies is recognizing the uses of efficiency "as serious attempts to apply a powerful and generalizable concept to an extended variety of human situations," as Jennifer Alexander (2008) argues. Straddling across management, design, engineering, science, technology, com-puting, and ethical discourses, efficiency is an authoritative boundary concept that coheres the work of engineers, managers, capitalists, politicians, and workers through shared though not entirely defined images of control, virtue, and discipline.

This is why references to "efficiency" were so central to the automation of financial markets: differing groups within and around the marketplace could anchor their claims and proposals of reform on the concept without losing their individual identities, diluting their interests, or engaging in endless definitional battles. Unlike "fairness," "efficiency" was a more general yet simultaneously less defined concept that, cloaked by technical language, was difficult to counter (Who, indeed, opposes efficiency?). While an eminently political and moralized object – any definition of efficiency necessarily implies a way of organizing the world and thus of allocating resources – uses of efficiency provided a more palatable point of articulation than other slightly more polemic rallying terms. For some actors, speaking in the language of efficiency allowed mobilizing a critique of the (inefficient) state and a theory of markets as the ultimate arbiters of values without making explicit the politics of their proposals (Mudge, 2007). Engineers and software designers similarly speak of efficiency, mobilizing and building into their systems lay theories of justice about what and who deserves attention in a "well designed" world (Eubanks, 2018). For market users, conversely, efficiency seems an obvious virtue, bolstering critiques of intermediaries not by stressing their failures but rather by highlighting the economic benefits on profits, savings, and the pragmatics of circulation and accumulation: efficiency is attractive because it makes transactions cheaper; that is its ultimate goal. Invoking efficiency means that there is no need for engaging in convoluted theological discussions or crafting detailed accounts of social order and its relation to some assumed morality. As a flexible placeholder, efficiency performs much of the same discursive work. This was of great importance for the automation of finance, as made clear in one emblematic case: the development of the first commercially successful electronic limit order book by an entity once called Institutional Networks Corporation, otherwise known as Instinet.

The founders of Instinet, Jerome M. Pustilnik and Herbert R. Behrens, were solving a problem that echoed Nymeyer's concerns. The rise of institutional investors in the 1950s and 1960s presented new problems for the market. In particular, this class of investors was captive to the structural forms of market control that positioned intermediaries in privileged positions across the transaction. Selling securities in the New York Stock Exchange required going through a broker who charged a commission on sales; it then entailed accepting the prices offered by market-making specialists on the floor of the exchange; and, finally, such an intermediated trade increased the risk that information about the transaction could be leaked, leading to an adverse price movement. For institutional investors, the situation was unwarranted, not the least because by the mid-1960s they had already internalized much of research and portfolio management, traditionally the two activities that had made up most of the value of intermediation. Why pay so dearly for trading? Paying for intermediation was exasperating at best, immoral at worst. Institutional Networks Corporation emerged from this context of struggle and competition.

The question was how to bypass the New York Stock Exchange. When Pustilnik and Behrens incorporated Institutional Networks in 1967, Nymeyer's patent was still in the making (it was only issued in 1971 and, even then, Nymeyer was far from Pustilnik and Behrens's Wall Street circles). In addition to dealing with the political and organizational might of the NYSE, their firm had to design a system from scratch to serve as the basis for an alternative trading mechanism. Institutional Network's trading system, known as Instinet, was arguably a fortunate consequence of a double coincidence of wants between Pustilnik and Behrens and the visionary computer scientist Charles W. Adams.

In the years that Pustilnik and Behrens set out to challenge the NYSE, Adams was a well-regarded professor at the Massachusetts Institute of Technology. Earlier in his career, Adams worked on Whirlwind, the ambitious project that resulted in the first real-time digital computer that utilized visual displays and that was subsequently reconfigured as the American air defense system SAGE (Edwards, 1997). In addition to his technical and scientific prowess, Adams was also a savvy entrepreneur interested in taking computing out of large organizations and into the core practices of the business world. Economics made this diffusion unlikely: in the late 1950s and early 1960s, owning computers was prohibitive for most small and medium-sized corporations. Even leases were too expensive for most firms: the IBM 1401, one of the most successful data processing systems available for business applications in the 1960s, came at an average cost of $2,500–$6,500 per month (or between $19,000 and $50,000 in current dollars). For most businesses, these expenses were unjustifiable. Although potentially useful for tasks like inventory management and account keeping, computers were simply too fast and were often idle. A potential answer was renting processing time as opposed to entire systems. Businesses interested in implementing some degree of office automation could buy time on a mainframe tailored to their specific requirements. This was part of the rationale behind Adams's enterprise. With his Whirlwind colleague, John T. Gilmore, he created Keydata Corporation in 1959 (originally called Adams Associates) as "the first to offer time-shared business data processing service" (Gilmore, 1969: 29–30).

INSTNET was born at this confluence of technical opportunity and managerial happenstance. When Adams, Pustilnik, and Behrens met in the mid-1960s to discuss the financing of Keydata Corporation, they discovered their mutually compatible interests. Pustilnik and Behrens found the technical expertise they needed in Keydata, while Adams found a chance to expand his firm into the corporate horizon of finance. As David Manns, an early programmer for Institutional Networks, recalls

> they thought to themselves, "wouldn't it be interesting to use this technology to let people trade with each other directly instead of going through these thieves at the New York Stock Exchange." So, they actually did start Instinet in 69, as a real live trading system. It ran on Keydata... Instinet got on the air in 1969 with about 60 or 70 institutional trading rooms connected, one broker-dealer, Weeden & Co. ... Charlie Adams had patented some of the basic ideas of electronic trading. So there was an Adams patent. That incarnation of Instinet ran quite successfully for several years.[6]

[6] Manns interview.

Like Nymeyer's, the patent that Pustilnik, Behrens, and Adams wrote was meant to answer a problem of justice in trading. The system was described as "an apparatus and method of automatically, anonymously, and *equitably* buying and selling fungible properties between subscribers" that permitted "institutional investors to communicate anonymously with each other for the purpose of arranging block trades" (Adams et al., 1971; emphasis added). By connecting users' terminals through dedicated private telephone lines to Keydata's UNIVAC 494 computer in Watertown, Massachusetts, Instinet bypassed the specialists of the New York Stock Exchange, creating an anonymous system for both negotiated transactions (buyers and sellers could decide on a price to trade) and automated execution (buyers and sellers could just select the best available price on the system). Its prices were free from the potential information leakages of the NYSE and the economic interference of its specialists. They were efficient.

Similar to Nymeyer's order book, Instinet was not simply a trading platform; it was also a political device that embodied an ethical critique of the marketplace. Admittedly, this dimension was not apparent in how Pustilnik and Behrens presented their service, although they did espouse its contributions to the market's welfare. For example, when Pustilnik testified before the House Subcommittee on Commerce and Finance in 1971, he spoke of Instinet as an example of automation "generating savings to the public every day" by "permitting institutional investors to deal directly with each other through the computer at a modest transaction charge" (House Subcommittee on Commerce and Finance, 1971: 3475). Someone else made the ethical character of Instinet explicit. Pustilnik and Behrens founded Institutional Networks, but did so with the support of a seminal figure in the automation of American stock markets: Donald Weeden.

Donald Weeden was born into a family of financiers, but not of Wall Street's stripe. The Weedens began working in the financial circles of San Francisco, where they opened a bond house in 1922 that concentrated on trading and underwriting Californian municipal securities – the type of local and state government debt instruments often used to finance public projects. As their firm expanded (in 1927 it opened offices in Los Angeles and Manhattan), so did the variety of the instruments in which they dealt. By the 1940s, Weeden & Co. were making markets in listed industrial common stocks – the so-called "third market," a loose collection of dealers of listed securities that operated outside the purview of stock exchanges through over-the-counter transactions. Two decades later, they were a recognized force in the third market, with Donald Weeden spearheading efforts to guarantee its survival in light of great regulatory challenges.

Weeden was also a keen investor in the emerging family of data processing and communication technologies that challenged the primacy of the New York Stock Exchange. Before Instinet, Weeden & Co. invested in AutEx, an electronic, computer-based bulletin board created by Alan Kay in 1968 that gathered and disseminated intentions to buy and sell large blocks of stocks from brokers.[7] Weeden also had a stake in Institutional Networks – and heavily so: at some point, his firm owned more than 90 percent of their shares, and even by the late 1970s had more than 70 percent of the corporation. This was certainly a reasonable bet. When Alan Kay sold AutEx in 1975, Weeden & Co.'s initial investment returned "a handsome profit" (Weeden, 2002: 59). But Weeden's interest in technology also stemmed from his moralized understanding of the securities markets. As he testified in 1971, exchanges were part of "an archaic system," he told the House Subcommittee on Commerce and Finance "involving a great many inefficiencies and a great many costs that are not necessary in this particular age of

---

[7] Although AutEx was the first computer-based trading system introduced to the US stock markets, trades were conducted over the phone; AutEx did not have an automated execution mechanism.

communications and electronic technology" (House Subcommittee on Commerce and Finance, 1971: 3647). David Manns recalled,

> [Weeden's] mindset was that the New York Stock Exchange was the evil Empire and was busy making sure that trading costs remained high, deliberately preventing markets from becoming more efficient. So they built this trading system and they encouraged Instinet. But Instinet to them was but a route to making electronic markets more efficient and also an outlet for their own market-making activity.

For Weeden, Instinet was a means to an end: challenging the dominant exchange in America. It demonstrated through cables and screens that the inefficiencies of traditional exchanges were entirely avoidable. Instinet was just one experiment within a larger sandbox of projects that explored novel designs for "efficient" markets. In addition to his investments in Autex and Institutional Networks, Weeden & Co. redeveloped the moribund Cincinnati Stock Exchange from a small regional organization into the first computerized stock exchange in the country. The system introduced in Cincinnati in 1976, initially called Weeden Holdings Automated Market (WHAM), was crafted by Donald's brother, Jack Weeden, who was "not only a tinkerer," but also a "perfectionist [who] knew computers inside and out" (Weeden, 2002: 122). Unlike Instinet's system, which allowed for both negotiated and automated trades among institutional investors, WHAM was a hard "consolidated limit order book": it worked as a central, automated repository that received and processed public orders (including those submitted by specialists and small investors) on an equal basis. Housed in "the smallest exchange in the nation," WHAM was the first fully operational electronic limit order book in an American stock exchange, and was "unquestionably the most controversial" system at the time, reported *The New York Times*. "To tinker with the viability of the New York Stock Exchange with the gimmickry of the Cincinnati Stock Exchange," specialist and NYSE member

Bernard J. Laskeris told reporters, "is nothing short of being either completely reckless or completely greedy or both." For Jack Weeden, Cincinnati's system was "a live market. We have brought the marketplace to the user rather than vice versa" (Sloan, 1978).

Throughout most of the 1970s, the struggle between supporters and detractors of the NYSE structured much of the national politics of American stock markets. These relatively polarized positions also defined the boundaries of automation: the computerization of trading almost always occurred as a challenge to the NYSE, triggering counter-reactions that involved taking control over technologies to defend the exchange's positions. Within this landscape, market participants, regulators, and technologists often referred to "economic, efficient, fair, competitive, and open" stock markets as proxies for automation. Among these, efficiency and its connections to automation were a particularly powerful discursive pivots. Speaking to Congress in 1971, for example, William Lupien, member of the Pacific Coast Stock Exchange and future president of Instinet, noted that a "federation of all market makers, tied together with a strong communications system, with equal access to all markets, would be a big step toward the most efficient and fair method of doing business" (Lupien in House Subcommittee on Commerce and Finance, 1971). For regulators, efficiency also mattered (Jovanovic, 2017). Consistent with Lupien and Weeden, they also referred to efficiency as desirable virtue of markets. The versatility of the concept across fields is also clear in how technologists used it to justify their designs. For David Manns, the idea of efficiency was connected to the type of markets and systems they built for Instinet. "Our background," he said in his interview, "was in thinking about how to use technology to make things work more efficiently."[8]

Manns's experience also demonstrates that the discursive capacities of efficiency were highly contingent and culturally situated.

---

[8] Manns interview.

When Instinet went public in 1971, it caught the attention of market actors across the world. In Britain, where the London Stock Exchange exercised control over much of finance, Instinet became an instrument for competition. In May of 1972, a group of investment banks announced that they would embark on the creation of a computerized dealing system named Automated Real-time Investments Exchange (ARIEL), providing "an inexpensive efficient trading market which will transcend national boundaries" (Kynaston, 2001). Developing a system from scratch was too expensive an option, and so the seventeen banks that founded ARIEL looked to the block-trading system pioneered by Instinet (Littlewood, 1998). A team from ARIEL's management traveled to the United States and

> realized they needed to be careful with the patents and so on. Pustilnik sold them a license to use the [intellectual property] in the patent... There was a user guide, which nobody ever looked at ..... But there was basically nothing. [These] bankers came back to London all chaffed with themselves that they had gotten an "off-the-shelf" system to do this stuff. But they quickly realized that they didn't actually know what they'd bought and there was nothing defining what they'd bought. This system was totally undocumented. So they hired some consultants to go and document it. This friend of mine ... went out to the States to document this thing [and] he pointed out to them that they really had to start from scratch to build something because there was just no way this was going to be of any use to them... And in the meantime, over in the States, the Instinet people realized they had to totally replace what they had, and get it onto screens, get out from under the time sharing service which was a huge constraint in all kinds of ways. [I joined ARIEL at the time, as] the real technical guy to take over this thing as it was built by [Capgemini] and handed over.[9]

[9] Manns interview.

Hired to develop ARIEL's trading system, David Manns reinvented the electronic order book in Britain. Then still in development, Instinet's second system (Instinet II) proved to be nothing more than "a demonstration ... it was all smoke and mirrors, and we actually suggested that we build the engine for it, the actual central piece, the matching system itself [in London] on a contract basis for them. Because we had started hiring some programmers at ARIEL and this was something for them to do and it could actually make us money. So, I had a team of about five people in London working on [Instinet's second] trading system."[10]

Although a tremendous technical achievement, ARIEL was "never terribly exciting." Efficiency might have been invoked in the early life of the system, but as it was rolled out into use in 1973, it became clear that, the accepting houses were "using technology as a political leaver ... over institutions like the [London] Stock Exchange [and] Bank of England."[11] "Not a huge amount happened," noted Manns.

> What ended up happening was that the usage was very spotty and minimal. It ended up really being used not as a limit order book for continuous trading. Probably 90% of its trading volume was bed-and-breakfast [or] taxless selling were at the end of the month institution A would sell a huge amount of stuff to institution B, and on the morning of the first they would buy it back from institution B so they've established their tax losses. And it was a significant volume of stuff, and obviously they didn't want to do it through the exchange because, you know, the trading costs were high enough to kind of offset the tax benefits significantly.

Moralities shape infrastructures, but they do not dictate how these are adopted or the success of their use. The link between electronic markets and references to efficiency provides an example. As both critique and pragmatic ideal drive the ethos of market technologists, efficiency's power was highly contextual. In the United States,

---

[10] Manns interview.   [11] Manns interview.

market engineers anchored their work on calls for efficiency that were common across the field. This made their embryonic designs of automated markets, however experimental, plausible, and applicable. Efficiency marshaled shared images of cheaper, virtuous, fair, equitable markets, free from the constraints of the NYSE and its specialists. In Britain, however, efficiency was less central to the imaginary of the marketplace, fizzling into a small element of a much more immediate political strategy to reduce the commissions charged by the London Stock Exchange. Efficiency did not capture imaginations; its ethics and virtues simply did not sell.

Much like infrastructural breakdowns, moments of reform and contestation become "occasions for remaking forms of political claims, technical adjustment in equipment, and realigning institutional and political relations" (Simone, 2012). The automation of financial markets occurred during such an occasion, positioning efficiency as a bridge connecting the marketplace and its machines with specific images of personal and collective virtue. The electronic limit order book was a central part of this story: as a technical construct, it tapped into the pragmatic ethics of market technologists; and as an economic object, it tapped into the imaginaries of regulators, investors, and market participants at large.

6.3 ARE ORDER BOOKS MORAL?

Three decades after the introduction of Instinet, order books became infrastructural to finance in two key ways. First, across countries and asset types, the majority of trading was increasingly routed through or executed in electronic limit order books. In the United States today, for example, at least 59.2 percent of the trades in equities are processed through order books (with a remaining 22 percent tied to manual yet essentially electronic forms of trading), as are 97.1 percent of the most common (G10) foreign exchange operations. Electronic limit order books are the undisputed standards for building markets – the technology of consociation for an automated world.

Second, and perhaps more importantly, action in the market is anchored in the way that order books work. Order books matter not only because they are operationally necessary to trade; their technical details define the space of strategies available to market participants. A cursory exploration of "practical" publications in algorithmic and high frequency trading exposes this well: unlike a previous generation of textbooks in financial economics – concerned mostly with determining risk adjusted equilibrium prices and the appropriate composition of portfolios on the basis of reported data – contemporary manuals peer into market microstructure, the operational dynamics of order books, and the effects of variations in market design on the profitability of specific trading strategies. Statistical arbitrage provides an illustration of how strategies take into account the architecture of order books. Techniques of statistical arbitrage involve buying and selling securities on the basis of quantitative signals reconstructed from the marketplace. Traditionally, these signals were primarily of two types: the prices and volumes reported by exchanges and trading venues. When transactions occurred on the floor, these were among the most precise types of publicly available market information. But order books afford a closer look at the market. They present, in particular, the interests and intentions of participants in the form of orders that have yet to be matched. In most electronic order books, orders to buy and sell stocks at prices above or below the best active quotes are not immediately executed and remain in the book until they are cancelled (Figure 6.2). As Irene Aldrige (2009: 39) writes in her guide to high frequency trading, these orders to buy and sell are often "assumed to be symmetrical about the market price, with the distribution of limit buy orders mirroring that of limit sell orders." But this assumption rarely holds, even in the most liquid and active stocks: there is almost always *some* asymmetry in the distribution of limit orders. This asymmetric queuing of orders, this positioning of time-stamped intentions in the book, provides signals that are more revealing in the short term than the prices and trading volumes of earlier forms of statistical arbitrage. These order book imbalances

Bid		Ask	
Price	Size	Price	Size
110.82	100	111.58	100
110.79	100		
110.56	100		
109.75	100		
109.00	100		

FIGURE 6.2 An illustration of the top of the order book for Apple Inc. on December 9, 2014, 9:01 AM.

allow seeing a proxy of the intentions around the market – revealing if there are more buyers than sellers or vice versa – and consequently predicting how prices might behave in the immediate future (more unfilled sell orders might suggest, for example, that the next movement in price will be negative). These statistical predictions require understanding the "interplay between incoming orders and the order book ... Market making strategies, optimal execution strategies, statistical arbitrage strategies, being executed at the individual level, all require a perfect understanding of the limit order book" (Abergel et al., 2016: 4). More generally, the algorithms animating contemporary markets are designed to fit the functionalities of specific devices, exploiting their different ways of handling orders, signaling information, modifying instructions, and executing trades (Balarkas and Ewen, 2007; interview with platform developer). The centrality of the order book to market action may well explain why, upon its diffusion, limit orders proliferated rapidly in forms. In addition to the plain limit order, contemporary order books process calendar spread orders (that instruct to buy one delivery month of a contract and sell another delivery month of the same contract, at the same time, and on the same exchange), deferred orders (that sit on the order book until triggered), hidden orders (that are not visible to other users), iceberg orders (that hide some of the volume to the marketplace), or any other of the 1,200 order types available in American financial markets across the sixteen national securities exchange recognized by the Securities and Exchange Commission (Mackintosh, 2014).

With its distinct codes, structures, and standards, the order book is a world in its own. And like the trading pits that occupied exchanges in the past, it is a particularly moral universe. The early automators of financial markets foresaw order books as ushering a fairer, more just, and more equal trading mechanism than the ones provided by humans on trading floors. Predictably, this is not the case: just as politics cannot be subtracted from machines, order books cannot be detached from their own ethical predicaments and moral asymmetries. The order book consociates – it brings trades together on one infrastructure – but it does not create community, honor, and a market ethics of itself. Order books do, however, introduce unexpected and controversial activities that unsettle the moral conventions of the market and provoke its dwellers to redraw their boundaries of acceptability. One set of practices is particularly relevant, specifically, forms of "market manipulation" where participants are said to knowingly alter prices with the intent of fooling others.

Market manipulation is a prominent example of the controversies surrounding high frequency trading, but there are many. Some important critiques, such as those highlighted by Michael Lewis (2015) in *Flash Boys*, are related to asymmetries in the architecture of markets – problems of equality of access that, as explored in the next chapter, have animated innovations in American stock market infrastructures for decades. The practice of co-location, whereby brokers and electronic market makers pay premium prices to place their computer servers as close as possible to the exchanges' matching engines, is a usual occurrence. So are "enriched" data feeds, offered by some trading venues at great costs, that provide a select set of market users with faster sources of information on the order book than what is contained in conventional feeds.

These inequalities matter but they are not what I want to focus on in the remainder of this chapter. My interest, rather, is in the actions considered unethical or illegitimate and that are made possible by the order book. I find one particularly relevant: spoofing, or the act of submitting orders not meant to be executed and that have the objective of eliciting reactions from other market participants to profit from market movements. Spoofing is a result of assuming that the orders placed in the book reflect actual, rather than fictitious, intentions to trade. Recall that one way of predicting price movements in the short term is by examining order imbalances: more buyers than sellers, even if their limit orders are below and above the best prevailing quotes, indicates that the next price move will be negative, that the intentions of the market are such that it is likely bearish rather than bullish. This depends, of course, on assuming that these passive limit orders are there for a reason, that they reflect the actual valuations that investors made of the stock. Submitting false orders can artificially fool algorithms that rely on this strategy, giving spoofers a brief though economically significant opportunity to profit from minute and predictable price movements. Because it unsettles confidence in what the electronic order book registers and is basically a form of market manipulation, spoofing corrodes marketplace ethics, and has consequently resulted in much regulatory and public attention.

In the United States, spoofing was only recognized as a crime under the Dodd-Frank Wall Street Reform and Consumer Protection Act of 2010. The first case of suspected spoofing was tried in 2011, when the American Commodity Futures Trading Commission and the British Financial Conduct Authority brought charges against Michael Coscia and his Panther Energy Trading for illegally manipulating markets on the Chicago Mercantile Exchange and the Intercontinental Exchange. Agreeing with the Department of Justice, a grand jury indicted Coscia in late 2014 on six counts of commodities fraud and six counts of spoofing. During the ensuing trial, the government argued that Coscia knowingly "entered large-volume orders that he intended to immediately cancel before they could be filled by other traders" (*US v. Coscia*, 2015a).

Coscia's trial revealed how the ethics and morality of action in electronic markets are bound to order books and their queues of intentions, stressing the techniques required to discern legitimate from the illegitimate trades. Coscia's defense relied on two arguments. First, that the trial was itself procedurally incorrect because existing statutes against spoofing were simply too vague, encompassing "much routine, innocuous conduct by commodities traders" (*US v. Coscia*, 2015b). Second, Coscia argued that both intent and manipulation were not evident. Since he never made an explicit false statement or material representation about when or how he would cancel the orders submitted to the market, he rejected that his actions amounted to frauds (*US v. Coscia*, 2015c).

For the prosecution, however, the matter of Coscia's intentions was clear cut: his strategy signaled an intent to cancel orders systematically, differentiating his conduct from other widely accepted and legitimate practices such as fill-or-kill and partial-fill orders. According to the government's legal team, Coscia manipulated the market by conveying "a misleading impression to customers" through his activity (*US v. Coscia*, 2015c). That he did not misrepresent his intentions beforehand was immaterial. Indeed, much of the proof offered by the prosecution consisted in highlighting the rationale behind Coscia's strategy, which consisted of so-called layering orders, that is, placing large orders to buy and sell instruments slightly above and under the best bids and offers in the order book, creating a "false sense of supply and demand." Through this, argued the prosecutors, Coscia affected the offers of other (mainly algorithmic) market participants and profited from market movements artificially created by his fictitious trades.

The central issue in the trial was establishing intent. Coscia's orders could have been part of a bona fide trading strategy; after all, 95 percent of all orders submitted to order book are cancelled before execution (Arnuk and Saluzzi, 2012). Evidence of intent had to be produced by opening up the Chicago Mercantile Exchange and Intercontinental Exchange's order books – by performing an infrastructural inversion, of sorts – to discern the nature of Coscia's actions. The indictment, for example, accused Coscia of knowingly transmitting "to a CME Group server Euro FX currency futures contract orders that he intended to cancel before execution, so he could purchase 14 contracts at a below-market price and then sell them immediately thereafter for a higher price, in order to obtain a profit of approximately \$175 in less than a second" (US v. Coscia, 2015a).[12] The intent of these orders was not established from confessions or other first-person statements, but rather inferred from the strategy followed by the defendant in the context of what was possible and expected within the order book. In addition to testimony by Coscia's programmer, the government relied on the expert testimony of Hendrick Bessembinder, a professor of finance at the University of Utah and specialist on market microstructure theory (O'Hara, 1995), whose account set much the tone for the trial. As Bloomberg reported, Bessembinder "went through data for the jury that showed that even after orders were filled there were attempts to cancel them by Coscia's algorithms" (Louis, Massa and Hanna, 2015). The construction of intent relied heavily on Bessembinder's representation of how order books work – on establishing a form of "second order" intentionality with respect to the infrastructure rather than an individual's state of mind (Muniesa, 2014). "The only way trading is generated in electronic markets," noted Bessembinder,

> is through order submission. So if one is seeking to generate trading, seeking to generate a reaction, the only way one could do that is by inducing people to change their order submissions. [The] high fill rates on the small orders [suggest manipulation]. They were not only very high relative to the fill rates on the large orders, they are actually remarkably high for fill rates for other high frequency traders, so the high fill rates on the small orders are certainly very much consistent with the idea that the reaction that was generated was to induce other traders to submit orders to trade against, interact with the small orders.

Bessembinder did not speak of Coscia's intentions; he did not "implicate intent as to any element of the crime charged"

---

[12] Though Coscia's indictment included only six counts of spoofing, none of which resulted in more than \$500 in profits, Coscia is thought to have engaged in multiple events, earning \$1.4 million over little less than three months.

(*US v. Coscia*, 2015c). Rather, Bessembinder's testimony suggested to the jury what is expected of *normal* order book dynamics, signaling that the only possible way of making sense of Coscia's orders was as fictitious, unethical dealings. The coupling was effective: in early November 2015, after a mere hour of deliberation, the Chicago jury found Coscia guilty on all twelve counts. The order book was not a guarantee of ethics, but it served as a platform linking native conceptions of intent and morality with the specific technical repertoires of market microstructure economics.

6.4   CONCLUSIONS

In this chapter, I explored some of the connections between infrastructures and market moralities that are relevant for understanding the automation of finance. The objective of this exercise was not to insist on the observation that moralities are important to markets (Fourcade and Healy, 2007; Shamir, 2008; Zelizer, 2017). What matters here is their location: moral struggles are simultaneously designed into and shaped by the devices, standards, and platforms that support transactions. If markets are moral projects, as sociologists, historians, and anthropologists have long argued, it is partly because their infrastructures incorporate and elicit particular frames of ethical evaluation.

That infrastructures matter in configuring ethical relations, that they create and shape the communities that exist on them (Star, 1998; Bowker and Star, 1999), can be seen perhaps by looking at the past as much as at the present. Consider the trading floor, an infrastructure that contrasts sharply with the queued logic of the order book. Whereas order books operate under strictly symmetrical rules of price-time priority with orders that index intentions, trading floors are spaces of asymmetric and opaque interaction. Order books are organized as queues of electronic messages; trading floors take the shape of crowds of traders. Order books are mostly anonymous while the dynamics of trading floors are characterized by interpersonal knowledge and embodied communications (Abolafia, 1996). Yet spoofing is native to both, receiving quite different treatments across each setting. In the digital domains of electronic limit order books, spoofing is an illegitimate, unethical transaction, a false relation that threatens the moral standing of the anonymous market. In trading floors, however, spoofing was at times tolerated, sort of like a joking relation (Radcliffe-Brown, 1940; Mauss, 2013) through which traders on the floor teased and tested their market-kin.

One example jumps to mind: a case similar to spoofing on the floor of the London Stock Exchange in the early 1980s. Then, prices were mostly verbal, sometimes represented through whiteboards propped on the pitches of market makers on the trading floor. Over interview, a once young trainee at one of the most reputable market makers in London recalled how visual representations were used to drive prices up. The individual in question was assigned to work on the Australian mining book, which consisted of a list of mining shares selected and managed by a senior partner. As part of his research, the senior partner traveled to Australia to inspect facilities, talk with managers and engineers, visit brokers in Sydney and Melbourne, and buy shares for the firm's inventory. On an occasion during which the trainee was on the pitch, the partner had returned from Australia, bringing shares of a newly found mining company. The market, as the trainee recalled, was "a bit frothy," yet the price of gold was "really going through the roof." Before the market opened at 9:30, the senior partner introduced his new finding to the firm's members and trainees in the pitch: "Alright. I've got this company called GEM Exploration, which I've bought 250,000 shares of ... and I've bought them for the equivalent price of 3p. [We'll] see what we can do with them." So he wrote "GEM" on the whiteboard and next to it he wrote "5" as the opening price for the share. Because it was written rather than printed on the board, it was clear for everyone in the market that this was a new share. And so, the first brokers were drawn to it. The first one to enquire about this strange new entry said "I see ... What's this GEM you've got up there? They look interesting. Tell me about that." As the one responsible for managing Australian mining shares, the senior partner replied: "Well, I went to Australia. I saw this company" and after explaining the business of the company, he mentioned he thought they were "a real prospect in the current market conditions." Intrigued, the broker asked for a quote. "They're 4 6" replied the senior partner. "What sized you'd like that?" asked the broker. "25,000" answered the market maker. "OK, well, thanks very much. I'll go away and have a think about that one," said the broker as he walked away from the pitch. Regardless of the fact that there had not been a transaction, the senior partner changed the price on the white-board, writing in blue the number 6. The next broker approached the pitch, seeing GEM Exploration on the board.

> "What are they this morning?" "Ah, well they're 5 7." "What's the size?" "Ah, well they're at bid for 25, offered in 10." Which showed that I'm a buyer, obviously. And he said "Oh, OK, well, I'll buy ten." The next guy comes along and literally, within half an hour, the things are trading at 25p. By the end of the day, they're trading at 40p, and we've turned over 2.5 million and we are long 350,000 shares instead of 250,000 shares.[13]

The case was plainly one of market manipulation: the representa-tions of prices on whiteboards were meant to elicit, like Coscia's orders, reactions within the market community. But any similarities obscure an important difference: these types of manipulations on the floor, although certainly contested, had an altogether different moral valence. To manipulate one's relative is one thing; to manipulate a stranger in an anonymous environment is quite another. Those were the days of the floor. As Gregory Meyer of the *Financial Times* wrote in 2015, technology "changes the nature of violations." But if it does so, it is necessarily because different technologies imply and enact different "mutualities of being," different ethics of participation and exchange (Carsten, 2013). The risk of spoofing is a risk of false, rather than joking, relations – a challenge to the legitimacy, morality, and

---

[13] Interview with former market maker.

senses of intentionality in modern electronic markets (Arnuk and Saluzzi, 2012).

Ethics and morality also matters at a larger scale: as factors that impinged on the contested evolution of financial infrastructures across the nation. Automation was not the removal of the dense moral orders of trading floors and their substitution by amoral electronic systems – this is certainly not a story about the end of *the* moral economy and its replacement by some fundamentally rational, capitalist regime, to paraphrase historian Edward P. Thompson (1971). Rather, the dynamics of how market organizations were automated was a tournament between competing ethical conceptions, a cacophony of moral economies, each of which fought for the salvation of finance. In the United States, three terms played a significant role in shaping this process: efficiency, equality, and fairness. Like the order book, the moral discourses anchored on these three contested terms shaped the course of infrastructures at large. This was the story of the creation of the national market system, to which I turn to in Chapter 7.

7   Rabbits Guarding the Lettuce

In *Flash Boys*, Michael Lewis (2015) tells the story of IEX, the Investors Exchange, an electronic trading platform founded upon the troubles and dilemmas of contemporary market structures. For Lewis and his informants, IEX is the private solution to the long-established problem of inequity of access in American finance. For Brad Katsuyama, the heroic character in Lewis's account who set up IEX at the height of controversies around automated trading, "there is systematic corruption in the market. A rigging, a rigging in the market. And it's the provision to high frequency traders of information that ordinary investors do not have [which is at the core of this form of corruption]" (Lewis, 2015).

Flash Boys is emblematic of a genre of writings critical of the inexorable automation of modern financial markets. Its theme suggests, like those developed by authors elsewhere, that financial markets, particularly those in the United States of America, are somehow skewed to the disadvantage of ordinary investors, rewarding material and technological innovations that befuddle our traditional imaginary of stock markets as institutions where knowledgeable actors congregated to collectively determine the value of diverse instruments. Stock markets and their technologically intensive forms of action, we are told by Paul Krugman (2014), are too full of socially wasteful innovations. A classic example is the seemingly Baroque pursuit of speed as a critical competitive edge for traders and intermediaries: at a cost of $200 million dollars, for example, Spread Networks, LLC's link between Chicago and New York increased the transmission between these two cities by a mere 2 milliseconds in 2010. More recently, Tradeworx's private microwave relay networks made 2 milliseconds closer to an eternity (MacKenzie et al., 2012; MacKenzie, 2018). The apparent opacity of these investments matter: as Fox et al. (2015: 194) note, recent polls suggest that about two-thirds of Americans agree with Lewis's informants in thinking that "the stock market unfairly benefits some at the expense of others."

Lewis and critics of automated finance are partly right: markets are, indeed, "rigged," but not in the way they so imagine. Automated trading and its technological arms race are not the result of fraudulent, manipulative, or distorting activities – of "being rigged" in Katsuyama's sense. Rather, these forms of market activity emerged from the jumbled creation of an environment that makes investments in speed profitable and morally permissible. This environment was not defined solely by technology and the power of a small group of institutions to shape the nature of trading but by market fragmentation as an endemic, fundamentally constructed feature of the American financial landscape. By market fragmentation, in particular, I refer to situations where trading for the same instrument is spread across numerous sites, creating arbitrage opportunities that, however individually small, are economically significant with the right technologies. Modern markets are notoriously fragmented: in the United States, trade is distributed among eleven public exchanges and more than fifty private dark pools.

In this chapter, I trace the history of stock market fragmentation in the United States of America by placing attention on the disjointed and unpredictable role of "politics" – national, institutional, and individual – in shaping the nation's critical market infrastructures. Specifically, the variety of market fragmentation that characterizes America's terrain encodes in its infrastructures multiple conceptions of efficiency, fairness, and equality, as well as shared imaginaries about the role that stock markets *should* play in the future of an increasingly financialized nation.

Although disparate, the multiple forces that fragmented markets shared a common concern: how best to build a single, national financial marketspace.[1] To understand the politics at play in the creation of this single market (formally called the National Market System, made up by the multiple trading venues, platforms, and communication networks that seamlessly route and execute the orders of investors throughout the United States of America), I return to the metaphors presented in Chapter 2 that link kinship and relation making to modern stock markets. If markets are communities of exchange then the project of building the National Market System was tied to the creation of a new form of relatedness that spanned the country, a variety of nationhood built around images of widespread financial participation. These market communities of the NMS required very different technologies of consociation from those that existed in the past. They needed, in particular, devices that made the vast spaces and distant places of mid-twentieth-century America intimately linked. Moreover, they required a different moral language, a technology of honor unbound to the constraints of the past. In building the National Market System, actors shifted the burdens of fairness and equality away from human intermediaries and their institutions onto the public order queue as an organizing principle of justice in finance.

7.1   THE OPPORTUNITIES OF AMBIGUITY

One of the most striking features of contemporary stock markets is their great level of fragmentation. While writing this, the market for Alphabet Inc.'s Class C stock (Google) existed in at least eleven US trading venues and seven European exchanges, not including dark

---

[1] I am borrowing the term "marketspace" from Alexander Engel (2015)" who identifies global markets as communicative spaces linked by the mutual observation of prices. Following Knorr Cetina's work on markets as interactional systems, Engel shows the emergence of global markets as a distinctly historical process that moved economic activity away from the physically constrained arena of the marketplace and into a global realm.

pools, private crossing networks, and numerous over-the-counter transactions.[2] In our hypermodern, capitalist world, the question of how much Google is worth does not have a simple answer. At any given moment, each market may trade at a different price, potentially creating 18 public valuations for the same stock (there is a large-ish cottage industry dedicated to visualizing the distributed prices of stocks, used by traders to identify the best deals available in the global marketplace). Such fragmentation is now taken for granted by most sophisticated market participants – it is one of the many naturalized facts of life that they deal with when designing strategies to buy and sell instruments. Fragmentation is so critical that entire life worlds are built around it: as a high frequency trader confessed over coffee in London some years ago, at any given point in time, his firm had to simultaneously observe and act in over 36 trading platforms to remain competitive in the industry.[3] Fragmentation is the name of their game.

For market participants, the fragmented structure of trading is both a problem and an opportunity. Investors looking for clarity in prices and transaction costs may see fragmentation as a matter of concern: they produce less efficient prices (economists might argue that the reduced volumes across the multiple trading venues can result in prices that are slightly off with respect to their "true" equilibrium values), making unknowable the "actual" value of stocks because there is no single market that serves as an undisputed reference. French anthropologist Alexandre Laumonier (2013) noted with some irony that in electronic markets only God truly knows how much stocks are worth: even with information moving at the speed of light, one simply cannot know the last transaction in the NYSE's matching engine in Mahwah, New Jersey, sitting nine milliseconds away in San Diego, California. By the time a person receives

---

[2] Data taken from Fidessa's Fragulator, http://fragmentation.fidessa.com/fragulator/ (accessed September 5, 2017).
[3] Interview with high frequency trader.

data on the NYSE's prices, these are stale by at least 9 milliseconds; on the far-away server, prices might already be different.

For others, though, fragmentation is a business opportunity. Where there is ambiguity there are profits and at least one algorithmic trading strategy relies on continued, minute price differentials across multiple marketplaces: so-called "latency arbitrage," the practice of trading assets across markets based on the ability to communicate with trading sites faster than competitors (Arnuk and Saluzzi, 2009). Latency arbitrage is the result of simple physics and engineering: information cannot travel faster than the speed of light and is often relayed by systems that require time to process and retransmit data. Finance takes time, whether in the form of a broker walking down the street with his customer's order or as a signal traveling across a communication network to reach the electronic order book of an exchange. A telling survey from 2008 shows some of the times involved in modern trades: the typical round trip of disseminating a price to preparing an order and executing it in the order book of an exchange takes between 110 and 140 milliseconds. Most of the time involves preparing orders through algorithms and transmitting them to the relevant exchange: for example, the transmission time between Chicago and New York is in the order of 7 milliseconds, but it takes an order about 35 milliseconds to travel from the West to the East Coast of the United States, moving at about two-thirds the speed of light through dedicated (though discontinuous) fiber optic cables. By installing systems that offer higher transmission speeds, investors can gain an edge over their competitors simply because they can execute their orders before others. With multiple marketplaces and large trading volumes, this strategy can become profitable: even with price differentials of a single penny and small lots of hundreds of stocks or less, trading millions of times a day adds up to sizable returns – as a study published in 2016 noted, the potential (though purely theoretical) return from latency arbitrage in the United States is as high as $3 billion dollars per year (though, of course, realized profits are quite likely much lower than this; Wah, 2016).

What is interesting about the type of market fragmentation that fuels automated, high frequency trading is that it occurred within a notably regulated industry. This is particularly true in the United States, where the Securities and Exchange Commission has held strong oversight of stock markets since its foundation in 1934 following the 1929 crash. The structure of American securities markets is undoubtedly the result of much profit-seeking and entre-preneurial activity – of organizational and technical innovations such as Nymeyer's never-realized patent and more concrete developments such as those at Instinet and Cincinnati. But stock markets also reflect the logics of the regulatory environments where they develop – of prevailing norms about appropriate behaviors, adequate institutional controls, and, importantly, how technologies *ought* to be linked in the marketplace. Fragmentation and the forms of automated trading that it promotes are as much the products of free enterprise as the (perhaps unintended) consequences of regulatory intervention. The question is: why did American markets fragment, despite developing within a strong regulatory environment?

7.2   A POLANYIAN TRANSFORMATION

Market fragmentation cannot exist without the concept of a national (or global) marketspace. Something can only be fragmented if it refers to an actually existing prior unit or some imagined whole to which the fragments correspond. For our case, this would correspond to a national market of some sort, where the bids and offers of investors interact to create a single reference, a national price. As Karl Polanyi (1944) famously noted, such whole, national markets are neither natural nor inevitable: they are produced, crafted, or, in the language of this book, infrastructured in concretely historical and political ways. Fragmentation is an acutely modern problem simply because a national market for stocks did not actually exist six or seven decades ago. This might seem odd, given our usual association between high-class finance and the remorseless expansion of capitalism (Giddens, 1971; Strange, 1986; Simmel, 2004 [1900]). Yet the fact remains that, in mid-twentieth-century America, there was very little competition or national exchange in even the most active stocks.

This observation derives from the history of how the key institutional sites of stock trading – exchanges – evolved as organizations. As discussed in Chapter 2, stock exchanges were built as relatively closed communities that sought to control access to their marketplace's membership and operations through a number of bureaucratic, physical, and cultural devices: from walls containing and isolating the trading floor to tropes of honor and belonging that gave their activities internal and public legitimacy. Exchanges are infrastructures of kinship, of closed-ness, of property and exclusion. This was also the case for the New York Stock Exchange and other organized trading sites in America. As the most important market in stocks in the United States, the NYSE was built to contain its members and their trades. Containment was necessary: from its foundation in 1816, the NYSE faced tremendous competition from challengers that emerged in close proximity to its floor – including bucket shops and curbstone brokers that threatened to cut into the exchange's business (Sobel, 1975; Hochfelder, 2006).

The NYSE used several mechanisms to discourage competition: tied to the issuing of stocks, the NYSE's specialist system gave market makers a unique level of control over the ebb and flow of trades; another well-discussed strategy was controlling the information of the ticker tape feeds to discourage the formation of outside, secondary markets (Preda, 2008); but notoriously, the exchange also made use of extensive internal regulations that kept the markets that it generated (that is, those in NYSE-listed stocks) firmly under its jurisdiction. One example of these regulatory devices was NYSE Rule 394 (renamed Rule 390 in 1977; Jarrell, 1984). A product of the NYSE's constitution, Rule 394 restricted members from "effecting a transaction in a listed stock off the Exchange, either as principal or as agent." Prior to the formulation of the rule in 1957, off-board trading restrictions were interpreted with some laxity: members could transact their client's trades off the floor of the exchange, if the transactions were made at better prices and in the benefit of the client's account. The growth of the so-called third or over-the-counter market in the 1950s, however, posed a particularly important threat – demonstrated by the histories of Instinet and Donald Weeden's efforts to digitize Cincinnati. As business moved away from the NYSE's floor, so did commissions on trades, threatening the profits of exchange's members. Rule 394 was introduced precisely when competition from over-the-counter dealers increased while the organization's tolerance for off-board trades dwindled and disappeared (Seligman, 1982).

Rule 394 was a blatant attempt by the exchange to exercise a monopoly over the trading of its stocks (D. Baker, 1976). Historically, this monopolistic strategy was interesting because it presumed the creation and maintenance of a "local" market. It was as if the NYSE was operating "without an economy," to use Polanyi's expression, subjected to "rituals and ceremonies which restrict[ed its] scope while assuring [its] ability to function [within] given narrow limits" (Polanyi, 1944). The exchange fostered a closed, almost traditional, economy of stocks, even if the instruments it traded were relatively sophisticated contractual agreements representing corporations with global operations. At this scale, the NYSE was a market *without* an economy, spatially anchored, and organizationally constrained. And while fragmentation and competition were emerging in the horizon – in the form of National Association of Securities Dealers (NASD) and the third market, for example – they were still far from shaping anything that could be thought of as a truly national "marketspace." For that, a Polanyian shift was needed: building a market to serve the nation as a whole.

7.3   THE SPOILS OF FAILURE

A central contribution of economic sociology is the insight that capitalist markets cannot exist without the state: for markets to operate, they need legal, institutional, and cultural supports that are crafted and reproduced through the authority of the state's policies and bur-eaucracies (Polanyi, 1944; Nee, 1989; Boyer, 1996; Fligstein and Mara-Drita, 1996; Fligstein, 2002; Block, 2003). Polanyi understood this well: in his work, he carefully noted that the fictitious commodities of modern capitalism were coined within the state's systems, though legal and administrative transformations that gave them weight and credence. The financial marketspace is no exception. The creation of a national system for trading stocks also required the explicit interven-tion of the state. Fragmentation and the forms of automated trading it fosters originated precisely in the nature of the decisions about how to set up this state-sponsored project.

Like most large projects, establishing a fully operational national market was a grueling task. We could think of it to be as complex and difficult as building the interstate highway system that now spans across the continental United States – a product of intense political battles to trace the paths that concrete, asphalt, and federal funding would follow across cities, wilderness, and fields (Karnes, 2009). Eisenhower's administration may have faced the elements and geological complexities of America's physical landscape to create the interstate highway system in the 1950s, but it certainly did not meet with the gargantuan obstruction of the New York Stock Exchange. As mentioned in the previous chapter, much of the logic of innovation within US stock markets was a reaction to the NYSE's dominant position and its institutional and cultural clout. Controlled by the powerful specialists – market makers that had the exclusive rights to run the books for listed stocks within the exchange – the NYSE was an engine designed to contain and limit the market. A national market challenged the NYSE and its construction required ample support, nothing short of a revolution.

By the mid-1960s, the conditions for a revolution were plentiful. Long-standing criticisms of the NYSE had intensified: large institu-tional investors including the increasingly influential pension and mutual funds deemed the NYSE's fixed commission structure costly and unpalatable. Competition from the National Association of

Securities Dealers (NASD) and the third market (including Weeden & Co.) questioned the necessity of the NYSE at the core of the American financial system. And since the early 1960s, regulators had kept an eye on reform, with the aim of materializing some of the most elusive promises of the 1934 Exchange Act – greater surveillance and guaranteed fairness for "average," small investors. Most crucially, however, the revolution was triggered by sociotechnical failure: following the market boom of the late 1960s, the rapid growth in trading volumes clashed with the largely invisible clearing and settlement systems of the NYSE, which exceeded its operational capacity and collapsed (daily activity grew from 6 million to 10 million traded shares per day between 1965 and 1968). This so-called paperwork crisis was immensely important: it was not an event that introduced uncertainty and economic losses; more fundamentally, it rooted automation at the organizational core of American finance.

Wyatt Wells (2000) offers what is perhaps the best account of how the paperwork crisis in settlement promoted transformations in stock markets for decades to come. Following a long bull market, the growth of trading outpaced investments in clearing and settlement both at the exchanges and the brokerage firms. At the time, settlement was siloed across numerous trading sites: each stock exchange settled its own trades, independently running operations with different practices, standards, and organizational routines. Thus, the New York Stock Exchange ran the NYSE Stock Clearing Corporation since the 1920s, as did the American Stock Exchange. Settlement was also intensely manual and required processing and physically transferring stock certificates, often-embellished pieces of paper that represented an investor's stake in a company (see Weiss, 1992). As Wells notes, stock certificates were usually produced in lots of 100 shares, and each time they were transferred they had to be registered individually by both parties to a transaction, notarized, and physically moved from the seller's to the buyer's agent. For brokers, this implied a complicated form of bookkeeping: in addition to accounting for the movement of monies, brokerages had to keep a second book documenting the transfer of certificates across transactions and marketplaces. The resulting complexity was great, as Wells note: each purchase could require up to 68 steps introducing an equally large number of opportunities for costly errors. As in London, furthermore, settlement was an invisible, lowly task. Poorly trained and overworked clerks oversaw the process, and the partners of brokerage firms rarely specialized on settlement (and when they did, they were seen as lesser members of the firm). Investments – symbolic, human, and material – were seriously lacking.

As a result of this complexity, the operational bottlenecks became critical when trading volumes grew. Brokerage firms "found themselves running days, or even weeks, behind current transactions," notes Wells (2000: 203), and the number of failures to deliver certificates on time raised tremendously: when these "fails" were surveyed in April 1968, the NYSE estimated its members had $2.67 billion in undelivered trades across all markets; by December, it had peaked at $4.12 billion fails. These were not simply delays: without receipt of the stock certificates, investors often did not pay for their trades, leaving brokerage firms holding large quantities of risky debt for unnecessarily long periods of time. At best, brokers had to pay interests over the debt until the transaction was settled. At worst, they were stuck with rapidly depreciating securities. The costs were significant: the Securities and Exchange Commission estimated that in both 1968 and 1969, firms incurred more than $1 billion in clerical and administrative expenses per year, compared to $600 million in 1966.

For numerous firms, computers were an obvious solution to the clearing and settlement conundrum, leading to heavy investments to mechanize their back-offices. As Wells reported, NYSE members spent $100 million on computer systems in both 1969 and 1970, well above the $25 million spent four years earlier. But as happened elsewhere, these investments were not backed by similar investments in expertise and organizational reform: the computers were placed amid chaotic and ill-prepared firms whose records were in complete disarray. Although powerful, the new systems could not cope with the disorderly transaction records, becoming greater financial liabilities than solutions in the short term: when markets fell in 1971 along with the commission income of brokerage firms, the large fixed costs of computers and settlement personnel remained. The small firms paid a dear price: with lower trading volumes, one-sixth of all the brokerage firms in New York could no longer maintain operations and either failed or were acquired by or merged with larger, better capitalized organizations.

When the dust of the paperwork jam settled, the buzz of computers echoed through Wall Street. As the industry developed expertise to better handle the machines in the basements, it also learned how to use their surplus processing power for other tasks (a broker quoted by Wells noted that computers did not reduce overhead costs but "did enormously increase the ability to process and handle business."). Settlement was soon but one of a multitude of activities automated through computerization. Others, from portfolio management to trading itself, would soon follow. Importantly, the forms of automation developed throughout the crisis created the conditions for a truly national market by establishing a platform that allowed settlement to occur (almost) seamlessly despite the great challenges of geography: the Depositary Trust Company, forerunner of the current Depositary Trust and Clearing Corporation.

National, internal markets require a very particular type of infrastructure to operate. For example, if local trades are to coalesce into a wide-reaching market, actors have to be equipped with technical and organizational devices that afford them communication across distance. In the early days of financial activity, price sheets served as means for communicating and coordinating markets across space, even if their transmission was slow and relatively cumbersome. More recently, the foreign exchange markets studied by Karin Knorr Cetina and Urs Brugger (2002) offer an additional example of the type of communication infrastructures that belie trade: currency trading requires digital systems connecting traders across the world, who share conventions about face-to-screen interaction that mediate the value, transmission, and ownership of money. But in addition to infrastructures that foster modes of communication, markets require systems to mobilize and process products, contracts, and trades – like containers that move things across the oceans and represent, in their standardized construction, a unit of accounting understandable to industry (Martin, 2013). Settlement provides this, a platform on which contracts, money, and property can be moved between buyers and sellers. As such, the design of a settlement system is extremely consequential to how the market evolves. When settlement was fragmented across stock exchanges and involved moving paper between businesses, it constrained the possibilities of both market growth and automation. A trading strategy based on arbitraging stocks across several exchanges was practically impossible: because clearing and settlement were so laborious, the trading costs of such strategy would probably outstrip its potential profits. Indeed, any form of high-turnover automated trading was unfeasible under this model of settlement.

The automation of the back-office was a turning point in the creation of a single, national settlement platform. In 1966, shortly before the paperwork jam, the New York Stock Exchange was working on the development of a settlement system that would dematerialize paper certificates among its membership – that is, a mechanism to substitute the documents stored in filing cabinets and scattered on the desks of notaries and brokers across Wall Street with neat electronic files residing on a single, central computer. The system introduced by the NYSE in 1968, the Central Certificate Service, allowed member brokers to deposit their investors' certificates with the exchange, who would then carry on settlement without physical delivery (papers remained stored in safes and the only thing that moved were electronic registers of ownership; Werner, 1971). This reduction in operational complexity was then taken as the template during the back-office crisis. As Wall Street firms struggled with extensive backlogs, the NYSE expanded the CCS's scope, eventually merging operations with the American Stock Exchange's clearing services and NASD's national network. This gave birth to the Depositary Trust Company (DTC) in 1973. The DTC was not simply a means for facilitating settlement through the NYSE-controlled computer-based book-entry delivery and payment architecture (similar to the type of systems that exist today; Depositary Trust Corporation, 1973; see also Millo et al., 2005). Critically, by including the largest exchanges and stock dealing services in the country, it established a *national* backbone for trading: the DTC did not only serve Wall Street, but, from its very introduction, "interfaced" with the clearing and settlement systems of other regional exchanges – from Boston and Detroit, to the Pacific and National stock exchanges. Contracts could now circulate, as electronic messages, without the need to move certificates back and forth through America's expanses. For financial markets, the DTC created the same type of opportunities that Eisenhower's highways created for interstate trade: it allowed for things to move; but unlike the interstate system, the movements on the DTC's infrastructure were digital.

More than evincing a common and collaborative digital future, the DTC expressed some of the politics of the markets to come. The settlement services of DTC traced their origin to the NYSE's efforts to dematerialize the certificates of its membership, and DTC itself remained wholly owned and operated by the exchange. As Robert Sobel notes, "the Exchange would not relinquish [leadership] under any circumstances," since controlling settlement was a proxy for controlling the course of the market (Sobel, 2000: 86), and settlement is a crucial technology of consociation, a form of producing and breaking the legitimate relations that belie every trade. Time would demonstrate that this was the preferred strategy for the NYSE: rather than leaving the design of market infrastructures to its competition or the state's bureaucracies, the exchange sought to command the development of some of the United States' most critical financial devices.

7.4 MECHANIZING MARKETS

While computers were in widespread use in stock markets by the early 1970s, they had existed, at least ideationally, as possible solutions to the woes of the American financial system writ large for over a decade. Well before the NYSE experimented with automation in their back-office, the Securities and Exchange Commission considered computers as mechanisms that could provide greater levels of transparency to some of the most dispersed markets of America.

For the SEC, digital electronic devices were attractive solutions for bringing order to the growing regional and over-the-counter markets that competed against the NYSE for trades. Although the NYSE could prohibit its members from trading outside of the exchange, it could not stop the trading of listed stocks within regional marketplaces or among independent dealers. The market was fragmenting in practice, creating an unwieldy regulatory challenge for the SEC. Anne Khademian (1992: 60) wrote that by the 1960s, securities markets were "bursting out of the old regulatory structure," and the SEC was simply ill prepared for the situation. The SEC was aware of its limitations and lobbied both President Kennedy's administration and the House Commerce and Senate Banking committees for additional funding to conduct a comprehensive study of the markets with a view to reforming its regulatory practice. The efforts of the SEC were successful, and the resulting mandate from Capitol Hill was broad. Milton Cohen, the commissioner responsible for leading the study at the time, recalled Congress' ample instructions: to "investigate anything and everything about the securities markets and report [their] conclusions and recommendations" by 1963 (M. Cohen, 1963).

The outcome was the *Report of the Special Study of Securities Markets*, the first comprehensive review of the structure and operation of a hitherto dislocated and little understood market system. The special study was momentous in at least two ways. On the one hand, its production required an organizational reinvention of the SEC, moving it slightly farther from its New Deal origins and into a

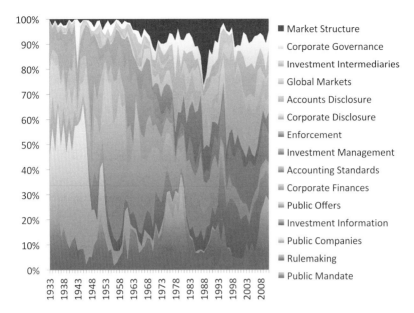

FIGURE 7.1 Graph representing the evolution of topics within speeches by
SEC commissioners, 1934–2011. This graph was generated by classifying
the texts of commissioner speeches into 15 themes through a technique of
automated text analysis known as topic modeling. Each theme is formed
by groups of co-occurring words refering to some particular topic. As the
graph shows, market structure – shown at the top – emerged as an
identifiable theme within the speeches in the early 1960s and peaked in
the 1980s, showing an expansion of the priorities of the SEC.

more technocratic mode of governance. For Yuval Millo (2004), the
process of researching, drafting and submitting the report "reinforced
the experts status that was granted to the SEC staff" who had to deal
with the most "up-to-date [analysis] of the [markets'] strengths and
problematic areas." This is particularly notable with respect to the
study's engagement with so-called market structure, namely, discussions about how the rules and organization of markets have effects on
pricing, trading, supply and demand. Whereas the SEC had occupied
most of its resources on matters of corporate and investment disclosure, the special study expanded its remit into discussions about the
legal, technical, and institutional organization of securities markets
(Figure 7.1).

On the other hand, the special study had long-ranging implications for the type of policies that the SEC pursued over the following fifteen years. For Joel Seligman, a noted legal scholar of American finance, this was "undoubtedly the single most influential document published in the history of the SEC" (Seligman, 1982: 299). In addition to strengthening the SEC's expertise, it established a blueprint for regulatory actions that sought to reorganize the United States' markets into a single, integrated national system.

For this chapter, a central aspect of the special study was that it married technology with discussions about changes to America's complex market structure. Specifically, while the SEC placed great scrutiny on the practices of established exchanges (NYSE and AMEX), it also dissected the operations and challenges of the over-the-counter market. As a loose network of brokers and dealers, the over-the-counter market was a difficult creature to regulate. Much was accomplished with the creation of the National Association of Securities Dealers in 1939, but the over-the-counter market remained "diffuse" and "heterogeneous" (two terms frequently used by the SEC to refer to OTC markets in the special study), and populated by a variety of mechanisms that were at times opaque to the regulator. How could the SEC guarantee that investors' interests were respected in a diffuse market without a clear trading center? How did it know that the NASD's dealers were providing their clients with the best possible prices? In New York, the floor of the NYSE and the different price and data collection systems created by the exchange provided some accountability and regulatory oversight. They were tangible technologies of consociation and honor that the SEC could audit and inspect. But in the distributed networks of NASD, there was less clarity over the nature and flow of transactions. The over-the-counter market was so complicated that in the early 1960s little information existed about its structure. As the SEC noted at the time, much of the data presented in the special study had "never been available before and that some of the areas covered have never been studied in the context of a total integrated view of the over-the-counter markets." But the special study was not only an opportunity to generate much needed data on the over-the-counter market. More importantly, it provided a chance to rethink its nature through the optics of automation.

This is why automation emerges in the special study not in connection to the NYSE and its settlement systems, but rather to the country's over-the-counter markets. Technology was a means for unifying and standardizing the "diffuse" and "heterogeneous" transactions of NASD and the third market, collecting information into a single, central point of reference. Inspired by private developments in quotation companies – organizations such as Scantlin and Ultronic that developed proprietary services providing investors with data on current market prices across the United States – the SEC noted strong reasons to believe

> that expanded electronic systems ... would be technically capable of processing information on every stock traded over the counter. These devices could receive and store, among other things, all bids and offers in each stock and reports of all consumated transactions. The information could be made instantly available for professional and public dissemination and compilation relating to price and volume could be prepared in permanent form.
>
> (Report of the Special Study of Securities Markets of the Securities and Exchange Commission, 1963: 657–658)

Unlike quotation companies, the real-time communication of current prices could be developed further, constituting a distributed national trading system. As the SEC indicated, it would be possible to design a "centrally located computer" that would

> select the best bids and offers, execute orders, and clear transactions. Transmitting and receiving units would be installed in the offices of all subscribing broker-dealers. Wholesale dealers and other broker-dealer subscribers could enter quotations (and size of market) into a central computer for indexing under the appropriate security and could interrogate the computer to

determine the highest bid and lowest offer, selected by the computer, together with the number of shares bid and offered at such prices … This would enable a broker-dealer to execute at the best prevailing price or, if he chose, to enter his own limit order in the hope of bettering that price. Thus, [in the view of the consultants] the principal barrier to the crossing of public orders – namely, lack of a central location – could be overcome by the use of a single, central computer.

The dream of a "single, central computer" became a key conceptual resource for the commission. In particular, it solved the problems of regulating a multi-sited market and guaranteeing that investors received both the best possible information on stocks and trades as well as the most current quotes of the national marketplace. The problem confronting the SEC was foundational, as Cohen noted in his recollections about the special study:

> Let me just mention five facts about the securities markets that, in combination, are of great significance, and some of which may come as a surprise to many of you. First, the major regional exchanges do most of their business in New York Stock Exchange listed stocks. Second, New York Stock Exchange member firms are the dominant members of the major regional exchanges. Third, the New York Stock Exchange firms also do more than half of the dollar volume of all over-the-counter business in stocks, even though they are numerically in the minority. Fourth, an over-the-counter business of growing proportions is conducted by non-New York Stock Exchange' members in New York Stock Exchange listed stocks. And fifth, the institutional share of the market has been increasing even though the number of individual public stockholders has also been increasing. (M. Cohen, 1963)

Cohen did not use the term fragmentation but nevertheless depicted its features: trades in NYSE-listed stocks were occurring *everywhere* and somehow had to be tallied and aggregated to produce the greater levels of "efficiency and economy" desired by both institutional investors and individual shareholders.

7.5 PRODUCING NATIONHOOD

A critical historical juncture for the infrastructures of financial markets came in 1971. Following a review of the role of institutional investors in securities markets (*Institutional Investor Study*, 1971), the SEC articulated its object of concern. "A major goal and ideal of the securities markets and the securities industry," wrote the SEC in its letter of transmittal to Congress, "has been the creation of a strong central market system for securities of national importance, in which all buying and selling interest in these securities could participate and be represented under a competitive regime." The SEC imagined a national, internal market enabled by "[recent] advances in communications and electronic data processing [that] make such representation technically feasible if the necessary systems are developed and used." The central market system (CMS) was not only a regulatory construct; it was, too, an object of technological investments and work. Donald Weeden made this clear in his 1972 testimony when he noted that "the Central Market Place today is no longer a geographical concept. It is a communications concept. With today's electronic miracles available to the industry, all market makers wherever located could be combined into a central, interrelated market for fast and efficient access by investors to all of its segments. The true Central Market Place demands access to all available pools of positioning capital for maximum liquidity" (Weeden in House Subcommittee on Commerce and Finance, 1971).

The central market system was also a project in constructing a form of financialized nationhood built upon a countrywide infrastructure of investor participation. Both regulators and market participants had placed much effort in expanding stock ownership in the country since the early twentieth century. Whether through marketing campaigns calling investors to "own [their] share of American business" (Traflet, 2003, 2013; Ott, 2011) or government policies that promoted indirect participation through investment funds (Krippner, 2011), institutions were placing stock ownership high in the identities of American citizens. The tacit objective was what Perry Mehrling calls the "Finance Society" in reference to Polanyi's "Market Society," a system where "social relations are ... structured in large part by a web of time-dated promises to pay, stretching from now into the future, and from here around the globe" (Mehrling, 2017). There were practical challenges for achieving this "investors' democracy," though: a fragmented marketplace limited the capacity of smaller, less capitalized investors from participating in the market; if anything, America was a financial democracy for the uniquely rich, rather than the modestly popular. Large institutions could use the power of their capital to leverage better commissions and more competitive deals from broking firms; and they could trade in large blocks of stocks through the third market, using the systems of Instinet and the like. But for an individual investor sitting in Omaha, Nebraska, the buy-in was high. Mobile apps that accessed the national markets with a few swipes of a screen were light years away. Even brokered access to the nation's capital markets was cumbersome and expensive. For a financial democracy to exist, participation had to be leveled, and the rights of every investor made equal. The SEC needed to create a form of egalitarian nationhood, if not civic then, at the very least, financial.

A useful way of examining the project of financial nationhood that belied the creation of a central market system is to explore it from the optics of relation making. More than anything else, the national system envisioned by Congress and the SEC implied a far-reaching set of mutual dependencies based on the ownership of financial investments – from stocks and debt, to the more speculative instruments emerging in the horizon. An investors' democracy was much more than a "purely" economic ideal: at its core, it was a form of financialized kinship that established relations through a common infrastructure of participation; a central mechanism for buying and selling stocks that could guarantee access to all potential investors, not only some fortunate financiers. This was not kinship as natural substance (Schneider, 1980). Rather, it was a web of relations built on laws, techniques, and an expectation of being a member of a larger project where individuals could shape their destinies by owning a bit of the national economy (Yanisago and Delaney, 1995).

For this, the SEC conceived of the central market system (CMS) as a key platform for participation. CMS was not simply a means for better regulation. At the core, it was an infrastructure that would have materialized the rights of countless investor/citizens – a technology of consociation to substitute the relatively hermetic stock exchanges of the past with a more accessible public platform for the future. "Markets in recent years have been taking new form at an incredible pace," wrote SEC Chairman Bradford Cook in 1973 in his presentation of the central market system to the New York Financial Writers Association.

> There have been many reasons: the surge in institutional trading, the emergence of new markets to handle big blocks of stock, the sudden and sweeping shifts in the pattern of securities trading, the upheaval in the economics of the securities business itself. Today, the result is that for many securities there are now many markets– both on the exchanges and off the exchanges in the offices of broker-dealers. At any given time, the public investor sees only part of this picture. He is looking at a goldfish bowl while really living in the middle of an aquarium … The major problem with all of this is that there is no way that an investor can be certain the investment process is working for him all the time, there is no way he can be sure his interests are being protected all the time, and that his order can be represented in all of these markets all of the time. This means that the public investor has no assurance that his broker is getting him the best available price on his order– wherever that may be. [There] is no way that a limit order left with a specialist on the floor of the New York Stock Exchange can participate in a transaction on the Pacific Stock Exchange – even if

the price on the Pacific Exchange moves to a level where that limit order could be satisfied.

The central market system solved these complications, placing "all limit orders [in] a closed, central electronic repository." Technology could connect multiple trading sites to form a single system "competitively based, with minimum restrictions on trade."

CMS challenged the powerful interests of the New York Stock Exchange and spoke to the concerns of both large investors – interested in lowering their operational costs – and entrepreneurial politicians – who sought to advance the rights and interests of the imaginary "everyday" investor. Assembled by the SEC, the Advisory Committee on the Implementation of the Central Market System published a preliminary statement outlining the design of the system in December of 1974. Representing exchanges, independent dealers, and users of the heterogeneous marketplaces, the committee's statement reads a bit like a constitutional agreement, identifying nine principles that should inspire the production of markets for the future. Under a central market arrangement, they wrote:

1. The best bid and offer, with size, of each specialist and other qualified market maker shall be available to all members of the system at all times.
2. There shall be maximum opportunity to improve on and displace the best bid and offer at all times.
3. There shall be an opportunity for public customers to meet through brokers at the best execution price without a dealer necessarily participating in the process.
4. Transactions for retail/individual customers shall be handled on an equitable basis with those for institutions.
5. All orders at a given price shall be executed on a time sequence basis, subject to public order preference.
6. All transactions in qualified listed securities shall pass through the central market system.
7. All qualified broker-dealers shall be permitted to become members of the system and have economic access to all specialists and other qualified market makers.

8. All member broker-dealers shall have an affirmative obligation to execute orders at the best possible price.
9. All participants shall be subjected to equitable regulation and prescribed capital requirements.

The plan was ambitious, to say the least. The principles identified by the Advisory Committee implied a new form of relation making for the marketplace that contrasted thoroughly with the dominant worldviews of the incumbent stock exchanges. It was a novel infrastructure of kinship, a distinct way of constructing communities around transactions and exchange. Consider, for example, how the principles behind CMS entailed a specific technology of consociation: rather than restricting the marketplace to floors and buildings, it envisioned a mechanism through which trading in all qualified listed securities could occur. To coordinate action and guarantee participation, the system would furthermore introduce a novel device, the National Best Bid/Offer, as a means for affirming value to the community. To substitute the interpersonal expertise of specialists and dealers as well as trust in intermediaries, a central market system would work on the principles of price and time priority (first come, first serve) and best execution, establishing an almost algorithmic technology of honor for the market's community. And to guarantee belonging, it enshrined the equality of institutions and individuals – on CMS, all orders are created and treated equally; this was not a system for institutions but for "public," perhaps even "the public's" orders.

The plans for CMS entailed a broad-reaching, totalizing infrastructure of access and participation: all those fragmented deals in NYSE-listed securities should be captured by the system, creating an unparalleled aggregator of prices and trades. The idea garnered support and when US Congress amended the 1934 Securities Act to modernize the SEC's capabilities in 1975, it incorporated the central market system as a prime objective for the regulator. From then on, the SEC would have the explicit obligation to "remove impediments to and perfect the mechanisms of a *national* market system for securities and a national system for the clearance and settlement of securities trans- actions and the safeguarding of securities and funds related thereto" (*Securities Acts Amendments*, 1975). At least in paper, the Polanyian national market was thus born: the National Market System acquired the force of law and legislative imagination.

7.6 CLOBBING TRADES

Paper plans do not always map neatly onto reality, and this was the case of the National Market System, NMS. Congress was clearly supportive of the concept. The 1975 Securities Act Amendments gave the SEC the legal teeth necessary for studying markets and guiding existing organizations to facilitate the establishment of NMS. The amendment also noted the strategic value of securities markets (they are "an important national asset which must be preserved and strengthened") as well as the crucial role of technologies in their operation ("[new] data processing and communications techniques create the opportunity for more efficient and effective market oper- ations"). Invariably, the makeup of the national market system was unspecified. What should a "strong central market system" to which "all investors [have] access" look like? Should it use the NYSE's trading floor as the basis for a national central exchange? Should it actively incorporate the third market and its burgeoning technologies of trade? Or should it challenge incumbents and foster new organiza- tional forms? The choices were multiple, contested and, in all instances, politically costly. Other than indicating that NMS should serve public interest, Congress left much of its design in the hands of the SEC.

The ambiguity created around the national market system was a clear opportunity for political entrepreneurialism. Third market advocates, for example, wanted to create a system that opened the NYSE's market makers to direct competition while preserving the heterogeneous structures of the national marketplace. The NYSE was more sanguine and used the moment to pursue a proposal it had presented in 1971 to create a National Securities Exchange, not surprisingly based on the NYSE's structure of operation (as a letter to the House Subcommittee on Commerce and Finance by 19 "especially well-qualified academicians" noted, the NYSE's proposal was "a little like having the rabbits guard the lettuce"[4]).

Without a specific design, the SEC had to defuse the tensions shaping the formation of NMS. But rather than taking the position of an informed and powerful architect, the regulator used a less direct form of bricolage as a politically sensible strategy of market construction. For this, the SEC relied on the existing mechanism of self-regulatory organizations to create the elements of the national system. Since the 1930s, the commission had delegated supervision and everyday enforcement to market organizations themselves: rather than observing the behaviors of each and every member of the NYSE, for instance, the SEC left it to exchanges to monitor their membership. The SEC was no Leviathan; it was, rather, an emboldened auditor. Instead of surveillance and control, the commission used registration and disclosure as means for regulating markets. And when it came to developing critical market infrastructures, the SEC leaned on the same tactic. The technologies of consociation, honor, and belonging of the national market system would not be created anew but forged amid the interested positions and capabilities of the incumbent exchanges – this was the key path dependency around which markets would organize (and eventually fragment) in years to come.

That technologies were built on interested histories was notable very early on, when the SEC sought to create the consolidated tape, one of the most critical devices of the American financial network. Whatever its ultimate shape, any national market system invariably required a data dissemination platform to communicate stock quotes

---

[4] The letter was signed by William Baumol, Fischer Black, Paul Cootner, Harold Demsetz, Donald Farrar, Lawrence Fisher, Milton Friedman, Michael Jensen, John Lintner, James Lorie, Birton Malkiel, Morris Mendelson, Franco Modigliani, Alexander Robicheck, Paul Samuelson, Myron Scholes, William Sharpe, Seymour Smidt, and George Stigler (Weeden, 2002: 82).

and trade confirmations in real time to investors across the country. This was the first principle of the central market system, and although several private firms offered such services, they did not cover the markets in their entirety and offered no standard of timeliness and delivery – and were not the basis for the egalitarian economy of investments that the SEC envisioned for NMS. The consolidated tape was different: it had to provide a common reference, serving as a public infrastructure rather than a private network – a utility, not a private service. The SEC did not build such infrastructure but delegated its making to others. Demonstrating a strategy that would characterize much of this period, the NYSE seized the opportunity and advanced the consolidated tape under its auspices. Working with NASD and the American Stock Exchange, the NYSE commissioned the production and maintenance of the consolidated tape to the Securities Industry Automation Corporation, the exchange's technical arm. The Consolidated Tape Association (CTA), formed by the NYSE, AMEX, NASD and the Pacific, Midwest and PBW exchanges, would then oversee the system's operation, under the same rules of self-regulation that characterized the SEC's approach to market governance. The CTA was also responsible for an equally important infrastructure, the Consolidated Quotation System, CQS. Whereas the tape reported transaction data, the CQS collected and disseminated the quotes to buy and sell securities from all of its members. As with the tape, the SEC neither designed not maintained the system, merely laying down the rules for its use: for example, to guarantee that the information on the quotation system was truly up to date, the SEC required exchanges and dealers in 1978 to collect and distribute "firm" quotations with their corresponding sizes. Other than this, its intervention in technical matters was at arm's length (that the SEC deferred to the exchanges was clear in the rules of the CTA: although the regulator had some say, the Association gave the NYSE veto power over changes).[5]

[5] Weeden, SEC Historical interview.

Together, CTA and CQS contributed to the type of scopic mechanisms (Knorr Cetina and Preda, 2007) that moved markets from floors to screens in years to come: by providing a standard infrastructure that rendered visible all of the prices and trades within the several national markets, both systems allowed investors far apart to interact as if they were in the same room. But to constitute a national market, these systems had to incorporate a trading facility for matching and executing the orders of investors located outside of specific trading floors: seeing a quote in Boston from Chicago was great, but without an efficient execution platform, it was of limited use.

Quote and trade data transmission could be centralized through the consolidated tape, but trading was slightly more difficult: in particular, it was a direct challenge to the role of the NYSE's powerful specialists and the growing networks of NASD's dealers. There were numerous options, of course, but it was clear that some form of centralization in trading was inevitable. As the president of the American Stock Exchange, Paul Kolton, argued at the time, a mechanism of trade aggregation was the only way of truly fulfilling the SEC's mandate by guaranteeing that "the public order that enters the system – that is, captured electronically … is switched to the best market … is assured of the best execution, [and is] executed within the framework of [a public] auction market system." The concept devised by the NMS's Advisory Board – the Consolidated Limit Order Book (CLOB) intended to do just that: centralize the limit orders submitted by investors into a single, consolidated trade execution and confirmation system.

As an abstract proposal, CLOB found great support across regulatory and market sectors. In 1975, for instance, the Advisory Committee on Implementation of a Central Market System noted that a CLOB based on the principles of "time, price, and public order priority" was an "essential element" of NMS. The SEC concurred, and noted in its Exchange Act Release 11,942 that the development of "a central electronic repository for limited price orders would be of special significance to ensure the integration of the markets and preservation of opportunity for public orders to meet without the participation of a dealer" (National Market Advisory Board, 1977). In 1976, the National Market Advisory Board strongly advocated a CLOB "linking the individual [trading] books of specialists" as a mechanism for increasing market competition and introducing much needed efficiencies to the national stock trading system. And similarly, as Donald Weeden recalled, even the Securities Industry Association's National Market System Committee, which had a strong participation of New York and American stock exchanges members, recommended some form of a CLOB as the "fairest trading mechanism which maximizes the opportunity of orders to meet" without intermediation.[6]

Supported in principle, much disagreement existed around how best to implement a CLOB. What form should this technology of consociation take? What kind of sociation should it produce? By the late 1970s, two designs dominated the discussion. The first largely mimicked the consolidated tape: rather than merging trading centers (an idea vehemently opposed by the leading exchanges and some members of NASD), NMS could rely on a "soft" CLOB that would offer "a composite quotation system and intermarket linkage [allowing for the] execution of orders left in the system only by specialists and qualified market makers" (National Market Advisory Board, 1977). A soft CLOB would maintain "the strengths of present markets," argued the National Market Advisory Board, but would overcome the problem of a physically fragmented trade mechanism through technology, generating a virtual trading floor out of a patchwork of different, interconnected venues. For the SEC, a soft CLOB was clearly an attractive solution; maintaining the "strengths of present markets" was synonym to political pragmatics: the commission could create an efficient, "fair and honest" national trading system without challenging powerful incumbents or straying too far from existing securities markets legislation.

[6] Weeden, SEC Historical interview.

A second option was more dramatic: it entailed physical centralization of trading in a computer file that would receive and execute all orders in the market under strict principles of price-time priority – a single, hardwired queue operating under the first-come first-served principle. This "hard CLOB," argued proponents, had the crucial advantage that "orders in the book would always have priority at a price over any other orders in the system at that price." As noted by the National Market Advisory Board, by guaranteeing a national standard of order routing and execution, hard CLOB would "contribute the most to reestablishing the confidence of individual investors," constituting the "fairest and most efficient" implementation of the NMS (National Market Advisory Board, 1977).

As "market devices" (Callon et al. 2007), the soft and hard CLOBs implied very different sortings of markets and society; they were dissimilar ways of making market-kin. They crystalized different political projects that, although begging for some degree of centralization, envisioned diverging notions of how fairness, equality, and polities are settled. The decision on which design to adopt was highly contentious, reflecting the politics that animated and shaped the project of an investors' democracy under the National Market System. The politics at play were not simply those of institutional interests and regulatory policies, though. Individual technologists and market engineers were also central to the debate. And like the designers of the first electronic limit order books, the local, contingent, and otherwise constrained actions of these technologists challenged scales of social action to transform markets for years to come.

7.7   JUNIUS PEAK AND THE LIBERAL ORDERS OF AMERICAN FINANCE

Enter Junius Peake, an economist, technologist, and entrepreneur that was central to the formulation of the NMS – and perhaps the staunchest proponent of the hard CLOB as a solution to the problems of justice in America's financial system. Born in 1932, Peake started in

Wall Street in 1950 when he joined the brokerage firm of Garvin, Bantel & Co. Peake's career touched on most aspects of the market's operation. He had first-hand experience of the difficulties of data dissemination, having taken care of Garvin, Bantel & Co.'s TransLux ticker machine. But he was also versed in the technicalities of the back-office, where he managed settlement and clearing operations and had a privileged "front row view" of the paperwork jam as a partner of Shields & Co. (Arnold, 2012).

Peake's experiences with computers at both Garvin, Bantel & Co. and Shields & Co. explain some of his affinities toward a particular model of market automation. While Peake had some opportunities to explore the applications of computers at Shields, he found an almost natural niche for publicizing the advantages of automation as a representative of his firm on NASD, where he served as a board member and eventually vice chairman. NASD provided Peake with two critical resources. On the one hand, it was a working example of a distributed market coordinated by telecommunications: since 1971 and as the self-regulatory organization for the over-the-counter market, NASD had operated its Automated Quotation service (NAS-DAQ), the pioneering online, real-time network that gave dealers the ability to interact with each other remotely (Ingelbresten, 2002). NASD demonstrated that makers could be made without a floor and at a national scale. But NASD was also important for a second reason: as the agent of the third market, it provided an institutional platform from which Peake could shape broader national policies and the course of markets, beyond the relatively modest symbolic and institutional capital he derived from his partnership at Shields.

Through NASD, Peake presented a bold and broad program of automation in congressional testimonies and letters to regulators and policymakers. One of the contributions he advocated in these communications is salient: his 1976 co-authored proposal to develop a "National Book System" to fully implement the NMS. The system proposed by Peake and his colleagues Morris Mendelson and Ralph Williams was essentially a hard CLOB. Instead of linking marketplaces through the consolidated tape, the composite quotation system, and some other order-handling device, Peake's design involved collecting the bids and offers of both professional market makers and individual investors and matching them in a central electronic file. Within this model, orders were anonymous and price-time priority of execution was guaranteed.

Peake's proposal differed from the SEC's soft CLOB in how it conceptualized the social purpose and technical components of an ideal market. For the SEC, fair markets were those that guaranteed price efficiency; technically, this translated into a system that fostered competition *between* trading venues within NMS. As a former staff member involved in the 1975 Amendments recalls, the SEC "clearly felt that the industry should be encouraged, nudged, and prodded to [implement intermarket competition] themselves" (Khademina, 1992). The SEC saw its responsibility as safeguarding efficient prices and fair markets by implementing "rule making when necessary" – leaving much of the market's operation in the hands of an institutionally fragmented field formed by several self-regulatory organizations. For Peake, in contrast, ideal markets were based on competition in prices *within a single* (even if abstract) setting. This matters both politically and technically: as Peake tellingly noted in 2003, the question of what a market is for him, had a clear answer: "Is a market a price or a place? I say it is a price" (Schwartz et al. 2006: 90). Whereas thinking of markets as competition in prices opened the possibility of broad direct participation, competition within a marketplace inherently restricted access. The national stock trading network, argued Peake, was a highly structured "'caste system' that severely restricts access to many of the facilities and functions [of the securities industry]" (Peake, 1978: 25). Though desirable, efficiency could not result from competition between trading venues but only from direct competition in prices in a standardized platform:

> An economist would require for a perfect national market system
> that all participants ... have an equal opportunity to vie for profit

on a fair field of competition, with equally available trading information and with equal access to the trading arena. The present market system is not perfect: Trading information is available to certain competitors instantly, and not available to others at all; the field is composed of membership organizations that restrict access to the game to members.

Rather than interconnecting heterogeneous mechanisms, wrote Peake, NMS "should be directed towards achieving the economist's dream": a single, unified market. Fragmentation, he noted,

> can be eliminated by a unitary system. While a single stock exchange would be a unitary system, it would also have a single market maker – and Congress wants fully competitive market makers. Fortunately, the technology now exists to construct a market mechanism in which all orders can interact and which preserves fully competitive market making. Computers have the speed and power to queue, display and match like-priced orders of investors, large and small, from all over the nation, and throughout the world.

Peake was not alone in advocating a centralized computer as a solution to questions of fairness and justice confronting American stock markets (some years earlier, Frederick Nymeyer had argued much the same). His activism was distinctive, however, because it placed center stage the politics that, for him and other market users, ought to have been key to the reorganization of finance. For Peake and colleagues, the problem was guaranteeing access and equality. Efficiency and competition were only valuable if they resulted from fair market organization. And as he argued, "if one class or group has access to necessary market facilities on more favorable terms than others, competition is not 'fair.' There is no justification, given today's level of technology, for limiting access to a favored few" (Peake, 1978). Equality necessitated a form of centralization unattainable with a soft CLOB: "while centralizing information flows or arbitraging between markets may equalize prices of a given security if the flow of information is maximized," wrote Peake's coauthor Morris Mendelson, "equity will not be produced. Without an execution focal point, there is no way for the first come to be the first served."[7] These politics were infrastructural: a soft CLOB maintained established intermediaries (such as the stock exchanges and dealers) at the center of the transaction, whereas Peake envisioned a different technology of honor – price-time priority – as the normative and operational core of the national market. As he wrote some years later,

> If a little broker-dealer in Tacoma, Wash., wanted to interject a superior bid or offer into the system, that little broker-dealer in Tacoma, Wash., would know that it would be first in line when the stock moved to that bid or offer. Merrill Lynch with all its size and all of its clout and all of its resources could never get ahead of them. The importance of price and time priority is that it places the little fellow in Tacoma, Wash. on the same footing as Merrill Lynch. (Peake, 2004)

For Peake, truly equitable markets required a hard CLOB. Seeking consensus with incumbents, the SEC's pragmatist attachment to the soft CLOB contrasted with Peake, Mendelson, and William's design of a single, centralized execution facility. The divergence was technical and ideological: a hard CLOB entailed "treating people as equals;" the SEC's soft CLOB implied "treating people equally" with respect to transparent and efficient price system as valuable resources for the marketplace. For the SEC, the ends of NMS were efficiency; for Peake, they were first and foremost instituting equality through technology.

7.8   ITS CHRISTOPHER KEITH

Just as the hard CLOB emerged from the affordances of technologies, its ultimate demise was similarly tied to the technical and

---

[7] See also Commissioner Milton Cohen's (1978) discussion of trading systems similar to Peake's.

organizational structures of American finance. Peake's proposal was perhaps far too radical for the SEC. Instead of building a hard central limit order book – which would have required a messy legislative challenge to the NYSE – the regulator could promote integration and competition between markets with a loose communication link-age of the country's existing trading sites. Soft CLOB was closer to the political logics of Washington where the SEC operated. Dan Schiller noted that delegating innovation onto industry organizations spoke to two broader government policies on telecommunications: first, that there be freedom to innovate, which the securities industry seized upon by setting its own standards and designs; and second, that the system maintain a "broad diversity of suppliers – to avoid an undue concentration of power in one entity [which] could adversely affect an industry as communication intensive as [finance]" (Vincent P. Moore in Schiller, 1982). But even this delegated solution required building some type of a system for routing the orders of investors across the different marketplaces that were part of NMS. The SEC was not a builder; it was a rule maker. The system would have to come from elsewhere.

The NYSE had a clear opportunity: if they could build a mech-anism for transmitting order across markets in real time, they could shape the course of NMS, much as they had done with the creation of the DTC for settlement, and the CT and CQS for data communica-tion. Peake might have had a bold, democratic, and entrepreneurial vision for the marketplace, but NYSE had a tremendous institutional clout. More importantly, though, NYSE had Christopher Keith, the exchange's very own technological visionary.

Keith was, like Peter Bennett in London, a self-made technolo-gist, trained within the bureaucracies of the dominant exchange's infrastructural teams; he was not "part of the establishment." A graduate in physics from Stanford, Keith joined Wall Street "as a virgin" in finance; although his previous graduate experience at Swarthmore and the Massachusetts Institute of Technology provided strong theoretical foundations, his practical training occurred as he worked his way through New York's emerging technological scene. Keith navigated this terrain with tremendous ability. By the 1970s, he had joined the Securities Industry Automation Corporation, where he would grow to occupy leading positions. "I was supposed to be the main guy who would manage the 'grand project,'" he recalled in an interview, referring to his role in producing the automated systems that solved the exchange's back-office crisis. Keith ultimately moved to the New York Stock Exchange in the late 1970s. His last assignment at SIAC was nevertheless of momentous importance: he was "to stop the [hard] CLOB" which he did by co-inventing the Intermarket Trading System (ITS).

If Peake was a proponent of the virtues of centralization, Keith was a thoughtful advocate of the necessity of fragmentation. "I thought CLOB was an absolutely terrible idea," he reminisced. A CLOB distorted prices, he argued, since distance from the site of execution and absence of a knowledgeable specialist invariably offset prices from their true, meaningful values. "In the perfect world of Junius Peake," noted Keith,

> the little old lady in tennis shoes in San Diego wants to get $21.76 for her order flow, so she sends it in, and it's just done [as] quickly and efficiently as in a perfect market. But [by the time the order arrives, the price has moved to] $21.78 [which is] the right price. [Peake] completely overlooked that. I mean, how do I know what the best price is when there is a time difference between the time [the order is sent and the time it] gets there?[8]

This was a "terrible myopia," in Keith's words, that could only be remedied by maintaining the specialist at the core of the transaction. The specialist, unlike the automated order book, could positively determine the correct price, gauging the patterns of the order flow and adjusting the prices of stocks accordingly. An open, all-visible and centralized order book did the contrary. It led to a race

---

[8] Interview with Christopher Keith.

for speed based on a distorted transparency in prices. "When I put an order on a CLOB," he argued "I'm giving everyone a free option and I have to get paid for the option, and automatically that's not the best price" CLOB is "dedicated to efficiency and getting most of the stuff done," not to producing trustworthy prices.

"Nationalizing the switch" was not an option for Keith or the NYSE. Rather than losing control of their listed markets, the exchange and its market makers could develop a system that would place them at the core of a national system, with prices that remained carefully discerned by human intermediaries on the trading floor. Fortunately for the NYSE, Keith and his team already had a system in place that could provide such service. From 1973 to 1976, SIAC developed a small but important system to process odd lots, that is, orders submitted in unconventionally small sizes and that, given their modest volumes, were unattractive to the NYSE's largest members (Bradford and Miranti, 2014): processing odd lots was as expensive as large transactions, but resulted in considerably lower commissions. This was not necessarily a problem for NYSE, since much of the odd lot activity occurred down the street in the American Stock Exchange. This concentration of activity in one exchange was nevertheless problematic. Fearing the intervention of the SEC – who might have considered AMEX's role in odd lots as potentially anticompetitive – NYSE and the AMEX linked their systems through an automated mechanism that transmitted customer orders for execution to the trading venue with the best prices (more often than not, NYSE's floor). Once created, this "common message switch" (CMS) offered a working operational linkage between two key trading sites of the National Market System, demonstrating in practice the possibilities of interconnectivity for fostering competition.

When time came to define the shape of the National Market System, the NYSE used its common message switch as the template to build a larger version, the Intermarket Trading System. Like the common message switch, ITS linked different marketplaces by routing the orders of investors to other national trading venues. And given the fact that it already operated at some scale, ITS quickly convinced the Securities and Exchange Commission about the feasibility of its expansion. The SEC, recalled Keith, "almost always yielded to our arguments if you made [them] basically sensible," and a working system was clearly more appealing than an imagined, nationalized behemoth – as MacKenzie (2018: 1662–1664) also notes – the SEC was wary of embarking on a risky technological project like CLOB. ITS quickly became the third cornerstone of the National Market System and, like the other two, was also designed and controlled by the incumbent NYSE. With only "a few weeks" of tinkering and bricolage, of retrofitting CMS for a national application, Keith eliminated the argument for CLOB and locked-in the design of NMS for years to come. It was an undoubted coup for the exchange: although ITS linked all the trading venues of the National Market System (initially with the exception of NASDAQ), it gave the NYSE priority over others. ITS was introduced to foment competition but, as Donald MacKenzie observes, it failed doing so (MacKenzie, 2018). A central operational feature of the Common Message Switch was replicated in ITS: when a trader in one of the NMS venues submitted an order to the NYSE in the form of a "commitment to trade," NYSE specialists had a set time to react, historically large enough to allow for human decision making (in the order of two minutes), serving as a cognitive and material barrier against the emerging threat of automated execution: as early as 1979, NASD was working on a Computer Assisted Execution System (CAES) that might have undercut the quotes of NYSE's specialists. NASD was not a founding member of ITS, so the connection between the Intermarket Trading System and CAES was only established through regulatory intervention. To guarantee price protection in trades in NMS stocks in the third market, the SEC mandated "a linkage between the ITS and over-the-counter market makers regulated by the NASD." A two-minute delay on the NYSE's trading floor effectively put a damper on any automated execution from NASDAQ, giving exchange specialists the opportunity to evaluate the flow of transactions before determining a price. ITS stemmed competition, which bolstered specialists at the core of the price formation process. It was clearly effective for, as late as 2005, 80 percent of the trades in NYSE-listed securities still took place on NYSE's systems.

7.9   SLOBs

The histories of CLOB and the various other elements of the United States' financial system underscore the difficulties of organizing infrastructural change and settling the contested politics of the National Market System. The path that markets took was not drawn on a table or planned in committees but infrastructured through the interests and capabilities of incumbent institutions, individual technologists, and the asymmetrically, built-up network of technical dependencies. Without the New York Stock Exchange's authority, some of the bolder proposals for centralization might have materialized. And without the Securities and Exchange Commission's historical reliance on self-regulation, a more forceful vision of the marketplace might have become a reality. The vexing difficulties faced in implementing projects that challenged the structure of stock markets are testaments to the entrenchment of interests, as much as to the inertia of the past. Infrastructures are built on what already exists, assembled from pieces that endured the test of time and the furnaces of institutional politics. These are, in practical, material, and institutional terms, the installed base on which infrastructures develop.

The National Market System's infrastructures were not only materializations of past politics, but, equally, they constrained the future spaces of innovation and action within the American financial system. One example is particularly salient: an attempt to create a stock exchange that worked outside of the parameters of NMS. The exchange, founded by Steven Wunsch in 1991, was initially called Wunsch Auction Systems Inc. and renamed the Arizona Stock Exchange (AZX) in 1992 (Muniesa, 2011). With a background in derivatives from the broking firm Kidder, Peabody & Co., Wunsch set out to create a mechanism for trading securities at a single consensus price. Recall that the logic of the National Market System was one of continuous trading: from the consolidated tape to ITS, infrastructures were meant to provide a live stream of data that investors could use to collectively value instruments in a distributed way. Wunsch's invention was fundamentally different, implying a single auction to determine price. There was an important rationale behind this design, informed by Wunsch' experience: derivatives require precise information about the value of their underlying instruments and a single price that is viewed as legitimate by the market is better, in this respect, than multiple prices achieved in discrete transactions through continuous trading on an order book. These "call auctions," in other words, generate credible public facts when compared to the individual transactions of continuous markets. While sensible in principle, AZX never truly worked. The Securities and Exchange Commission eventually treated the AZX as a public exchange, but under tight constraints (though it exempted it from registration due to low trading volumes; for some time, AZX's documentation included a disclaimer noting that it was not a "registered exchange"). "They gave us permission to operate only at times when nobody would want to use us," Wunsch told me in interview. Politics mattered in this decision, but so did technical interconnection standards: "all the barricades that we faced came about because it was too difficult for the SEC to deal with the incompatibilities of a different price setting auction independent of the National Market System and its price and time priority."[9] The problem was a consequence of systems architecture, interconnectivity, and the path dependency of infrastructures. The National Market System required a continuous, real-time flow of orders organized through the principle of price-time priority; Wunsch's auction did not fit.

Although constraining, infrastructures also generate unexpected conditions and novel terrains. The forms of algorithmic trading that we observe today and are central to discussions about rigged

[9] Interview with Steven Wunsch.

stock markets are products of NMS and its implementation. While the NYSE's relative control over the National Market System was a source of stability and permanence for a period of time, it was also generative of an environment that made latency arbitrage possible and profitable, as the forms of automation that had started at the fringes of the marketplace – in Instinet, Autex, Cincinnati, and elsewhere – diffused and standardized. NYSE could not resist automation forever, and as market participants moved towards computer-based execution of trades, they made the fragmentation of the national market materially apparent and economically exploitable.

Much of this rested on the type of politics encoded into the infrastructures of NMS. Between the introduction of ITS in 1979 and the consolidation of automated trading in the past decade, the idea of centralizing markets through technology reemerged numerous times though but was invariably defeated in public debates, showing the resilience of the political settlement at the core of the National Market System. Some of this was tied to the affordances of technologies. Throughout this period, communication technologies were fast enough to avoid the more visible problems of fragmentation in the marketplace. For all intents and purposes, venues were linked in real time; the National Market System worked – if heavily under NYSE's control. When revived, mentions of a hard CLOB were more often rhetoric devices aimed at nudging regulatory change than serious calls for instituting systemic transformations. Consider how CLOB reemerged from the dustbins of history in 1994, when the SEC revised the operation of the country's stock markets almost two decades after the 1975 Securities Act Amendments. Written in response to "concerns about possible market fragmentation, inadequate disclosure of market information, and uneven regulation among competitors," the SEC's *Market 2000* report reviewed CLOB as a possible market design, recognizing that although it might "allow for improved price discovery and best execution for customer order[s]," it would also "expose market makers to greater risk" (Securities and Exchange Commission, 1994) without particularly meaningful gains in liquidity. In other words, a CLOB would make the lives of specialists and market makers more difficult without improving the quality of markets. Rather than pursuing a centralized CLOB and a radical transformation of the nation's market structure, the SEC resolved keeping ITS and altering markets incrementally through rulemaking and the agency's standard apparatus of registration and disclosure. ITS "is not, and was not intended to be, a complete intermarket linkage," recognized the SEC, but it also noted that "it is not necessary at this time to expand [the system] into a CLOB or to require automated executions of commitments … [By] enhancing ITS to improve its efficiency and reliability," a system similar to a soft CLOB could be created by "a web of portal executions coming together that allow functionally the transparency of a central limit order book" (Securities and Exchange Commission, 1994: AII-12). A national market could be built "without dictating a particular structure," wrote the commission. "[T]rading venues a thousand miles apart but linked electronically are as much a single market today as were broker-dealers across the room from each other yesterday. The market they comprise cannot be described as fragmented."

The Intermarket Trading System was effectively locked into the operation of the National Market System. For over two decades, it was one of the most palpable triumphs of the NYSE in moving public policy. Even when Electronic Communications Networks (ECNs) emerged to reshape American stock markets in the mid-1990s, ITS remained an undisputed solution to the problem of market competition. During this period, hard CLOB resurfaced as a possible solution to problems of efficiency and equality under multi-sited marketplaces exacerbated by ECNs. Like the inter-broker platform provided by Instinet decades before them, ECNs were services that gave users the ability to trade with others directly through an electronic limit order book, without a market maker standing in the middle of the transaction. Unlike Instinet, ECNs were built on a far more accessible technology of public participation – the Internet – creating at least the possibility for rapid expansion – and fragmentation. These small and entrepreneurial challengers distilled the aura of Internet technologies into the infrastructures of stock markets: they provided ample entry to small investors (mostly day and retail traders that operated outside the established institutional order of Wall Street); they were transparent and accessible (the code for the matching engine of Island ECN it still available on the website of its creator, Josh Levine); and they were vehemently oppositional, challenging the logic of established exchanges by introducing incentive structures that made away with established roles in the marketplace (for example, Island ECN introduced the so-called liquidity rebates, payments made to users who were providing liquidity to the system rather than taking it away; such incentives eliminated the need for specialists and other market makers by providing a constant and competitive stream of limit orders into the book).

ECNs were disruptive and for both the SEC and incumbent trading venues, not the least because they were a potential source of deleterious forms of fragmentation: if trading moved away from established exchanges and onto electronic trading platforms, markets would invariably fragment, potentially reducing the quality and efficiency of prices in the National Market System (in particular, specialists on the floor of the NYSE would not be able to resolve the direction of the market with as much accuracy as before because the order book would be dispersed, rather than concentrated). Just imagine having not one large central market where most supply and demand meets, but multiple little marketplaces where trade arrives almost randomly and haphazardly, creating multiple and less credible prices. Well aware of this problem, Congress called for hearings on the state of NMS at the turn of the century in 2000. The resulting document, *Competition in the New Electronic Market*, laid down much of the regulatory groundwork upon which algorithmic trading flourished in subsequent years (US Congress, 2000).

The hearings behind *Competition in the New Electronic Market* indicated widening fissures within the political settlement that had prevailed over the infrastructures of the marketplace. In particular, they showcased the rise of an entrepreneurial, almost libertarian imagery within the debates about equity market structure in America. Unlike previous discussions that placed great emphasis on ITS as the NMS's critical backbone, the hearings in 2000 stressed the remarkable powers of digital technologies to produce interconnectivity across the marketplace *without* a central coordinating force. This worldview was particularly clear among the founders of the new electronic marketplaces who defended intermarket competition as a uniquely virtuous contribution of their platforms to the public good. Unlike earlier generations of market innovators who considered some version of the CLOB as a common solution to fundamental problems of equality, the later generation of market technologists privileged private innovations and vehemently clashing with centralization owing to its anticompetitive nature. As Kevin Foley, Chief Executive of Bloomberg Tradebook argued, creating a CLOB to deal with fragmentation was erred. A central black box

> runs contrary to the operation of state-of-the-art modern telecommunications, the Internet being the best model. The innovations that ECNs have brought to the market … could not occur under an industry sponsored CLOB, an industry-sponsored black box … It creates a centralized single point of failure, and it creates a single decision-making apparatus that is resistant to change.
>
> *(Foley in US Congress, 2000: 14)*

For Foley, furthermore, discussions on fragmentation only reinforced the anticompetitive practices of established trading venues. As he told the congressional committee, "[w]hen the status quo laments the impact of 'harmful fragmentation' be careful – often it is really bemoaning beneficial competition." The moral imperative of competition reverberated across the new generation of market technologists: Cameron Smith, General Counsel of Island ECN, stressed that the "fundamental issue" confronting markets was not competition between orders within a single CLOB – as outlined two decades earlier by Junius Peake. Rather, "We believe that there should also be competition between markets."

Smith's comments indicate a qualitative change in the financial democracy envisioned at the turn of the twentieth century. His politics contrasted starkly with those of the entitled, age-old institutions that considered themselves guardians of the public interest. ECNs foregrounded a profound transformation of what "the exchange" meant as a market actor, an organization, and a business. A stock exchange was no longer a trading floor; it was no longer a social apparatus that produced trade, honor, and belonging. In the financial democracy of the late twentieth century, competition was produced through a second-order economic system, a market for plug-and-play digital marketplaces where financialized citizens could choose a design of their predilection to pursue their interests and ideals (for an important account of this shift, see Castelle et al., 2016). Both CLOB and the NYSE's control over ITS were incompatible with this new landscape. As the co-founder of Island ECN Matt Andresen evoked, the "reality" of an American financial democracy was a necessary argument against any solution implying centralization. While in 1980 only one in ten Americans invested in the stock market, observed Andresen,

> Today that number is over 52 percent. While these investors have new-found access to market research and market data, some proposed taking a giant step backwards from these innovations by calling for a central limit order book or so-called CLOB. Its advocates claim that the CLOB would cure the fragmentation allegedly attributable to [ECNs]. I argue that ECNs have, in fact, consolidated the markets … What would the effect be of a government-installed CLOB? One of the most immediate effects would be to eliminate a market participant's ability to compete on the basis of speed, reliability and cost, in essence, dumbing down the innovative technology, which has so benefited investors.
>
> (Andresen in US Congress, 2000: 6)

The ECNs' philosophy stressed private spaces of innovation and entrepreneurialism over the potentially obstructive and centralized (almost pejoratively "statist") hard CLOB. This was perhaps most notable in John Schaible's testimony. President of NexTrade, Schaible argued that

> [the] competitive for-profit model exemplified by ECNs has had a proven, beneficial impact on our markets. In 1998 alone, the cost of a trade on NASDAQ fell 23 percent and spreads fell 41 percent. While ECNs have helped investors, this progress is minimal in comparison to the benefits that will be derived from the privatization of stock exchanges. Privatization will result in exchanges that are more competitive and will respond better to the needs of the investors. New for-profit exchanges will enable the United States to maintain its position as the preeminent global market.
>
> *(Schaible in Securities and Exchange Commission, 1994)*

For these actors, fragmentation neither resulted in inequality nor generated inefficiency. On the contrary, it was the *raison d'être* of the new electronic marketplace: talking to the *LA Times*, broker Charles Schwab summarized the logic, "What some call fragmentation ... we call competition."

The operational fragmentation of markets worked relatively well until about 2005, when not too many surprises emerged from the nation's financial infrastructures. The argument made by Keith and the NYSE to the SEC in the 1970s was still valid, given the speed of technology and legal constraints in the early twenty-first century: a National Market System could exist through interconnection and, although far from optimal, ITS provided an essential backbone for the country's shared project of a financial democracy. CLOB was simply disproportionate to this end. Through a series of order-handling rules, the SEC could foster a particular materialization of NMS by creating what economist Craig Pirrong (2013) calls a Simulacrum Limit Order Book – SLOB, a virtual, multi-exchange system that shared many of the characteristics of CLOB without centralized order execution.

By late 2005, however, the alignment between technology and market structure broke, and the conjoined yet fragmented landscape built through the institutional power of the NYSE's ITS transformed the marketplace. Recall that ITS was built around the NYSE's trading floor: as a product of the Common Message Switch, the system was designed to provide specialists with enough time to gauge the direction of transactions in order to determine the prices that would clear their books in the most efficient way possible. The NMS of 1975 ultimately relied on human market makers to clear the market. But the National Market System of 2005 was simply too slow for the faster paced orders of electronic customers who had grown accustomed to the affordances and logics of Electronic Communication Networks. The SEC was caught between habit and possibility: its strategy of innovating through self-regulatory institutions worked in the past but was no longer appropriate for the technologies of the present; a SLOB simply could not meet the objectives of the National Market System: as long as the NYSE held the central position in the marketplace, intermarket competition was unattainable. Something else was needed: rules establishing the principles for guaranteed access and execution across the entire marketplace.

The rules came in 2005 under the title of Regulation National Market System (Reg NMS), a set of directives introduced by the SEC that sought to deliver the project of a leveled, interconnected national market. Regulation NMS coalesced discussions about organizational and technological changes in the industry, addressing four key aspects of the country's national stock markets: first, it sought to create clear standards around how market data should be handled; second, it established rules that improved access to market quotations within NMS; third, it created a standard for quotations, banning those of less than one penny increments; and fourth, it introduced the so-called order protection rule, which guaranteed that the orders submitted by investors to the NMS would be routed to the venue offering the best possible price – orders were protected from so-called "trade throughs," where they were executed within an exchange and at a level inferior to the National Best Bid/Offer (Securities and Exchange Commission, 2005).

RegNMS was a relatively small and historically coherent change. At a fundamental level, it simply reproduced the principles of the once proposed central market system. Apparently predictable, RegNMS had surprising material consequences for the structure of American finance. The unexpected transformation came from how the rules of RegNMS interacted with the physically and organizationally fragmented structure of the National Market System. A key result of RegNMS was precisely what the NYSE feared since the early 1970s, namely, an erosion of its position as the cornerstone of stock trading in the country. Until 2005, most of the activity of NYSE-listed shares still occurred on the trading floor of the exchange, where specialists controlled the price formation process. But decimalization, competition, and the elimination of trade throughs meant that the once rather manual process of executing trades and clearing the book was now economically unviable. Electronic Communication Networks introduced a new temporality to financial markets, a mode of existence and structure of incentives that privileged the automatic execution of small batches of stocks across a distributed network of trading sites. In this world, there was little patience for human intermediaries: they had to go.

In response to RegNMS, the NYSE tried a "hybrid" approach, providing specialists with real-time technologies on the floor to better visualize the fast-paced marketplace. ITS also disappeared, replaced by the Common Customer Gateway that promised to handle trades in hundreds, and eventually dozens, of milliseconds. But these proved inadequate: the high costs of the NYSE's peculiar automation process were offset neither by a greater market share nor increased revenues (Beunza and Millo, 2015). The incumbent was far behind the frontline of automation, and there was little it could do to catch up. The pressures to adapt were high and tradition was too costly: by 2007, the NYSE had no other choice than to emulate the model of its

challengers, the ECNs, embracing electronic limit order books, automating core operations, and becoming a demutualized exchange – a
public corporation like so many other, listed on the market that it
itself provides. The NYSE's community was unmade. The exchange
was one more digital rabbit in the burrow of ECNs.

Facilitated by RegNMS, the changes at the New York Stock
Exchange were fertile grounds for the rise of automated trading. Without the ability to control the flow of orders through ITS, the organizational behemoth was outrun by smaller challengers that, with a
couple of wires and nifty code, could draw business away from the
specialists and into their servers: from commanding 80 percent of
trading in NYSE-listed stocks in 2005, today, the exchange has less
than a quarter of the market's share – mirrored by growing volumes of
algorithmic trading across markets (Figure 7.2). Charles Schwab's

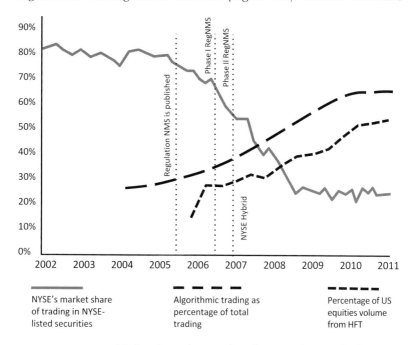

FIGURE 7.2 Market share of NYSE plotted against the growth of
algorithmic trading. Data for this graph was obtained from Celent
(Easthope, 2009), The Economist (2009), and Angel et al. (2011).

vision became a reality: competition for order flows between trading venues transformed fragmentation into profitable business opportunities. High frequency trading was tied to this new environment, as much as to the founding ideals of NMS: with pressure to make better, more competitive prices – made possible, in part, by the novel incentive structures introduced by ECNs and their electronic limit order books (MacKenzie and Pardo Guerra, 2014) – market participants had to compete on time, rather than solely on price. For the most liquid stocks in the market, where competition often reduces spreads to a mere penny, fulfilling a buy or sell order is a matter of speed. Combined with price-time priority, the technology of honor meant to guarantee a level playing field for the country's financial democracy, technology and telecommunications further fragmented a marketplace for which alternatives were imagined but ultimately defeated.

7.10   CONCLUSIONS

The history of market fragmentation problematizes some dominant accounts of financial automation. First, while it supports the critics of automated trading in suggesting that American markets are "rigged" (Lewis, 2015), it does so reservedly. The fragmented markets that made possible some of the most prominent and controversial forms of electronic trading were not engineered through deceit or manipulation. They were the product of the numerous technical and institutional tensions that coexisted within the design of the National Market System. This jumbled structure of NMS followed from the attempts to hastily assemble a single, internal market. Although created by congressional mandate, the actual process of erecting the NMS was fraught with contrasting politics – from Peake's visions of equality of access to the radical individualist logics of Andresen, Smith, and Schwab – that were condensed in assorted and contradictory technologies. Markets were rigged, but only as a sail is rigged in makeshift fashion to take advantage of unexpected winds.

A second lesson refers to the role of politics in shaping the evolution of market structures. If market fragmentation was not designed, it was similarly not driven by a single political project. Debates around how best to organize the national marketplace were framed by distinctly moralized repertoires. Efficiency, equality, and fairness figured prominently in discussions on the nation's stock markets. But they did so in the context of tremendous ambiguity. Congress' instructions in the 1970s were broad and left much of the work in the hands of the Securities Exchange Commission, its historical reliance on self-regulation, and its emerging dreams of automation. This provided an environment where the NYSE could shape much of how stock market infrastructures were built and interconnected. In its attempt to retain control of the market, for example, the NYSE set the templates for the Depositary Trust Company, the consolidated tape and the Intermarket Trading System, so defining much of the architecture of late twentieth-century stock markets. The NYSE's control was only temporary, fading as innovations at the fringes of finance – electronic limit order books that were changing the expectations of behaviors of traders and investors – conquered more of the marketplace.

This does not mean that politics were absent. A significant lesson in the history of market fragmentation is that there was always a choice, sometimes quite explicitly so. Regulators and market participants elected to build an integrated marketplace driven by a form of competition reliant on geographic interconnection in place of order aggregation. The possibility of building a consolidated limit order book, however radical, was technically, organizationally and even politically realistic – so thought the NYSE: the 1971 report by former president William Chesney Martin Jr. proposed effectively transforming the exchange into the nation's prime trading site, granting it control over the trading of any stocks deemed of national importance. The issue was never whether centralization was possible, but the type of centralization that best fitted the interests of incumbents. Infrastructures are difficult to wrangle, and they develop through trajectories often tied to the messy paths of organizations, fields, and struggles. Politics matter here, as in every point of interconnection, in every moment of decision, in every design rejected, investors, regulators, and exchanges selected a fate for their financial democracy, its constituencies, and its excluded citizens.

More speculatively, we can draw this chapter to a close by observing the unintended consequences stemming from the efforts to contain and shape the scope of market fragmentation. The Regulation National Market System that eroded the New York Stock Exchange's dominance and propelled high frequency trading transformed the world in more than one way. To establish the level playing field that inspired the National Market System, the Securities and Exchange Commission fostered novel subjecthoods in the marketplace that dovetailed the assemblages of digital infrastructures and the new relations they produce. Earlier, the regulator had governed the market through a combination of self-observance, disclosure, and registration. By examining incoming generations of broker-dealers and requiring organizations to report on the activities of their members, the Securities and Exchange Commission oversaw the integrity of markets by guaranteeing the judgment, discretion, and fiduciary ethics of its human inhabitants and the rules they followed. Regulation NMS was designed for the altogether different situation where human intermediaries sit on the edges of a fast, electronic marketplace (MacKenzie, 2018). As such, it did not protect investors directly, but rather their orders or "indications of a willingness to buy or sell," requiring trading centers to "establish, maintain, and enforce written policies and procedures that are reasonably designed" to prevent trade throughs (situations where an order is fulfilled at prices inferior to the National Best Bid/Offer). But if orders are relationships (as argued in Chapter 6), then this shift positions the United States closer to Melanesian legal logics. As anthropologist Marilyn Strathern suggests, Euro-American law "does not recognize a relationship as a legal subject ... in Melanesian ways of thinking relationships are the equivalent of a legal subject, insofar as they are embodied [and] subjected to politico-ritual protocols and public attention." Order protection moved the focus further away from the fiduciary protection of investors as bounded, complicated agents and closer to the protection of orders as objects of legal attention and protocol. These ethics of order protection were political, too, reframing the rights and responsibilities of the human individuals of the past into a panoply of technical details about the electronic order of the present. I will now turn to some of the consequences of these uncanny politics of queues.

8 Infrastructures, Kinship, and Queues

Why did stock markets automate? Previous chapters suggest not one, but multiple tentative answers. The motives for automation were numerous, from organizational battles encoding the politics of class and expertise between newcomers and established members of the marketplace, to national contests meant to define the scope of action of financial citizens and the shape of their economized democracy. Automation was a process that transected multiple histories, knitting infrastructures across space, organizations, economic cultures, and the politics of equality, belonging, personhood, and nation. In closing this book, I want to highlight three theoretical themes stemming from these stories.

8.1 THEME ONE: INFRASTRUCTURES MATTER

The historical and institutional contingency of infrastructures is one of the recurring threads connecting cases throughout this book and the automation of financial markets more generally. Stock markets did not automate following a pregiven template – there was no single paradigm driving the computerization of stock exchanges initially – but did so in piecewise fashion, responding to local demands, constraints, and situated expectations about the operation of the market, its standing in society, and its weight in the political world. Consider, as an illustration, key differences between the early automation of the London Stock Exchange and the sociotechnical imaginaries promoted by the Securities and Exchange Commission of the late 1960s. Both British and American markets were mature settings, populated by sophisticated investors and intermediaries who shared similar technical horizons. In principle, and as far as technologies were concerned, there was nothing inhibiting a rapid convergence in models of automation. The Automated Real-Time Investment Exchange, intro-duced by British banks in the early 1970s, serves as a notable example: connected to Instinet through the technical work of David Manns, it placed electronic limit order books at the core of an exchange. A similar system *could* have colonized both American and British financial markets from then onward, but only did so much later: in Britain, after Tradepoint forced the LSE to change its strategy and culture, and in America, only after multiple Electronic Communications Networks disrupted the ecology of the National Market System. This was, of course, not the only opportunity for a dominant design to emerge. The occasions for convergence in technological trajectories were multiple, particularly given how knowledge about the innovations happening elsewhere in the financial field traveled between infrastructural workers. The technologists of the London Stock Exchange were not acting in vacuum but rather within networks of collaboration and competition with other engineers and members of the industry nurtured as they built the systems for the organization. Bennett, Hayter, and their colleagues were entirely networked, as were their colleagues overseas. Sitting in my office in London some years ago, David Manns observed a poster on my wall (Figure 1.1) and asked about its authorship. I mentioned it had been a gift from Peter Bennett, who used it to sell the project of a satellite-based global price communication system to the stock exchange's council. Manns quickly recognized both the content of the poster and its author, noting that although he had never met Bennett, he knew of his work. Bennett and Keith were similarly acquainted, having established what seems to have been a lasting friendship based partly on the respect of their techno-organizational prowess. But despite these global networks of experts and machines, automation was ultimately shaped by local concerns. Networks mattered, but mostly around decisions for procurement and hiring, and largely within the proximity of each market organization. At the end of the day, markets were not automated through the attractive forces of electronic limit order books as dominant designs in financial markets – an argument made, for example, by economist Lawrence Glosten (1994), who wrote of the order book as potentially "the only stable institution . . . within the set of economic environments and trading structures" of late twentieth-century finance. The market engineers that wrangled together the technologies of finance only made the allure of order books visible after much infrastructural buildup, institutional work, and countless roadblocks and surprises. In effect, for much time, the devices populating the financial system did not even reflect all the dreams of market technologists. In London, the systems that made the trading floor redundant were planned as Bailey bridges instead of products of careful foresight, and remained in use well beyond their estimated expiry date; and in the United States, the systems that retained the NYSE's control of the market were not monuments to automation, but instead resulted from minor innovations at the fringes of the market. If infrastructures seemed to have coalesced into a dominant design, it is probably because of the slow, path-dependent accumulation of systems, regulations, expertise, and cultural commitments through time.

The difficulties, frictions, and messy contingencies associated with the automation of financial markets may well be connected to the nature of the objects that circulate through their systems: orders, intentions, contracts, and stocks. Trading floors are not like factories, and automating stock markets was not "simply" a project in finding more efficient forms of matching some stable, preexisting things called "orders" on a computer. On the contrary, the process implied transformations across the entire lifecycle of deals – from their messy origination with investors to their finalization in the bureaucratized spaces of clearing and settlement. For the National Market System to come into existence, it required a centralized clearing body based on the dematerialization of paper certificates. And in much the same way, for Tradepoint to hit the market, it necessitated legislation that introduced the practices and legal frameworks of central counterparty clearing to Britain.[1] Even today, degrees and patterns of automation are modulated by these "infrastructures of infrastructures": as Robert Barnes commented in his interview, much of the competitive pressure in European equities markets derives from how the continent's multiple exchanges and clearinghouses are interconnected. Because each clearinghouse adds costs to transactions, consolidation at this level promotes savings in transaction costs between exchanges and, consequently, more incentives for automated, high-volume trading strategies.[2] Taken to the extreme, if each transaction were processed at a different clearinghouse, trading costs would be so prohibitive that they would make activities like high frequency trading impossible. The situation is similar for information dissemination: the forms of automation we know today are unthinkable without the consolidation and standardization of data feeds from trading sites to market users. Most of these processes, however, developed with at least some degree of cultural and organizational independence from each other: both in London and New York, back- and front-office operations were often disconnected through knowledge, design preferences, and status.

There is an important consequence of this contingency that I want to illustrate with a theoretical flashback. More than a century ago, Max Weber wrote two pamphlets for the Göttingen Workers Party to address questions concerning stock and commodities exchanges and their role in speculation and crisis. The world that Weber inhabited was dramatically different from our current, hyperconnected present, and the exchanges that he studied seem to be light years away from the technological behemoths of automated finance. Weber's analysis, however, remains relevant for understanding contemporary markets in general and exchanges in particular, with or without their fancy technologies.

In *Die Börse*, Weber positioned exchanges against a well-known account of the growth and rationalization of economies (Weber, 2000

---

[1] Waller-Bridge and Wilson interviews.   [2] Barnes interview.

[1894]). Starting with traditional forms of production and bartering, trade grew and consolidated into larger networks or exchange: "no cotton threads will be spun or woven within the regional economy in which it was harvested; no iron ore will be smelted by the mine owners who first took it from the earth" (Weber, 2000 [1894]: 309). Exchanges emerged within this expanded transregional economy as sites where "the business of selling transpires [with deals] struck over a set of goods that are not present, and often 'in transit' somewhere, or often yet-to-be-produced; and it takes place between a buyer who usually does not himself wish to 'own' those goods (in any regular fashion) but who wishes – if possible before he receives them and pays for them" (Weber, 2000 [1894]: 309–310). This "thumbnail history of commerce" presents exchanges – and in particular commodities exchanges – as indispensable for facilitating the distinctive economic patterns of industrial capitalism. How well does this represent automated exchanges more than a century later?

Weber's account rests several observations, one of which matters to the infrastructural perspective advocated in this book: he sees organized exchanges as concrete and tangible market mechanisms to negotiate prices and effectuate trades. Importantly, Weberian markets are positioned against the abstractive economic concepts that were already prevalent in the literature of the late nineteenth century. For example, whereas Cournot's market is defined analytically as "the whole of any region in which buyer and sellers-are in such free intercourse with one another that the prices of the same goods tend to equality easily and quickly" (Cournot, 1838; see also Marshall, 2014 [1890]), Weber's markets are places where bilateral transactions occur between agents: local or "smaller markets," as Weber writes, are "almost always [between] producers and users who trade directly with each other." Exchanges are markets, providing physical and spatially bound settings where securities are traded between buyers and sellers on behalf of investors. For Weber, the localized character of markets facilitates the meeting of the "outstretched hands" of supply and demand. This has consequences for the institutional characteristics of exchanges: they are necessarily organizations defined by "place."

Placeness is unusually persistent for stock and commodities exchanges. As Ruben Lee notes in his classic *What is an Exchange?* (1998), much of the dynamics of exchanges over the past half century centers on the erosion of institutional structures traditionally associated to place (with its distributed networks, electronic trading stands as a prime example). For Lee, much of this transformation is the consequence of adopting information technologies across the financial services industry, questioning and reinventing the functional characteristics of exchanges: as Lee (1998) argues, a key feature of exchanges is that they operate as trading systems (rather than places) that route, match and execute investors' orders – making technologies that emulate these functions without the fixity of place solutions to the problem of trade. In the late nineteenth century, trading required technologies that were deeply anchored and embedded in space, from trading floors where dealers met to conduct their daily business, to buildings that condensed the symbolic weight of finance in a nascent financialized international economy. But through their affordances, information technologies displaced these previous generations of technologies, making space, situations, and place apparently irrelevant. This shift is perhaps best captured by Richard O'Brien's (1992) once notable metaphor of the "end of geography" in financial services, or in the very popular discourse of "disintermediation" that targets the needlessness of brokers, dealers, and exchanges for trading.

As I've examined throughout this book, exchanges were certainly altered through technology, but it would be incorrect to locate the effect of this transformation on the elimination of "placeness." Quite the contrary, the current geography of trading suggests that stock and commodities exchanges are far less mobile than what the radical images of liberating information technologies once promised. The world's major stock exchanges, for example, populate the same sites of trading that were once inhabited by their previous analog incarnations – New York, Chicago, London, Toronto, Paris, Sao Paulo, Tokyo. That a challenger has not emerged from a circuit board in Nebraska can be perhaps attributed to the fact that exchanges are intertwined with the fabric of global cities (Sassen, 2013), requiring their deep roots of social and cultural capital, sunken infrastructural investments, and highly mobile elites. But the relevance of place is also an expression that the key function of exchanges – to provide a mechanism for trading – has to occur *somewhere*. For the New York Stock Exchange, this may not the building on the corner of Wall Street and Broad Street in Lower Manhattan but rather its "liquidity center" in Mahwah, New Jersey, where the firm's matching engines are located. Even today, when the only constraints on technology seem to be those imposed by physics, stock and commodities exchanges remain tied to space, and perhaps even more so than in the past: the introduction of digital systems that either emulate or substitute the floor create incentives for competing on speed in the execution of trades that render relativistic space crucial. This is the case of electronic limit order books. Like the trading floors of the past, electronic order books are the devices that allow the long hands of demand and supply to meet. Since they operate as any other standard computational device, these systems process "one message at a time, completing all requisite actions from the instruction (e.g., update the order book, execute trades, publish quote updates) before processing the next message" (NYSE, 2018). All other things held equal, the most effective strategies for traders consist of reaching the servers of the stock exchange before others, making their message the first in the queue. This form of so-called latency arbitrage, whereby competition is primarily based on the minimization of the time it takes messages to travel in the network, is necessarily tied to transmission speed and the topography of data communications. This is also true for other similarly speed-sensitive strategies. The materialities of modern electronic exchanges inflect space in particular ways: trading floors made ties to cities and the proximity to brokers and investment agents crucial, dynamically shaping much of the urban setting of analog finance; order books similarly hinge on proximity, not primarily to the symbolic investments of the past but to global hubs of digital connectivity and the topologies of data transmission. A focus on infrastructures thus implies rekindling the concept of market*places* as relevant to sociological analysis. Exchanges are not "just" trading mechanisms or entities reducible to computational processes (Lee, 1998; Mirowski, 2002) in the same way that markets are not just competitive arenas of mutual observation and strategic action. They are situated organizational objects, defined as much by their capacity to provide mechanisms to match transactions, communicate messages, and process information, as by their bureaucracies, interests, politics, moralities, and the infrastructures where these are crystalized.

8.2 THEME TWO: RELATIONS ARE PRODUCED

Recognizing the role of infrastructures and technologies in the operation of stock markets and the organizational dynamics of exchanges is relatively straightforward. A slightly less obvious theme is the comparison between markets and kinship that I advance in this book. This argument is based on two points: first, a Weberian conceptualization of markets as communities of exchange where participants are bound through ethical principles that structure how transactions occur. More broadly, this echoes a larger social scientific literature in the sociology and anthropology of markets that suggests exchange as deeply modulated by cultures, expectancies, and diverse behavioral codes (Garfinkel, 1967; Geertz, 1978; Gudeman, 1998; De la Pradelle, 2006; Nathaus and Gilen, 2011). Taking this a step further, thinking of markets as sites of sociation casts transactions as forms of semi-durable social relations where agents are never entirely quits (Bearman, 1997; Callon, 1998; Mauss, 2000; Slater, 2002; Healy, 2010). Here again, these arguments mirror the contributions of sociologists that stress economic action as modulated by social relations (Zelizer, 2010).

The twist in these pages comes from introducing a second theoretical point: economic transactions are certainly defined and shaped by social relations, but it may be useful to go a step further and think of how relations themselves are produced through know-ledge, categorical work, and their infrastructures. Kinship enters the stage here, with the work of social anthropologists who study family, homes, and courts as sites where relations are fabricated through affect, expertise, and institutional power (Franklin and McKinnon, 2001; Carsten, 2004; Strathern, 2005). My use of kinship is primarily metaphorical, but it points to a more general statement about how social scientists conceptualize relations. Relations are not natural occurrences, stemming instead from how actors are enabled and con-strained by the mutually constituted, asymmetric fields they inhabit. As an example, consider how relations are made objects of analysis by social network scholars (Erikson, 2013). On the one hand, we can think of social networks as expressions of some underlying structural feature of the world, be it general laws governing how agents create ties, the way they fall within organizational divisions, or logics guiding patterns of exchange. On the other hand, we can think of social networks as products of historically situated experiences of social agents that coalesce into dynamic formations. In both cases, however, the capacities of actors to create connections (or to become related to each other in some meaningful way) are indexed by the infrastructures they use to stabilize their social worlds: to close a triad, closure must be afforded within the system, whereas to develop relations through interactions and familiarity requires a platform that makes intersubjective experience possible. This is how infrastruc-tures matter to relations. They make possible categorical comparisons that provide both resources and constraints for establishing the exist-ence of "meaningful connections," potentially shaping the scope and breadth of relational systems themselves (Star, 1999). These infra-structures may come in many forms, from formal organizational hierarchies and communities (I am "related" to colleagues by virtue of being in the same department), to highways and telecommunica-tions that make long-distance relations possible and tractable (I am "related" to friends through social media), to contractual agreements that establish a distribution of rights and responsibilities across their parties (I am "related" to my bank and other debtors through my mortgage). In any case, the existence of relations is both mediated and resolved by infrastructures and the forms of knowledge connected to their operation – as explored in Chapter 6, where market microstructure theory was used to distinguish legitimate from illegitimate relations in electronic limit order books. These relations didn't exist "out there." They were not obvious. They were made.

This joint metaphor of kinship as an infrastructural phenomenon should not be read as excluding politics from markets, that is, as an attempt to naturalize exchange as simply constitutive of community building or to internalize the tensions, interests, and power imbalances in marketplaces, their organizations, and their ecologies. Quite the contrary, this metaphor calls for rethinking politics beyond the extremes of pro- and anti-market positions. Kinship is political, an expression of hierarchies, segregations, and exclusions as much as it is of connections and ties; kinships "exclude as well as include" (Haraway, 2016: 207), and by defining the limits of group membership, they create as much as it moderate inequalities. Indeed, kinship is a political project by definition, involving institutions that define the scope of legitimate and illegitimate relations, the parameters under which one can be considered kin, and the ultimate rationale for relatedness. Take the promise of the financial democracy that symbolically underlies much of the automation of stock and commodities exchanges. Ideas of financial citizenship, inclusion, and literacy are premised on a kinship-like system of connective, interdependent, mutual responsibilities. But these are not apolitical, reflecting the historical retreat of the state from the provision of welfare (Krippner, 2011; Streeck, 2014), nor are they uniformly distributed, with some persons possessing more value and protections from hazards than others (Fraser and Gordon, 1994; Mirowski, 2013). Perhaps the best way of thinking about the forms of relatedness established in current forms of financial citizenships is through segregation rather than inclusion. While members of the community, most financialized citizens lack the safety nets that market intermediaries possess, and are segregated from protective instruments through law, regulation, and infrastructural capacities (see Parsons, 1943; Young and Wilmot, 2013; for a fascinating discussion of segregation with inclusion, see Accominotti et al. 2018.)

The language of kinship matters, partly because it appeals to the productive possibilities of mutuality in markets. At stake is not whether markets in the abstract or in their particular instantiations are "moral" but, rather, how, among whom, and in which directions they trace relations of dependence and responsibility. The contrast with discussions about "families" serves as an example. In some sense, families are moralized in similar ways to markets (see Fourcade and Healy, 2007), as forces of civilization, mechanisms of destruction, or feeble structures of social life. We write of some families as positive sources of capital for offspring (Harker, 1984; Parcel and Menaghan, 1994; Coleman, 1998) or symbolic anchors of nationhood and civilization (McClintock, 1993); of others as sites for the propagation and reproduction of vices (Gove and Crutchfield, 1982; Chernikov and Giordano, 1987); and of others as structures that should have little explanatory power over social outcomes (McDonough, 1994). Yet adopting a pro- or anti-family position seems analytically and politically pointless. What matters is thinking about conditions of felicity, redefinitions, and structures of relatedness and obligation that lead to desirable outcomes. Politics and the possibility of intervention are about shaping the networks of responsibility of market kin. (A relevant example is offered by Greta Krippner's (2017) recent work, presenting possessive collectivism as an alternative to current forms of economic citizenship.) This is, perhaps, both a practical and theoretical frontier for a new type of "market design" (Roth, 2002) that places less emphasis on seemingly technical questions of engineering and efficiency and more on public, deliberative discussions of how markets should be constrained, altered, expanded, and retooled to serve our collective, kindred interests.

8.3   THEME THREE: MARKETS ARE INDICATORS

I close this book with a more tentative suggestion. The automation of stock markets is more than a historical curiosity or a topic relevant only to those interested in finance and the economy more generally. As I argued before, markets are entangled with societies and their organizational forms. The metaphor of embeddedness (Granovetter, 1985) often used to understand markets' relation to society, while insightful and important, reproduces an artificial divide between "the economic" and a residue; it renders markets distinct from an external "society" that affects them from afar. This is a theoretical mistake. Markets are not objects "embedded" in a larger social sphere as rough diamonds are embedded to rocks. Social structures do not "shape" economic action, as a child forcing Play-Doh into individual forms. And markets are not abstract collections of transactions modulated by social relations that are external to economic logics. More than embeddedness, markets mirror the societies they inhabit, partially reflecting their tensions of knowledge, class, power, inequality, and interests. This is why the automation of stock markets matters: it reflects broader processes that are not confined to stocks or trading but extend to multiple realms of social life. This is the third theme of this book: finance is a canary in the coalmine of contemporary capitalism.

What does stock market automation say about the present and future of capitalism and its infrastructures of relation making? To answer this question, I turn to the work of E.P. Thompson whose analysis of the origins of industrial capitalism offers a suggestive tactic for understanding the complex relations between technology and the emergence of novel economic and social formations. In his celebrated essay, "Time, Work Discipline, and Industrial Capitalism," Thompson (1967) poses a fascinating puzzle. Shifts in the appreciation and understanding of time are quite old in modern European societies. For some of Thompson's contemporaries, these shifts traced to refinements in the design of clockworks from the fourteenth century onward. So went the argument, the proliferation of standardized, publicly visible timepieces afforded a move from traditional forms of task-orientation to the more exacting forms of clock-orientation that were necessary for transforming labor into capital. Capitalism emerged at this intersection, between technological advancements and the capacity of clocks to slice time for monetization. As a sophisticated historian, though, Thompson was careful in assigning causality to clocks and self-governing agency to innovation. The "time-sense in its technological conditioning" certainly mattered, but so did the growing social imperative of "time-measurement as a means of labor exploitation" (Thompson, 1967: 80). Clock-time was not autonomous but reflected a concern to perfect the means for extracting rents from labor in capitalism's early historical trajectory.

Market automation is similarly Thompsonian. Computers and data processing equipment existed in different forms and configurations well before stock exchanges automated. The very notion of a computer was itself historically entangled with the organizational trajectories finance – think, for instance, of how Charles Babbage's definition of a computer derived from his observations of the Banker's Clearing House in 1830s London. Finance, too, existed well before the mechanical forms of ranking, commensuration, quantification, and valorization that authors often associate with expansive, neoliberal financialization (Lapavitsas, 2013; Chiapello and Walter, 2016). Automation indicated a specific convergence of wants and desires, a way of organizing relations through machines and for society at large. This convergence occurred around a specific aspect of the design feature of modern computers – particularly, those associated to the real-time communication and data processing systems that populated banks and stock exchanges from the 1970s onward: the queue.

The queue is rationalizing critique of a key modern institution, the crowd. Crowds have always existed, of course, but their significance and visibility changed considerably over time. Sociologist Christian Borch (2012) argues that understanding the political imaginaries of the past two and a half centuries requires examining the changing appreciation for crowds in social life. Prior to the late 1700s, crowds connoted pollution and moral impropriety. The civil revolts of the eighteenth century had a catalytic effect: in the semantic register, crowds became agents of change through which politics could be challenged, deconstructed, and reinvented (Thompson, 1971; Rude, 2005; Le Bon, 2009). By the end of the nineteenth century, crowds acquired new significance as registered within the burgeoning fields of social theory. Positioned between reason and irrationality, between the emotional mob and the thoughtful thinker, they were reconceptualized as a "distinct germ of society," to use the words of Gabriel Tarde (2010). Modernity was a time of crowds.

Borch's argument is much more erudite and detailed than what I can present in a single paragraph – his work traces with great care the shifting connotations of crowds among early European and American sociologists, highlighting the centrality of the concept in the making of a new theoretical apprehension of society followed by its peculiar rejection within the literature in the mid-twentieth century. Importantly, his argument echoes a similar, contemporaneous rehabilitation of the way market congregations were evaluated in popular and academic thought. During the middle ages, for example, market gatherings were judged with a great degree of suspicion. Markets were necessary though ambiguous points of encounter where, as historian James Davis (2000) explores, "every man was a devil to himself," challenged by the temptations of "professional traders, marginal retailers, part-time hucksters, peasant producers and sundry consumers" meeting under the market cross. Market crowds were anything but virtuous. They were uncouth and antithetical to the purity of the godly and, later, to the order of reason. But this was not so by the nineteenth century, when these same crowds were cleansed of their moral impropriety. Market gatherings were sanitized, organized, and enclosed; they moved from streets and self-organized meetings in piazzas and squares into highly regulated and architectured spaces for trading and exchange. Market crowds became respectable. They became exemplars of a spanning modernity.

Consider how stock trading moved from the margins of morality in the days of Jonathan Swift and the Exchange Alley and into the organized and revered national institutions of the early twentieth century. Consider how stock trading bodies inflected the space around their activities, away from the rowdy coffee houses and haphazard gatherings in lanes and streets and into highly ritualized places that, like Wall Street and the City of London, are now emblems of capitalism and industry. Think of how trading crowds changed from collections of speculative agents of intrigue into fountains of knowledge and truthful valuations (Poovey, 2002; De Goede, 2005). Observe how these crowds inspired, too, the abstraction of markets, be it through Leon Walras's auctioneer – perhaps inspired by the Paris Bourse (Walker, 2001) – or Alfred Marshall's (2014) perfect market – imagined under the shadow of the London Stock Exchange. And consider how stock markets came to symbolize, in Frederick von Hayek's (1945) metaphors of the price system as a switching board or Eugene Fama's (1970) repertoire of informational efficiency, mechanisms for collective deliberation – processors animated by the wisdom of crowds rather than their individual moral and cognitive failings.

But the physical and logical design of the computers and the real-time systems that structure finance simply negates the possibility of crowds. Authors may speak of "crowds of algorithms" or high frequency traders "crowding the market" (Lange and Borch, 2014), but these are inadequate metaphors for understanding what happens when orders to trade hit the market's silicon substrate. Computers are designed around architectures of discreteness, as input–output systems that address data sequentially rather than collectively (Treleaven et al. 1982; Flynn, 1995). Like other forms of electronic data, market orders are not simply dumped into computers as sacks of wheat fed into a mill, but instead trickle in, one-by-one, grain-by-grain, bit-by-bit. In computers, the asynchrony of crowds can be simulated but never truly reproduced. The only possible configurations are serially ordered data types upon which logical operations are performed. And among these, one data structure is characteristic of the automation of stock markets: the queue, an ordered linear method for organizing data, commands, or routines into a calculable, computable list.

Queues are to electronic automated financial markets what crowds were to trading floors. This is for one simple reason: the electronic limit order books that animate activity in most modern stock markets are essentially complex queuing systems either in time (as in the time-price priority mechanisms that are common in stocks) or in volume (as in the pro-rata mechanisms of derivatives and money markets) (Chan, 2005; Cont et al. 2010; Lipton et al. 2013; Muni Toke, 2015). The queue-ness of these digital marketplaces results from how they arrange and process the incoming orders from participants. Think of the systems based on the principle of price-time priority. In their most basic configuration, these order books receive, time stamp, and then enqueue limit orders onto a list that is subsequently matched and cleared.

The queues of financial automation are not ancient capitalism repackaged for the digital age. If time-discipline characterized early forms of industrial capital as a proxy for the transformation of the labor process (Biernacki, 1995), queue-discipline binds the operational logics of automated capital by establishing a functional system of priorities through which resources, rights, and values are allocated according to given attributes and classes. Queue-discipline is not primarily about the politics of production, where time-discipline argu-ably governs behaviors and expectations, but rather concerns ordering, position, and arbitrage as sources of value. What matters here are logistics and inventory management, rather than the qual-ities of the objects produced and consumed within the market. Queues are about extracting value from circulation, rather than cre-ation; they are about efficiencies in the timing and coordination of movements, instead of manufacturing or the forms of human capital it requires. Automated financial markets are closer to modern super-markets than to the crowds of the old trading floors (LeCavalier's, 2016) prioritizing high sales volumes over markups. This is, for instance, the logic of high frequency trading. Profits are derived not from creating artificially large spreads (marking up or down the prices of stocks), but from how well an actor is able to process market information, route orders and cancellations, and effectuate trades that individually result in miniscule profits. Using fine-grained transaction-level data, for example, some economists placed the profits of HFT strategies at about $0.25 per contract traded in 2010 (Baron et al. 2012). In the following years, markets became much more competitive. Data obtained from the initial public offer of the firm Virtu in 2014 placed the profits for high frequency trading at an average of $0.0027 per trade. The value proposition of HFT is finding excess returns from individual stock – emulating investment funds that purportedly outperform a market benchmark. Value in HFT is couched in the semantics of volume. For Virtu to pay for its expensive 4.7 millisecond latency between Carteret, New Jersey, and Aurora, Illinois, it has to multiply its small profits many times, every single day. Indeed, by the estimates of one analyst, Virtu trades about 160 million contracts daily (Laughlin, n.d.), churning about 5 percent of US securities markets.

Financial automation suggests some relevant concepts for thinking about queues in contemporary societies. The cases explored in this book point to three. The first concerns the making of queues as material, organizational, and social interventions to reorganize the world. The second refers to how queues generate unexpected forms of value. And third relates to how the proliferation of queues may require novel narratives of politics and moralities. I explore these three themes below.

8.3.1   *Queues as Sociotechnical Achievements*

Queues do not emerge naturally but are deliberate interventions to achieve particular ends by specifying how interactions *should* take place within a certain setting (Taylor and Lyon, 1995; Ritzer, 1998; McKenzie, 2012; Waring and Bishop, 2015). Whether rational reactions to problems of resource allocation or cultural projects of globalized discipline-making, queues require infrastructures that equip and constrain how their users communicate, act, exchange, and move within their social spaces. Because of these sociomaterial arrangements (barriers, legal constraints, service desks, formatted spaces, specialized software; Vargha, 2014), any account of how queues matter must address their making. Queues are manufactured; they are organized into being – and the process of assembling the infrastructures of queuing requires further attention.

One possibility is thinking about the actors who make queues possible, what I call queue-smiths. This concept provides theoretical traction for explaining why queues propagated as organizational forms throughout fields, proximal and distal. Inspired by E.P. Thompson's clock-smith, I think of queue-smiths as the type of quasi-invisible engineers, managers, technologists, regulators, and similar infrastructural workers that labor to automate different arenas of social life by organizing solutions to scarcity and inefficiency into queues. Queue-smiths may be particularly relevant sets of actors because of how they create "hinges" across fields (Abbott, 2005), deploying strategies that operate and are rewarded simultaneously across differing sites. As "biological tails" of organizations,[3] queue-smiths create connections across different sites of practice, implementing similar strategies of automation that collectively speak to the importance of queues without making explicit a shared logic or ideology. Consider how electronic bulletin boards propagated throughout very different stock markets in Britain in the 1980s. Designed for the main market on the basis of an existing price reporting system – the Market Price Display Service – the Stock Exchange's EPIC database and its associated price visualization service (TOPIC) originally operated only for British stocks traded on the LSE. But as another ecology emerged – namely, the international stock market that grew under the shadow of the stock exchange and was populated by firms that were foreign to the traditional City of London – the same technologists implemented

---

[3] This metaphor was kindly suggested to me by Yuval Millo.

their system there. The result was SEAQ International, a hinge that linked two very different ecologies – the traditional British stock markets and the local markets in overseas shares – with the same type of device. Consider, also, the more provocative example of the interconnections between the gaming industry and finance. A technologist working for a large London hedge fund hinted this to me in interview. Trained in computer science and engineering, this interviewee first worked as a network programmer for large online multiplayer games. His greatest challenge was the fact that the Internet is not instantaneous: when a player sends a command to execute an action, it takes time for the signal to reach the computer server and interact with the commands of other players. For the game to be realistic, such delays have to be taken into account when rendering reality on the screen. The challenge for the network programmer is to make these asymmetries as invisible as possible so that the game seems "equitable to everyone."[4] The problem is similar in finance, where the physical distance from the stock exchange's matching engines matters tremendously, requiring a similar solution to the problem of latency: simulating the most likely state of the order book on the firm's computers in order to estimate the most advantageous strategies or the firm's trading algorithms. Gaming and finance are linked not through an institutional imperative of culture or capital – or even a strategy, as such – but rather through the more mundane and lowly problems of how to *fairly* manage latency and connectivity.

8.3.2   Queues as Displacements of Value

Queue-smiths also matter because their work dislocates, even if momentarily, how value is discussed and constructed away from objects and exchange and onto their organization and circulation. Queues hence refer to what Marion Fourcade (2016) identifies as a ubiquitous logic of ordinality of late capitalism based on comparisons

---

[4] Interview with HFT developer.

and judgments of worthiness dictated by the relative position of actors and objects rather than on perceived qualities or assumed essences. Wine, colleges, graduate programs, music, financial instruments, et cetera, are increasingly valued not according to individualized judgments but rather to where they fall within an ordered set of classifications. These forms of ordinalization create resources and inequalities derived as much from established asymmetries in access as from the implicit logics of the algorithms that perform and reproduce classification systems (Fourcade and Healy, 2013). Queues matter because they are particular ways of operationalizing the ordinal, by arranging data, objects, and actors to determine value. Consider how data is introduced to order books. The dominant mechanism – first in, first out – places emphasis on speed and timeliness as a way of accessing the market since, as economists note, control of queue position in the order book is paramount in electronic markets (Moallemi and Yuan, 2014; Flint, 2017). The ability to control queue position affords actors predictability over order flows, execution costs, and market impacts. Focusing on how things are enqueued and how designs are said to promote virtues and values matters for appreciating the forms of worth displaced in these systems. Speed is costly, after all, and any financial system that privileges latency necessarily stimulates specific types of firms, actors, and forms of knowledge. There is nothing neutral or apolitical about how we queue. Quite the contrary, queues are all about the implicit politics designed into the line.

8.3.3 Queues and Algorithmic Moralities

This leads to a third theme: how queues materialize moralities and politics through design, use, and acceptance. Here, existing sociological work provides some insights. For Erwin Goffman (1983), for example, the interactional, local arrangement of service queues prevents "certain externally based influences at certain structural points," generating a sense of equal treatment even when such does not exist. Confronted with delays, agents in the queue do not identify structural features as the origins of the unequal distribution of waiting times but rather speak of "bad luck" as the explanation for their woes. As Harold Garfinkel notes, queues emerge in the context of shared expectations of moralized behavior: the line is a visible, witnessable object, actively constituted by its participants through the knowledge they have of how a queue *should* operate (Garfinkel and Livingston, 2003). A line is made up of ways of acting, of positioning bodies, of controlling voices, of directing stares, and reacting to others. As Barry Schwartz writes, queues index society at large, reproducing broader structures of divisions and inequality (Schwartz, 1974). Waiting times are rarely equally distributed, and sub-queuing (or the formation of several queues for the same process) is often related to preexisting classes of actors in society. For Leon Mann (1969), queues are miniature social systems in their own right.

Previous sociological work often studied queues as local interactional achievements, placing these phenomena at a micro-scale of analysis. The pervasiveness of queues as organizational forms and solutions, however, might require thinking of these as macro-scale forms of politics and governance. Cultures of queue-building, for example, are intensely political. Most of the queues studied in the social scientific literature are defined by the principles of first-in, first-out (FIFO), partly because these reflect a specific form of egalitarian, impersonal rationality (cutting in line, circumventing the queue, or jumping positions are read as forms of indiscipline, disruptions of shared norms and expectations of equal treatment; Goffman, 1983). The FIFO culture of queue-making has deep historical roots. Citing cases that span more than a century and a half, legal scholars Ronen Perry and Tal Zarsky (2013) identify FIFO as an "omnipresent and overarching principle in the law," closely associated to a canonical rule of conflict resolution based on the concept that the first in time is the first in right (this applies to liens, for instance). Legal scholar Kevin Gray (2007) also argues that FIFO is central to modern legal thought, serving as a proxy for fairness and equality, a "great leveler of humankind." A first-in first-out queue, writes Gray, could even be thought of as a Rawlsian "veil of ignorance," agreed upon by agents before allocations are made to produce the most equitable result possible. This principle is at play in finance: the creation of the National Market System, and the recent controversies about high frequency trading in the United States, are both anchored on the perceived virtue of a FIFO queue. As Junius Peake wrote to the Securities and Exchange Commission in 2004 in relation to the making of the NMS, first come first serve was "the only way" to solve the problems of privileged access in American stock markets (Peake, 2004).

But real-world queues are controlled by much more than simple variants of the first-in, first-out principle. The "service disciplines" used to decide how to enqueue and dequeue items are numerous. First-in first-out might dominate our social imaginary, but it shares space with other service disciplines that infrastructure governance. In data communications, first-in first-out can lead to poor outcomes: a customer that demands a long service time increases waiting times for others, creating bottlenecks for critical processes and communications. Most network applications thus use a processor sharing discipline where each of the n customers using the system receives $1/n$ of the service effort. Other applications rely on a last-in, first-out (LIFO) mechanism that assigns priority inversely to waiting time (some forms of accounting prefer LIFO to better represent tax liabilities rather than book value; Mills, Newberry, and Trautman, 2002). Closer to everyday lives, priority disciplines enqueue and dequeue objects on the basis of assigned status (think, for example, of how packages are sent through postal services or of the more mundane and uncomfortable experience of boarding a plane).

These organizational forms condense and reproduce visions of society and perform categories and relations into existence. Unlike the self-patrolled queues described by Goffman and Garfinkel, many of these service disciplines are hardwired into the infrastructures of experience. Think, for example, of the allocation of tasks among workers with flexible contracts. The increased tracking and monitoring of employees through the internal record keeping systems of modern commercial organizations may well create unequal opportunities for distributing scheduled work-time. A young and childless employee who can work during hours of peak demand, seldom reports in sick, and has an above-normal sales record and may be easily prioritized over a worker who, having to tend for a family or commute great distances, is deemed less effective. It is by no means farfetched to think of how scheduling might differ between these two imagined workers, reproducing broader inequalities and asymmetries through how algorithms and organizations enqueue their access to work-time.

In substantiating categories, queues are fundamentally a project in redefining kinship, relatedness, community, and rights. People in a queue are related, even if artificially – queues produce communities of interactions and effects, of belonging and behavior; they elicit moralities and shared ethics. Understanding how queues are fashioned by infrastructures to produce effects and communities is part of the task at hand. As scholars, we need to place more attention on how the service disciplines regulating queues, coded into their infrastructures, and performed in organizations, get enacted both *in silico* and *in vivo*. This is where novel moralities, politics, and contested forms of worth are built today; but these are also sites for the reproduction of old differences and inequalities, dressed under new garbs. The history of financial markets provides some suggestions – it highlights the invisible queue-smiths that thread the marketplace and the assumptions, politics, commitments, and imagined futures. And as with finance, our task is to make visible the mundane, boring, and taken for granted, placing infrastructures, the societies they bring into being, and the societies they fail to deliver, as visible objects of collective deliberation.

Appendix: A Note on Sources

This book combines a variety of sources on the historical development of market infrastructures in and across stock exchanges. The evidence is of two broad types: the first consists of semistructured interviews with individuals involved in the automation of stock exchanges and other trading sites between c. 1965 and 2014; the second is formed by materials collected in archives, libraries, and private collections.[1] Given the paucity of microhistories of market engineers – of the individuals that were involved in automating trading venues throughout the second half of the twentieth century – I adopted an iterative sampling strategy that provided access to this historically opaque sphere of technological and organizational action. Interviewees were identified and reached through a process that combined research on the histories of firms and institutions with traditional snowball sampling techniques. Initially, I conducted documentary research in specialist archives, trade publications, and other periodicals on finance and technology to identify the names of individuals involved in the automation of specific stock exchanges. Data from this phase was used to organize a first round of interviews leading to a second list of names not identified in the initial iteration. Archival research into this second set of names produced a new list of actors around which a second round of interviews was organized. This proceeded for five rounds until I reached a point of theoretical saturation – while always enthralling, the overarching narratives conveyed by different informants eventually converged.

The sample I obtained through this process is predominantly male (I only interviewed one woman). This should not be read as a characteristic of the population, but, rather, as a reflection of the dynamics of organizational memory and career trajectories (e.g., Hicks, 2017)—in the documentary archives, women emerge

---

[1] The documentary sources used in this study include the London Stock Exchange's records at Guildhall Library, London; numerous trade magazines and journals consulted at the British Library and the National Library of Scotland; digitalized copies of Frederick Nymeyer's works (which are dispersed through numerous online repositories); private documents provided by interviewees and informants; the archives of the London School of Economics and Political Science; John Maynard Keynes's archives at King's College, Cambridge; parliamentary records of the United Kingdom; the online archives of the US Securities and Exchange Commission; documents compiled by SEC Historical; archived US Congressional Hearings; and the online records of the Cincinnati Stock Exchange.

as critical actors in the process of market automation and their omission from the narratives that I present is a methodological limitation for which I wholeheartedly apologize. The organizational locations of my informants are, however, a closer reflection of the hierarchies of automation in financial institutions: 9 interviewees were senior managers of stock exchanges or brokerage firms; 24 were technology developers, some of whom also occupied senior management positions in the past; 7 were traders with some involvement in technology; 4 were economists and/or regulators; and 2 were journalists or consultants. The interviews took place between October 2006 and May 2016 in various sites in the United Kingdom, New York, and California. I conducted three interviews over the phone, and transcribed all recordings.

My methodology was to use interviews as sources of oral histories of actors involved in different stages of the process of market automation. This approach was valuable insofar as it allowed peeking into a microcosms that are otherwise inaccessible through archival and documentary research. But this empirical approach also poses a challenge: as representations of reality, the interviews that informed this study are patently false. Human minds are fallible recording instruments and are embedded in constellations of interests and concerns that shape the structure, meaning, and purpose of personal narratives. These are valid arguments typically adopted by critics of oral histories in historical research (Roper, 1996). Oral histories, however, are tremendously valuable in providing detailed accounts of everyday relations, of organizational and familiar interactions, and due to their situated character, of subjective and lived experiences that can be queried in dialogue with the interviewee – a luxury in other forms of historical research. Indeed, oral histories are empowering because they capture the lives of actors often marginalized in print historical sources – from miners and laborers, to women and engineers (Perks and Thomson, 1998). In buttressing the value of these oral histories, accounts were "triangulated" across interviews and the available secondary sources on market automation – including newspapers and the extant literature in financial management and economics.

The oral histories used in this book are peculiar: they mostly deal with the taken-for-granted sphere of infrastructural work which, due to its very invisibility, makes cumbersome identifying creators, designers, genealogies, and politics. Perhaps the single most challenging aspect of this study was gaining access to a field that, for many decades, was symbolically neglected by narratives of the financial services industry. For example, until the recent expansion of technology-intensive operations in finance, the type of infrastructural workers studied in this book occupied modest positions within their organizations. The interviewees that informed this study were hence individuals that obtained some prominence within

Table A.1 *Affiliations of interviewees*

AFFILIATION	NUMBER OF INTERVIEWS
LONDON STOCK EXCHANGE	
Management	9
Technology*	11
Members*	10
TECHNOLOGY PROVIDERS	3
FOREIGN TRADING VENUES	
US	3
Europe	2
OTHER UK PRACTITIONERS	
Traders	6
Market analysis/Economists/Journalists	4
REGULATOR	1
TOTAL	**49**

the market – people who started as trainees and, with time, became managers reaching the highest possible levels in management. The histories they offer are thus tinted with heroic overtones – although this may be, too, a consequence of microhistories, as discussed by Carlo Ginzburg and Jacques Revel (1995). Together, these microhistories recover the politics and struggles that made automated finance, the conflicts and affinities, calculated plans and emergent surprises that transformed markets into today's digital, high-frequency domains.

Bibliography

Abacus. (1962). "The age of machinery." *Stock Exchange Journal*, 7: 12–14.

Abbott, A. (2005). "Linked ecologies: States and universities as environments for professions." *Sociological Theory*, 23(3): 245–274.

Abergel, F., Anane, M., Chakraborti, A., Jedidi, A., and Muni Toke, I. (2016). *Limit Order Books*. Cambridge: Cambridge University Press.

Abolafia, M. (1996). *Making Markets: Opportunism and Restraint on Wall Street*. Cambridge, MA: Harvard University Press.

Accominotti, F., Khan, S., and Storer, A. (2018). "How cultural capital emerged in gilded age America: Musical purification and cross-class inclusion at the New York Philharmonic." *American Journal of Sociology*, 123(6): 1743–1783.

Adams, C.W., Behrens, H.R., Pustilnik, J.M., and Gilmore, J.T. (1971). "Instinet communication system for effectuating the sale or exchange of fungible properties between subscribers." US Patent 3573747, issued April 6.

Ahrne, G., Aspers, P., and Brunsson, N. (2015). "The organization of markets." *Organization Studies*, 36(1): 7–27.

Aldridge, I. (2009). *High-frequency Trading: A Practical Guide to Algorithmic Strategies and Trading Systems*. New York: John Wiley & Sons.

Alexander, J. (2008). "Efficiencies of balance: Technical efficiency, popular efficiency, and arbitrary standards in the late progressive era USA." *Social Studies of Science*, 38(3): 323–349.

Angel, J.J., Harris, L.E., and Spatt, C.S. (2011). "Equity trading in the 21st century." *The Quarterly Journal of Finance*, 1(1): 1–53.

Anonymous. (1960). "Towards mechanization: Methods of providing bargain information to machine systems." *Stock Exchange Journal*, 5: 8.

Anonymous. (1966). "House notes." *Stock Exchange Journal*, 11: 1.

Anonymous. (1969). "House notes." *Stock Exchange Journal*, 14: 1–3.

Anonymous. (1970a). House notes. *Stock Exchange Journal*, 15: 1.

Anonymous. (1970b). House notes. *Stock Exchange Journal*, 20: 26–27.

Anonymous. (1970c). Stock exchange information computerised. *Accountancy*, 81: 606–607.

Anonymous. (1974). "The stock exchange's new computer. *DataSystems*, 15: 10–12.

Anonymous. (1986a). "City Systems." *Accountancy*, 129: 128.

Anonymous. (1986b). "Monday is D-day for the stock exchange." *Computer Weekly*, October 23.

Anonymous. (1986c). "A huge sigh of relief was heard throughout the City of London." *Computing*, October 2.

Anonymous. (1987). "London to end trading floor." *The New York Times*, March 13.

Anonymous. (1988). "*Computer Weekly* looks at computerisation and the stock exchange." *Computer Weekly*, November 24.

Anonymous. (1991). "Stock exchange changes its management structure in bid for new customer-focused organization." *Computing*, May 30.

Anonymous. (1992). "Stock exchange faces flak over decision to outsource information technology to Andersen Consulting." *Computing*, April 23.

Arnold, L. (2012). "Junius Peake, early advocate of electronic securities trading, dies at 80." *BloombergBusinessWeek*, February 13. Accessed March 22, 2012, www.bloomberg.com/news/articles/2012-02-13/junius-peake-early-advocate-of-electronic-trading-dies-in-colorado-at-80

Arnuk, S. and Saluzzi, J. (2009). "Latency arbitrage: The real power behind predatory high frequency trading," Themis Trading LLC White Paper (December 4). Accessed October 10, 2013, www.themistrading.com/article_files/0000/0519/THEMIS_TRADING_White_Paper_-_Latency_Arbitrage_-_December_4_2009.pdf

Arnuk, S. and Saluzzi, J. (2012). *Broken Markets: How High Frequency Trading and Predatory Practices on Wall Street Are Destroying Investor Confidence and Your Portfolio*. New York: FT Press.

Aspers, P. (2011). *Markets.* Cambridge: Polity Press.

Attard, B. (2000). "Making a market: The jobbers of the London Stock Exchange 1800–1986." *Financial History Review*, 7: 5–24.

Babbage, C. (1856). *An Analysis of the Statistics of the Clearing House during the Year 1839*, London: John Murray.

Baker, D. (1976). "Antitrust law and policy in the securities industry: A tale of two days in June." The Business Lawyer, 31(2): 743–753.

Baker, W.E. (1984). "The social structure of a national securities market." *American Journal of Sociology*, 89(4): 775–811.

Balarkas, R. and Ewen, G. (2007). "Algorithms to help you trade aggressively." In Patel, B. (ed.), *Algorithmic Trading Handbook*, 2nd ed. London: TRADE.

Barber, B. (1977). "The absolutization of the market: Some notes on how we got from there to here." In Dworking, G., Bermat, G., and Brown, P. (eds.), *Markets and Morals*. London: Hemisphere.

Barley, S.R. (1986). "Technology as an occasion for structuring: Evidence from observations of CT scanners and the social order of radiology departments." *Administrative Science Quarterly*, 31(1): 78–108.

Barley, S.R. and Bechky, B.A. (1994). "In the backrooms of science: The work of technicians in science labs." *Work and Occupations*, 21(1): 85–126.

Baron, M., Brogaard, J., and Kirilenko, A. (2012). "The trading profits of high frequency traders." Unpublished Manuscript.

Bearman, P. (1997). "Generalized exchange." *American Journal of Sociology*, 102(5): 1383–1415.

Becker, G. (2009). *A Treatise on the Family*. Cambridge, MA: Harvard University Press.

Beckert, J. (2009). "The social order of markets." *Theory and Society*, 38: 245–269.

Bennett, M. (1959). Putting the house in order: Junior members' views expressed by M. Bennett. *Stock Exchange Journal*, 4: 7–10.

Bennett, P. (1984). "U.K. stock exchange information services developments: A statement of intent" (memorandum). Information Services Division, Stock Exchange, London.

Berman, H.D. (1963). *The Stock Exchange: An Introduction for Investors*, London: Pitman & Sons.

Beunza, D. and Millo, Y. (2015). "Blended automation: Integrating algorithms on the floor of the New York Stock Exchange." London School of Economics and Political Science. Unpublished manuscript.

Beunza, D., Millo, Y., Pardo-Guerra, J.P., and MacKenzie, D. (2011). "Impersonal efficiency and the dangers of a fully automated securities exchange." *Foresight Driver Review*, 11. Department for Business, Innovation and Skills, UK.

Biernacki, R. (1995). *The Fabrication of Labor: Germany and Britain, 1640–1914*. Oakland: University of California Press.

Black, F. (1971). "Toward a fully automated stock exchange, Part I." *Financial Analyst Journal*, 27(4): 28–35.

Block, F. (2003). "Karl Polanyi and the writing of the Great Transformation." *Theory and Society*, 32(3): 275–306.

Böhm-Bawerk, E. (1891). *Capital and Interest*. London: MacMillan.

Boltanski, L. and Thévenot, L. (2006). *On Justification: Economies of Worth*. Princeton, NJ: Princeton University Press.

Borch, C. (2012). *The Politics Of Crowds: An Alternative History of Sociology*. Cambridge: Cambridge University Press.

Bourdieu, P. (2005). *The Social Structures of the Economy*. Cambridge: Polity Press.

Bourdieu, P. (2013). *Distinction: A Social Critique of the Judgement of Taste*. London: Routledge.

Bowker, G. (2015). "Temporality:" Theorizing the contemporary. *Cultural Anthropology*. Accessed September 24, 2016, www.culanth.org/fieldsights/723-temporality.

Bowker, G., Baker, K., Millerand, F., and Ribes, D. (2010). "Toward information infrastructure studies: Ways of knowing in a networked environment." In Hunsinger, J., Klastrup, L., and Allen, M. (eds.), *International Handbook of Internet Research*. New York: Springer.

Bowker, G. and Star, S.L. (1999). *Sorting Things Out: Classification and Its Consequences*. Cambridge, MA: MIT Press.

Boyer, R. (1996). "State and market." In Boyer, R. and Drache, D. (eds.), *States Against Markets: The Limits of Globalization*. London: Routledge.

Bradford, P.G. and Miranti, P.J. (2014). "Technology and learning: Automating odd-lot trading at the New York Stock Exchange, 1958–1976." *Technology and Culture*, 55(4): 850–879.

Brown, M. (1986). "The Big Bang: When the heat is on." *The Sunday Times*, October 26.

Brynjolfsson, E. and McAfee, A. (2014). *The Second Machine Age: Work, Progress, and Prosperity in a Time of Brilliant Technologies*. New York: W.W. Norton.

Burk, J. (1988). *Values in the Marketplace: The American Stock Market under Federal Securities Law*. Berlin: Walter de Gruyter.

Burk, K. (1992). "Witness seminar on the origins and early development of the Eurobond market." *Contemporary European History*, 1(1): 65–87.

Callon, M. (1998). *The Laws of the Markets*. Oxford: Blackwell.

Callon, M., Millo, Y., and Muniesa, F. (2007). *Market Devices*. London: Wiley-Blackwell.

Callon, M. and Muniesa, F. (2005). "Economic markets as calculative collective devices." *Organization Studies*, 26(8): 1229–1250.

Carruthers, B. (1999). *City of Capital: Politics and Markets in the English Financial Revolution*. Princeton, NJ: Princeton University Press.

Carruthers, B. and Espeland, W. (1991). "Accounting for rationality: Double-entry bookkeeping and the rhetoric of economic rationality." *American Journal of Sociology*, 97(1): 31–69.

Carsten, J. (2004). *After Kinship*. Cambridge: Cambridge University Press.

Carsten, J. (2013). "What kinship does—and how." *HAU: Journal of Ethnographic Theory*, 3(2): 245–251.

Cassis, Y. (2010). *Capitals of Capital: The Rise and Fall of International Financial Centres 1780–2009*. Cambridge: Cambridge University Press.

Castelle, M., Millo, Y., Beunza, D., and Lubin, D. (2016). "Where do electronic markets come from? Regulation and the transformation of financial exchanges." *Economy and Society*, 45(2): 166–200.

Cernkovich, S.A. and Giordano, P.C. (1987). "Family relationships and delinquency." *Criminology*, 25(2): 295–319.

Chan, Y. (2005). "Price movement effects on the state of the electronic limit-order book." *Financial Review*, 40(2): 195–221.

Chiapello, E. and Walter, C. (2016). "The three ages of financial quantification: A conventionalist approach to the financiers' metrology." *Historical Social Research/Historische Sozialforschung*, 41(2)155–177.

Clark, G. (2000). *Pension Fund Capitalism*. Oxford: Oxford University Press.

Clark, M. and Thomson, R. (1986). "Big Bang anger over faults on rehearsal day." *The Times*, October 20.

Clemons, E.K. and Weber, B.W. (1990). "London's Big Bang: A case study of information technology, competitive impact, and organizational change 1." *Journal of Management Information Systems*, 6(4): 41–60.

Clemons, E.K. and Weber, B.W. (1997). "Information technology and screen-based securities trading: Pricing the stock and pricing the trade." *Management Science*, 43(12): 1693–1708.

Coase, R.H. (1937). "The nature of the firm." *Economica*, 4: 386–405.

Cobbett, D. (1986). *Before the Big Bang: Tales of the Old Stock Exchange*. Portsmouth: Milestone Publications.

Cobbold, C.F. (1955). "Foreword." *The Stock Exchange Journal*, 1: 3.

Cohen, M. (1963). "Reflections on the special study of the securities markets." Speech read at the Practicing Law Institute, May 10.

Cohen, M. (1978). "The National Market System – A modest proposal." *George Washington Law Review*, 46(5): 743–789.

Cohen, N. (1995a). "Fancy footwork to ward off blows." *Financial Times*, March 27.

Cohen, N. (1995b). "A city flea waits to draw blood." *Financial Times*, September 4.

Coleman, J.S. (1998). "Social capital in the creation of human capital." *American Journal of Sociology*, 94(S): 95–120.

Collins, R. (1986). *Weberian Sociological Theory*. Cambridge: Cambridge University Press.

Competition in the New Electronic Market. (2000). 106th Congress, Second Session, House Doc. No. 106,111.

Cont, R., Stoikov, S., and Talreja, R. (2010). "A stochastic model for order book dynamics." *Operations Research*, 58(3): 549–563.

Cortada, J. (2003). *The Digital Hand: How Computers Changed the Work of American Financial, Telecommunications, Media and Entertainment Industries*. New York: Oxford University Press.

Council of the Stock Exchange. (1951). *My Word Is My Bond: The Stock Exchange, Some questions and Answers* (pamphlet) London: St. Clements Press.

Council of the Stock Exchange. (1974). "Comments on the Labour Working Party Green Paper on the reform of company law and its administration." Council of the Stock Exchange, London.

Council of the Stock Exchange. (1984). *The Stock Exchange: A Discussion Paper*. London: Stock Exchange.

Cournot, A.A. (1838). *Recherches sur les principes mathématiques de la théorie des richesses par Augustin Cournot*. Paris: L. Hachette.

Courtney, C. and Thompson, T. (1996). *City Lives: The Changing Voices of British Finance*. London: Methuen.

Cox, P. (1985). "SEAQ International: The birth of an electronic marketplace." In *Computers in the City: Financial Trading Systems. Proceedings of the International Conference*. London: Online Publications.

Crane, D. (2000). *Fashion and Its Social Agendas: Class, Gender, and Identity in Clothing*. Chicago: University of Chicago Press.

Crockett, B. (1990). "European stock exchanges to build shared network: PIPE net will link major exchanges on continent." *Network World*, January 8.

David, P. (1985). "Clio and the economics of QWERTY." *American Economic Review*, 75: 332–337.

Davis, G.F. and Kim, S. (2015). "Financialization of the economy." *Annual Review of Sociology*, 41.

Davis, J. (2000). *Medieval Market Morality: Life, Law and Ethics in the English Marketplace, 1200–1500*. Cambridge: Cambridge University Press.

Davison, J. (2009). "Icon, iconography, iconology: Visual branding, banking and the case of the bowler hat." *Accounting, Auditing & Accountability Journal*, 22(6): 883–906.

Day, M. (1956). "The mechanized office: New methods for old problems." *Stock Exchange Journal*, 2: 13.

De Boever, A. (2018). *Finance Fictions: Realism and Psychosis in a Time of Economic Crisis*. New York: Fordham University Press.

De Goede, M. (2005). *Virtue, Fortune, and Faith: A Geneaology of Finance*. Minneapolis: University of Minnesota Press.

De La Pradelle, M. (2006). *Market Day in Provence*. Chicago: University of Chicago Press.

Depositary Trust Corporation. (1973). *Annual Report*. New York.

Doherty, B. (2009). *Radicals for Capitalism: A Freewheeling History of the Modern American Libertarian Movement*. New York: Public Affairs.

Domowitz, I. (2002). "Liquidity, transaction costs, and reintermediation in electronic markets." *Journal of Financial Services Research*, 22(1): 141–157.

Domowitz, I. and Steil, B. (1999). "Automation, trading costs, and the structure of the securities trading industry." *Brookings-Wharton Papers on Financial Services*, 2: 33–92.

Duguid, C. (1913). *The Stock Exchange*. London: Methuen.

Durkheim, E. (1976). *The Elementary Forms of the Religious Life*. London: Allen and Unwin.

Easthope, D. (2009). "Demystifying and evaluating high frequency equities trading: Fast forward or pause? Celent. Accessed December 18, 2017, www.celent.com/insights/318327835

Edwards, P. (1997). *The Closed World: Computers and the Politics of Discourse in Cold War America*. Cambridge, MA: MIT Press.

Edwards, P. (2003). "Infrastructure and modernity: Force, time, and social organization in the history of sociotechnical systems." In Misa, T.J., Brey, P., and Feenberg, A. (eds.), *Modernity and Technology*. Cambridge, MA: MIT Press.

Edwards, P. (2010). *A Vast Machine: Computer Models, Climate Data, and the Politics of Global Warming*. Cambridge, MA: MIT Press.

Edwards, P., Bowker, G., Jackson, S., and Williams, R. (2009). "Introduction: An agenda for infrastructure studies." *Journal of the Association for Information Systems*, 10(5): 364–374.

Emirbayer, M. (1997). "Manifesto for a relational sociology." *American Journal of Sociology*, 103(2): 281–317.

Emirbayer, M. and Johnson, V. (2008). "Bourdieu and organizational analysis." *Theory and Society*, 37(1): 1–44.

Emmet, D. (1956). "Prophets and their societies." *The Journal of the Royal Anthropological Institute of Great Britain and Ireland*, 86(1): 13–23.

Engel, A. (2015). "Buying time: Futures trading and telegraphy in nineteenth-century global commodity markets." *Journal of Global History*, 10(2): 284–306.

Erikson, E. (2013). "Formalist and relationalist theory in social network analysis." *Sociological Theory*, 31(3): 219–242.

Escott, T.H.S. (1906). *Society in the Country House*. London: T. Fischer Unwin.

Eubanks, V. (2018). *Automating Inequality: How High-Tech Tools Profile, Police, and Punish the Poor*. New York: St. Martin's Press.

Evans, S. (2011). *Life Below Stairs: In the Victorian and Edwardian Country House*. London: National Trust Books.

Fama, E.F. (1970). "Efficient capital markets: A review of theory and empirical work." *The Journal of Finance*, 25(2): 383–417.

Fedida, S. and Malik, R. (1979). *The Viewdata Revolution*. New York: Halsted Press.

First Principles in Morality and Economics. (1960a). "Announcement regarding 'First Principles in Morality and Economics.'" December 6(12): 353–354.

First Principles in Morality and Economics. (1960b). "An analysis to show who gets the 'profit' from new automation machines." June 6(6): 184–192.

First Principles in Morality and Economics. (1960c). "How economics separates the two questions, relation of men to things and the relation of men to men." April 6(4).

First Principles in Morality and Economics (1960d). "Subjects on which theologians and economists can and should get together." April 6(4).

First Principles in Morality and Economics. (1960e). "Determination of price with two-sided competition." November 6(11): 330.

First Principles in Morality and Economics. (1960f). "Justice and injustice in price determination under four different circumstances." December 6(12): 359.

First Principles in Morality and Economics. (1960g). "Determination of price with one-sided competition among sellers." October 6(10): 317.

First Principles in Morality and Economics. (1960h). "Some inquiries about the business outlook in 1960." January 6(1): 8.

Fligstein, N. (1996). "Markets as politics: A political-cultural approach to market institutions." *American Sociological Review*, 61(4): 656–673.

Fligstein, N. (2001). *The Architecture of Markets: An Economic Sociology of Twenty-First Century Capitalist Societies.* Princeton, NJ: Princeton University Press.

Fligstein, N. (2002). *The Architecture of Markets: An Economic Sociology of Twenty-First-Century Capitalist Societies.* Princeton, NJ: Princeton University Press.

Fligstein, N. and Goldstein, A. (2015). "The emergence of a finance culture in American households, 1989–2007." *Socio-Economic Review*, 13(3): 575–601.

Fligstein, N. and Mara-Drita, I. (1996). "How to make a market: Reflections on the attempt to create a single market in the European Union." *American Journal of Sociology*, 102(1): 1–33.

Fligstein, N. and McAdam, D. (2011). "Toward a general theory of strategic action fields." *Sociological Theory*, 29(1): 1–26.

Flint, A. (2017). "Order placement strategies across different trading platforms: an empirical approach." PhD thesis, University of Wollongong.

Flynn, M. (1995). *Computer Architecture: Pipelined and Parallel Processor Design.* Burlington, MA: Jones & Bartlett Learning.

Fourcade, M. (2009). *Economists and Societies: Discipline and Profession in the United States, Britain, and France, 1890s to 1990s.* Princeton, NJ: Princeton University Press.

Fourcade, M. (2016). "Ordinalization: Lewis A. Coser Memorial Award for Theoretical Agenda Setting 2014." *Sociological Theory*, 34(3): 175–195.

Fourcade, M. and Healy, K. (2007). "Moral views of market society." *Annual Review of Sociology*, 33(1): 285–311.

Fourcade, M. and Healy, K. (2013). "Classification situations: Life-chances in the neoliberal era." *Accounting, Organizations and Society* 38(8): 559–572.

Fox, M.B., Glosten, L.R., and Rauterberg, G.V. (2015). "The new stock market: Sense and nonsense." *Duke Law Journal*, 65: 191.

Franklin, S. and McKinnon, S. (2001). *Relative Values: Reconfiguring Kinship Studies*. Durham, NC: Duke University Press.

Fraser, N. and Gordon, L. (1994). "A genealogy of dependency: Tracing a keyword of the US welfare state." *Signs: Journal of Women in Culture and Society*, 19(2): 309–336.

FSG. (1957). The Stock Exchange 'I' corps: Some sidelines on the collection and distribution of information." *Stock Exchange Journal*, 2: 104–106.

Garfinkel, H. (1967). *Studies in Ethnomethodology*. Englewood Cliffs, NJ: Prentice-Hall.

Garfinkel, H. and Livingston, E. (2003). "Phenomenal field properties of order in formatted queues and their neglected standing in the current situation of inquiry." *Visual Studies*, 18(1): 21–28.

Geertz, C. (1978). "The bazaar economy: Information and search in peasant marketing." *The American Economic Review*, 68(2): 28–32.

Geisst, C. (2012). *Wall Street: A History*. Oxford: Oxford University Press.

Gibson, G. (1889). *The Stock Exchanges of London Paris and New York: A Comparison*. New York: G.P. Putnam's Sons.

Giddens, A. (1971). *Capitalism and Modern Social Theory: An Analysis of the Writings of Marx, Durkheim and Max Weber*. Cambridge: Cambridge University Press.

Giddens, A. (1984). *The Constitution of Society: Outline of the Theory of Structuration*. Oakland: University of California Press.

Gilmore, J. (1969). "A panel session-on-line business applications." In *Proceedings of the Spring Joint Computer Conference*, May 14–16, Boston, MA.

Glaisyer, N. (2006). *The Culture of Commerce in England, 1660–1720*. Woodbridge, UK: Boydell Press.

Glosten, L.R. (1994). "Is the electronic open limit order book inevitable?" *The Journal of Finance*, 49(4): 1127–1161.

Goffman, E. (1983). "The interaction order: American Sociological Association, 1982 presidential address." *American Sociological Review*, 48(1): 1–17.

Goodison, N. (1986). "The Big Bang: Taking on the world." *The Sunday Times*, October 26.

Gorham, M. and Singh, N. (2009). *Electronic Exchanges: The Global Transformation from Pits to Bits*. New York: Elsevier.

Gove, W.R. and Crutchfield, R. (1982). "The family and juvenile delinquency." *The Sociological Quarterly*, 23(3): 301–319.

Graham, G. (1996). "Exchange delays order-driven trading." *Financial Times*, March 22.

Granovetter, M. (1985). "Economic-action and social-structure – The problem of embeddedness." *American Journal of Sociology*, 91(3): 481–510.

Grant, A. (1983). "Computing and Dealing Decisions in Stocks and Shares." In *Computers in the City: Proceedings of the International Conference*. London: Northwood Online.

Gray, K. (2007). "The legal order of the queue." Unpublished Manuscript, University of Cambridge.

Greaves, B.B. (2006). "Preface." In Von Mises, L. *The Anti-Capitalist Mentality*. Indianapolis: Liberty Fund.

Grimm, E. (1977). "London Town." *IBM THINK Magazine.*

Grundfest, J. (1988). *International Cooperation in Securities Enforcement: A New United States Initiative*. Washington, DC: US Securities and Exchange Commission.

Gudeman, S. (1998). *Economic Anthropology*. London: Edward Elgar.

Hales, C. (1795). *The Bank Mirror; Or, a Guide to the Funds, &c. J.* London: Adlard.

Hamilton, A. (1986). *The Financial Revolution*. New York: Free Press.

Hamilton, J.D. (1968). *Stockbroking Today*. London: Macmillan.

Hamilton, J.D. (1986). *Stockbroking Tomorrow*. London: Palgrave Macmillan.

Haraway, D.J. (2016). *Staying with the Trouble: Making Kin in the Chthulucene*. Durham, NC: Duke University Press.

Hargrave, T. and Van de Ven, A. (2009). "Embrace of contradiction." In Lawrence, T.B., Suddaby, R., and Leca, B. (eds.), *Institutional Work: Actors and Agency in Institutional Studies of Organizations*. Cambridge: Cambridge University Press.

Harker, R.K. (1984). "On reproduction, habitus and education." *British Journal of Sociology of Education*, 5(2): 117–127.

Hayek, F.A., von (1945). "The use of knowledge in society." *The American Economic Review*, 35(4): 519–530.

Hayek, F.A., von (1948). *Individualism and Economic Order*. Chicago: University of Chicago Press.

Hayter, G. (1983). "The stock exchanges integrated data network – A service for the securities industry." In *Computers in the City: Proceedings of the International Conference.* London: Online Publications.

Hayter, G. (1984). "The New Market Machinery: System Strategies for a Changing Market Place." *The Stock Exchange Quarterly.*

Hayter, G. (1993). "Telecommunications and the restructuring of the securities markets." In Bradley, S., Hausman, J., and Nolan, R. (eds.), *Globalization, Technology and Competition: The Fusion of Computers and Telecommunications in the 1990s.* Cambridge, MA: Harvard Business School.

Healy, K. (2010). *Last Best Gifts: Altruism and the Market for Human Blood and Organs.* Chicago: University of Chicago Press.

Hertz, E. (1998). *The Trading Crowd: An Ethnography of the Shanghai Stock Market.* Cambridge: Cambridge University Press.

Hertz, E. (2000). "Stock markets as 'simulacra': Observation that participates." Tsantsa, 5: 41–50.

Herzog, J. (1984). "Computers in market-making and accounting: an example." In *Computers in the City: Proceedings of the International Conference.* London: Online Publications.

Hicks, M. (2017). *Programmed Inequality: How Britain Discarded Women Technologists and Lost Its Edge in Computing.* Cambridge, MA: MIT Press.

Hirst, F.W. (1911). *The Stock Exchange: A Short Study of Investment and Speculation.* London: Thornton Butterworth.

Hobbs, D. (1974). "The development of a practical share evaluation model. *The Statistician*, 23: 31–56.

Hochfelder, D. (2006). "'Where the common people could speculate': The ticker, bucket shops, and the origins of popular participation in financial markets, 1880–1920." *The Journal of American History*, 93(2): 335–358.

House Subcommittee on Commerce and Finance. (1971). "Hearings on securities market structure." October 19, Washington, DC.

Hughes, M. (1971). Shares prices by push button catch on. *Stock Exchange Journal*, 21: 24–25.

Hülsmann, J.G. (2007). *Mises: The Last Knight of Liberalism.* Auburn, AL: Ludwig von Mises Institute.

Ingebretsen, M. (2002). *NASDAQ: A History of the Market that Changed the World.* Roseville, CA: FORUM.

Institutional Investor Study: Report of the Securities and Exchange Commission (1971). 92nd Congress, 1st Session, House Doc. No. 92–64, Part 8, p. xxv.

Investors Chronicle. (1961). *Beginners, Please.* London: Eyre and Spottiswoode.

Jacquillat, B. and Gresse, C. (1998). "The diversion of order flow on French stocks from CAC to SEAQ International: A field study." *European Financial Management*, 4: 121–142.

Jamison, A. (1989). "Technology's theorists: Conceptions of innovation in relation to science and technology policy." *Technology and Culture*, 30: 505–533.

Jarrell, G. (1984). "Change at the exchange: The causes and effects of deregulation." *The Journal of Law and Economics*, 27(2): 273–312.

Josephs, M. (1979). *Technology and the Future of Stockbroking: A Prospect for the 1980s*. London: London Stock Exchange.

Jovanovic, F. (2017). "Beyond performativity: How and why American courts should not have used efficient market hypothesis." In Chambost, I., Lenglet, M., and Tadjeddine Fourneyron, Y. (eds.), *The Making of Finance*. London: Routledge.

Kandiah, M.D. (1999). "Witness seminar I 'Big bang': The October 1986 market deregulation." *Contemporary British History*, 13(1): 100–132.

Karnes, T. (2009). *Asphalt and Politics: A History of the American Highway System*. Jefferson, NC: McFarland.

Keen, G. (1966). "Stock exchange computer one." *Stock Exchange Journal*, 11: 12–13.

Keith, C. and Grody, A. (1988). "Electronic automation at the New York Stock Exchange." In Guile, B. and Quinn, J.B. (eds.), *Managing Innovation: Cases from the Services Industries*, Washington, DC: National Academy of Engineering.

Kerr, R. (1864). *The Gentleman's House: Or, How to Plan English Residences, from the Parsonage to the Palace*. London: John Murray.

Khademian, A. (1992). *The SEC and Capital Market Regulation: The Politics of Expertise*. Pittsburg, PA: University of Pittsburgh Press.

Kirzner, I. (1996). *The Meaning of Market Process: Essays in the Development of Modern Austrian Economics*. London: Psychology Press.

Knorr Cetina, K. (2003). "From pipes to scopes: The flow architecture of financial markets." *Distinktion: Scandinavian Journal of Social Theory*, 4(2): 7–23.

Knorr Cetina, K. and Bruegger, U. (2002). "Global microstructures: The virtual societies of financial markets." *American Journal of Sociology*, 107(4): 905–950.

Knorr Cetina, K. and Preda, A. (2007). "The temporalization of financial markets: From network to flow." *Theory, Culture & Society*, 24(7–8): 116–138.

Krippner, G. (2011). *Capitalizing on Crisis: The Political Origins of the Rise of Finance*. Cambridge, MA: Harvard University Press.

Krippner, G. (2017). "Democracy of credit: Ownership and the politics of credit access in late twentieth-century America." *American Journal of Sociology*, 123(1), 1–47.

Krugman, P. (2014). "Three expensive milliseconds." *The New York Times*, April 14.

Kynaston, D. (1994). *The City of London: A World of Its Own 1815–1890*. London: Pimlico.

Kynaston, D. (2001). *The City of London: A Club No More 1945–2000*. London: Chatto & Windus.

Lander, R. (1986). "Rehearsal for Big Bang: 3,000 shares will be 'traded.'" *The Times*, October 18.

Lange, A. and Borch, C. (2014). "Contagious markets: On crowd psychology and high-frequency trading." Unpublished Manuscript.

Lapavitsas, C. (2013). "The financialization of capitalism: 'Profiting without producing.'" *City*, 17(6): 792–805.

Larkin, B. (2013). "The politics and poetics of infrastructure." *Annual Review of Anthropology*, 42: 327–343.

Laughlin, G. (n.d.). "Insights into high frequency trading from the Virtu initial public offering." Accessed December 13, 2016, https://online.wsj.com/public/resources/documents/VirtuOverview.pdf

Laumonier, A. (2014). *6: Le Soulèvement des machines*, Paris: Zones Sensibles.

Latour, B. (1992). "Where are the missing masses?" In Bijker, W. and Law, J. (eds.), *Shaping Technology/Building Society: Studies in Sociotechnical Change*. Cambridge, MA: MIT Press.

Latour, B. (2012). *We Have Never Been Modern*. Cambridge, MA: Harvard University Press.

Law, J. (1987) "Technology and heterogeneous engineering: The case of Portuguese expansion." In Bjiker, W., Hughes, T., and Pinch, T. (eds.), *The Social Construction of Technological Systems: New Directions in the Sociology and History of Technology*. Cambridge, MA: MIT Press.

Le Bon, G. (2009). *Psychology of Crowds*. Southampton: Sparkling Books.

LeCavalier, J. (2016). *The Rule of Logistics: Walmart and the Architecture of Fulfillment*. Pittsburgh: University of Minnesota Press.

Le Dantec, C. and DiSalvo, C. (2013). "Infrastructuring and the formation of publics in participatory design." *Social Studies of Science*, 43(2): 241–264.

Lee, R. (1998). *What Is an Exchange? The Automation, Management, and Regulation of Financial Markets*. Oxford: Oxford University Press.

Lee, R. (2002). "The future of securities exchanges." *Brookings-Wharton Papers on Financial Services*, 1: 1–33.

Leith, P. (2007). *Software and Patents in Europe*. Cambridge: Cambridge University Press.

Lévi-Strauss, C. (1983). "Histoire et ethnologie." *Annales*, 38(6): 1217–1231.

Lewis, M. (2015). *Flash Boys: A Wall Street Revolt.* New York: W.W. Norton.

Lipton, A., Pesavento, U., and Sotiropoulos, M.G. (2013). "Trade arrival dynamics and quote imbalance in a limit order book." arXiv preprint, arXiv:1312.0514.

Lisle-Williams, M. (1984a). "Beyond the market: The survival of family capitalism in the English merchant banks." *British Journal of Sociology*, 35(2): 241–271.

Lisle-Williams, M. (1984b). Merchant banking dynasties in the English class structure: Ownership, solidarity and kinship in the City of London, 1850–1960. *British Journal of Sociology*, 35(3): 333–362.

Littlewood, J. (1998). *The Stock Market: 50 Years of Capitalism at Work.* London: Pitman Publishing.

Louis, B., Massa, A., and Hanna, J. (2015). "From pits to algos, an old-school trader makes leap to spoofing." Bloomberg, November 12. Accessed December 11, 2018, www.bloomberg.com/news/articles/2015-11-12/from-pits-to-algos-an-old-school-trader-makes-leap-to-spoofing

Lupton, T. and Wilson, C.S. (1959). "The social background and connections of 'top decision makers.'" *The Manchester School*, 27(1): 30–51.

Ma, D. and Van Zanden, J. (2011). *Law and Long-Term Economic Change: A Eurasian Perspective.* Palo Alto, CA: Stanford University Press.

MacKenzie, D. (1984). "Marx and the Machine." *Technology and Culture*, 25(3): 473–502.

MacKenzie, D. (with Elzen, B.) (1996). "The charismatic engineer." In *Knowing Machines.* Cambridge, MA: MIT Press.

MacKenzie, D. (2005). "Opening the black boxes of global finance." *Review of International Political Economy*, 12(4), 555–576.

MacKenzie, D. (2008). *An Engine, Not a Camera: How Financial Models Shape Markets.* Cambridge, MA: MIT Press.

MacKenzie, D. (2011). "The credit crisis as a problem in the sociology of knowledge." *American Journal of Sociology*, 116(6): 1778–1841.

MacKenzie, D. (2018). "Material signals: A historical sociology of high-frequency trading." *American Journal of Sociology*, 123(6): 1635–1683.

MacKenzie, D., Beunza, D., Millo, Y., and Pardo-Guerra, J.P. (2012). "Drilling through the Allegheny Mountains: Liquidity, materiality and high-frequency trading." *Journal of Cultural Economy*, 5(3): 279–296.

MacKenzie, D. and Millo, Y. (2003). "Constructing a market, performing theory: The historical sociology of a financial derivatives exchange." *American Journal of Sociology*, 109(1): 107–145.

MacKenzie, D. and Pardo-Guerra, J.P. (2014). "Insurgent capitalism: Island, bricolage and the re-making of finance." *Economy and Society*, 43(2): 153–182.

Mackintosh, P. (2014). "Demystifying order types." KCG Working Paper. KCG, New York.

Mahoney, J. and Thelen, K. (eds.) (2009). *Explaining Institutional Change: Ambiguity, Agency, and Power*. Cambridge: Cambridge University Press.

Malkiel, B.G. and Fama, E.F. (1970). "Efficient capital markets: A review of theory and empirical work." *The Journal of Finance*, 25(2): 383–417.

Mann, L. (1969). "Queue culture: The waiting line as a social system." *American Journal of Sociology*, 75(3): 340–354.

Marshall, A. (2014 [1890]). *Principles of Economics*. London: Palgrave.

Martin, C. (2013). "Shipping container mobilities, seamless compatibility, and the global surface of logistical integration." *Environment and Planning A*, 45(5): 1021–1036.

Maurer, W. (2017). "Blockchains are a diamond's best friend." In Bandelj, N., Wherry, F., and Zelizer, V. (eds.), *Money Talks: Explaining How Money Really Works*. Princeton, NJ: Princeton University Press.

Maurer, B. and Swartz, L. (eds.) (2017). *Paid: Tales of Dongles, Checks, and Other Money Stuff*. Cambridge, MA: MIT Press.

Mauss, M. (2000). *The Gift: The Form and Reason for Exchange in Archaic Societies*. New York: W.W. Norton.

Mauss, M. (2013). "Joking relations." *HAU: Journal of Ethnographic Theory*, 3(2): 321–334.

McClintock, A. (1993). "Family feuds: Gender, nationalism and the family." *Feminist Review*, 44(1): 61–80.

McDonough, P.M. (1994). "Buying and selling higher education: The social construction of the college applicant." *The Journal of Higher Education*, 65(4): 427–446.

McKenzie, R. (2012). *The New World of Economics: A Remake of a Classic for New Generations of Economics Students*. Berlin: Springer Science & Business Media.

Mehrling, P. (2017). "Financialization and its discontents." *Finance & Society*, 3(1): 1–10.

Mendelson, M. and Peake, J.W. (1979). "The ABCs of trading on a national market system." *Financial Analysts Journal*, 35(5), 31–42.

Mendelson, M., Peake, J.W., and Williams, R.T. (1977). *Towards a Modern Exchange: The Peake-Mendelson-Williams Proposal for an Electronically Assisted Auction Market*. New York: Salomon Brothers Center for the Study of Financial Institutions.

Meyer, J.W. and Rowan, B. (1977). "Institutionalized organizations: Formal structure as myth and ceremony." *American Journal of Sociology*, 83(2): 340–363.

Michie, R. (1998). "Insiders, outsiders and the dynamics of change in the City of London since 1900." *Journal of Contemporary History*, 33: 547–571.

Michie, R. (1999). *The London Stock Exchange: A History*. Oxford: Oxford University Press.

Miller, D. (2008). *The Comfort of Things*. Cambridge: Polity Press.

Millo, Y. (2004). "Creation of a market network: the regulatory approval of Chicago Board Options Exchange (CBOE)." Unpublished manuscript, Centre for Analysis of Risk and Regulation, London School of Economics and Political Science.

Millo, Y., Muniesa, F., Panourgias, N., and Scott, S.V. (2005). "Organized detachment: Clearinghouse mechanisms in financial markets." *Information and Organization*, 15(3): 229–246.

Mills, L., Newberry, K.J., and Trautman, W.B. (2002). "Trends in book-tax income and balance sheet differences." Paper presented at the 2002 IRS Research Conference. Accessed May 20, 2017, www.irs.gov/pub/irs-soi/bktxinbs.pdf

Mirowski, P. (1988). *Against Mechanism: Protecting Economics from Science*. New York: Rowman and Littlefield.

Mirowski, P. (1991). *More Heat than Light: Economics as Social Physics, Physics as Nature's Economics*. Cambridge: Cambridge University Press.

Mirowski, P. (2002). *Machine Dreams: Economics Becomes a Cyborg Science*. Cambridge: Cambridge University Press.

Mirowski, P. (2013). *Never Let a Serious Crisis Go to Waste: How Neoliberalism Survived the Financial Meltdown*. London: Verso Books.

Mises, L., von (1974). *Planning for Freedom and Twelve Other Essays and Addresses*. South Holland, IL: Libertarian Press.

Mises, L. von (1998 [1949]). *Human Action: A Treatise on Economics*. Auburn, AL: Ludwig von Mises Institute.

Moallemi, C. and Yuan, K. (2014). "The value of queue position in a limit order book." In Abergel, F., Bouchaud, J.P., Foucault, T., Lehalle, C.A., and Rosenbaum, M. (eds.), *Market Microstructure: Confronting Many Viewpoints*. London: Wiley-Blackwell.

Morgan, D. (2005). "Class and masculinity." In Kimmel, M., Hearn, J., and Connell, R.W. (eds.), *Handbook of Studies on Men and Masculinities*. Thousand Oaks, CA: SAGE.

Mudge, S.L. (2007). Precarious progressivism: The struggle over the social in the neoliberal era. PhD Dissertation, University of California, Berkeley.

Muniesa, F. (2003). "Des marchés comme algorithmes: Sociologie de la cotation électronique à la Bourse de Paris." PhD Thesis, École Nationale Supérieure des Mines de Paris.

Muniesa, F. (2011). "Is a stock exchange a computer solution? Explicitness, algorithms and the Arizona stock exchange." *International Journal of Actor-Network Theory and Technological Innovation*, 3(1): 1–15.

Muniesa, F. (2014). *The Provoked Economy: Economic Reality and the Performative Turn*. London: Routledge.

Muniesa, F. and Callon, M. (2005). "Economic markets as calculative collective devices." *Organization Studies*, 25: 1229–1250.

Muni Toke, I. (2015). "The order book as a queueing system: Average depth and influence of the size of limit orders." *Quantitative Finance*, 15(5): 795–808.

Musson, J. (2009). *Up and Down Stairs: The History of the Country House Servant*. London: John Murray.

Nathaus, K. and Gilgen, D. (2011). "Analysing the change of markets, fields and market societies: An introduction." *Historical Social Research/Historische Sozialforschung*, 36(3): 7–16.

National Market Advisory Board. (1977). *Report to the Securities and Exchange Commission from the National Market Advisory Board*. Washington, DC.

Nee, V. (1989). "A theory of market transition: From redistribution to markets in state socialism." *American Sociological Review*, 54(5): 663–681.

Nightingale, R. (1985). "Electronics in the city." In *Computers in the City 1985. Retailing Financial Services: Proceedings of the International Conference*, London.

Nymeyer, F. (1971). "Auction market computation system," US Patent 3,581,072, filed Mar. 28, 1968, and issued May 25.

NYSE. (2018). "Technology FAQ and best practices: EQUITIES." Accessed February 10, 2018, www.nyse.com/publicdocs/nyse/markets/nyse/NYSE_Group_Equities_Technology_FAQ.pdf

O'Brien, R. (1992). *Global Financial Integration: The End of Geography*. London: Royal Institute of International Affairs.

O'Hara, M. (1995). *Market Microstructure Theory*. Cambridge, MA: Blackwell.

Orlikowski, W. (1992). "The duality of technology: Rethinking the concept of technology in organizations." Organization Science, 3(3): 398–427.

Orlikowski, W. and Scott, S.V. (2015). "The algorithm and the crowd: Considering the materiality of service innovation." MIS Quarterly, 39(1): 201–216.

Ott, J. (2011). *When Wall Street Met Main Street: The Quest for an Investors' Democracy*. Cambridge, MA: Harvard University Press.

Pagano, M. (1985). "The Big Bang will really be a series of small pops: Analysis of technology and the stock exchange." *The Guardian*, April 3.

Parcel, T.L. and Menaghan, E.G. (1994). "Early parental work, family social capital, and early childhood outcomes." *American Journal of Sociology* 99(4): 972–1009.

Parsons, T. (1943). "The kinship system of the contemporary United States." *American Anthropologist*, 45(1): 22–38.

Peake, J. (1978). "The national market system." *Financial Analysts Journal*, 34(4): 25–28, 31–33, 81–84.

Peake, J. (2004). Email to the Securities and Exchange Commission, re: Subject: NYSE SR-2004–05 Release: 34–50173. March 15, 2014, www.sec.gov/rules/sro/nyse/nyse200405/jwpeake092204.pdf

Peake, J. (2006). "Entropy and the national market system." *Brooklyn Journal Corporate, Financial and Commercial Law*, 1(2): 301–315.

Peebles, G. (2010). "The anthropology of credit and debt." *Annual Review of Anthropology*, 39: 225–240.

Perks, R. and Thomson, A. (1998). *The Oral History Reader*. London: Routledge.

Perry, R. and Zarsky, T.Z. (2013). "Queues in law." Iowa Law Review, 99: 1595.

Pipek, V. and Wulf, V. (2009). "Infrastructuring: Towards an integrated perspective on the design and use of information technology." Journal of the Association of Information Systems, 10(5): 306–332.

Pirrong, C. (2013). "SLOB v. CLOB." Streetwise Professor, August 10. Accessed May 7, 2014, http://streetwiseprofessor.com/?p=7530

Polanyi, K. (1944). *The Great Transformation*. Boston: Gower Beacon Press.

Poovey, M. (2002). "Writing about finance in Victorian England: Disclosure and secrecy in the culture of investment." *Victorian Studies*, 45(1): 17–41.

Powell, W.W. and Colyvas, J.A. (2008). "Microfoundations of institutional theory." In Greenwood, R., Oliver, C., Sahlin, K., and Suddaby, R. (eds.), *The SAGE Handbook of Organizational Institutionalism*. London: SAGE.

Preda, A. (2006). "Socio-technical agency in financial markets: The case of the stock ticker." *Social Studies of Science*, 36(5): 753–782.

Preda, A. (2008). "Technology, agency, and financial price data." In Pinch, T. and Swedberg, R. (eds.), *Living in a Material World*. Cambridge, MA: MIT Press.

Preda, A. (2009). *Framing Finance: The Boundaries of Markets and Modern Capitalism*. Chicago: Chicago University Press.

Progressive Calvinism. (1955). "The character of the Progressive Calvinism League." January 1(1): 2–15.

Progressive Calvinism. (1956a). "Max Weber, sociologist." September 2(9): 259–265.

Progressive Calvinism. (1956b). "The natural sciences and the praexological sciences." November 2(11): 337–339.

Progressive Calvinism. (1956c). "One phase of economics – The relationship of men to men." July 2(7): 196.

Progressive Calvinism. (1956d). "What is the Protestant ethic?" September 2(9): 286.

Pryke, M. (1991). "An international city going 'global': Spatial change in the City of London." *Environment and Planning D: Society and Space*, 9(2): 197–222.

Radcliffe-Brown, A.R. (1940). "On joking relationships." Africa, 13(3): 195–210.

Radcliffe-Brown, A.R. (1952). *Structure and Function in Primitive Society*. Glencoe, IL: Free Press.

Ranger, T. and Hobsbawm, E. (1992). *The Invention of Tradition*. Cambridge: Cambridge University Press.

Ransom, J. (2014). "Stockmaster – The service that revolutionised Reuters." The Baron. Accessed September 2, 2016, www.thebaron.info/archives/technology/stockmaster-the-service-that-revolutionised-reuters

Reader, W. and Kynaston, D. (1998). *Phillips & Drew: Professionals in the City*. London: Robert Hale.

Reed, M. (1975). *A History of James Capel & Co*. London: Longman.

Rehmann, J. (2013). *Theories of Ideology: The Powers of Alienation and Subjection*. Leiden: Brill.

Report of the Special Study of Securities Markets of the Securities and Exchange Commission. (1963). 88th Congress, 1st Session, House Doc. No. 95, Pt. 7.

Revel, J. (1995). "Microanalysis and the construction of the social." In Revel, J. (ed.), *Histories: French Constructions of the Past: Postwar French Thought*. New York: New Press.

Ricardo, D. (1891). *Principles of Political Economy and Taxation*. London: G. Bell.

Riles, A. (2011). *Collateral Knowledge: Legal Reasoning in the Global Financial Markets*. Chicago: Chicago University Press.

Ritzer, G. (1998). *The McDonaldization Thesis: Explorations and Extensions*. Thousand Oaks, CA: SAGE.

Roper, M. (1996). "Oral Histories." In Brivati, B., Buxton, J., and Seldon, A. (eds.), The Contemporary History Handbook. Manchester: Manchester University Press.

Roth, A. (2002). "The economist as engineer: Game theory, experimentation, and computation as tools for design economics." *Econometrica*, 70(4): 1341–1378.

Royal Commission. (1878). *Report of the Royal Commission on the London Stock Exchange*. London: UK Parliament.

Rude, G. (2005). *The Crowd in History 1730–1848*. New York: John Wiley & Sons.

Sassen, S. (2013). *The Global City: New York, London, Tokyo*. Princeton, NJ: Princeton University Press.

Schiller, D. (1982). *Telematics and Government*. Westport, CT: Greenwood Publishing.

Schneider, D. (1980). *American Kinship: A Cultural Account*. Chicago: University of Chicago Press.

Schoeters, T. (1970). "Electronic systems have much to offer." *Financial Times*, April 17: 11.

Schwartz, B. (1974). "Waiting, exchange, and power: The distribution of time in social systems." *American Journal of Sociology*, 79(4): 841–870.

Schwartz, R.A., Byrne, J.A., and Colaninno, A. (eds.) (2006). *Call Auction Trading: New Answers to Old Questions*. Berlin: Springer Science & Business Media.

Schwartz, R.A. and Weber, B.W. (1997). "Next-generation securities market systems: An experimental investigation of quote-driven and order-driven trading." *Journal of Management Information Systems*, 14(2): 57–79.

Securities Acts Amendments of 1975. (1975). Public Law 94–29, 94th Congress, 1st Session.

Securities and Exchange Commission. (1994). "Market 2000: An examination of current equity market developments." SEC Division of Markets Regulation, Washington, DC.

Securities and Exchange Commission. (2005). "Regulation NMS." SEC Release 34–51808 (June 9).

Securities and Exchange Commission. (2015). "Equity market structure advisory committee meeting." Washington, DC.

Seligman, J. (1982). *The Transformation of Wall Street: A History of the Securities and Exchange Commission and Modern Corporate Finance*. New York: Houghton Mifflin.

Sennholz, H. (2007). "Memories of Ludwig von Mises." In Grove City College Conference on the Legacy of Ludwig von Mises, February 23–24.

Shamir, R. (2008). "The age of responsibilization: On market-embedded morality." *Economy and Society*, 37(1): 1–19.

Shaw, W. (1906). "The 'Treasury Order Book.'" *The Economic Journal*, 16(61): 33–40.

Simmel, G. (1972). *On Individuality and Social Forms*. Chicago: Chicago University Press.

Simmel, G. (2004 [1900]). *The Philosophy of Money*. London: Psychology Press.

Simone, A. (2012). "Infrastructure: Introductory commentary by AbdouMaliq Simone." Curated Collections, *Cultural Anthropology*, November 26.

Sinn, R. (n.d.). "Reminiscences of a stock quotation system: The real story of Ultronic Systems Corporation." Unpublished manuscript.

Slater, D. (2002). "From calculation to alienation: Disentangling economic abstractions." *Economy and Society*, 31(2): 234–249.

Slater, D. and Tonkiss, F. (2005). *Market Societies: Markets and Modern Social Theory*. Cambridge: Polity Press.

Sloan, L. (1978). "Automated trading debated." *New York Times*, June 19.

Sobel, R. (1975). *NYSE: A History*. New York: Weybright and Talley.

Sobel, R. (2000). *Inside Wall Street*. New York: Beard Books.

Sombart, W. (1924). *Der moderne kapitalismus*. Munich: Duncker & Humblot.

Star, S.L. (1998). "Working together: Symbolic interactionism, activity theory, and information systems." In Engestrom, Y. and Middleton, D. (eds.), *Cognition and Communication at Work*. Cambridge: Cambridge University Press.

Star, S.L. (1999). "The ethnography of infrastructure." *American Behavioral Scientist*, 43(3): 377–391.

Star, S.L. and Bowker, G. (2006). "How to infrastructure." In Lievrouw, L. and Livingstone, S. (eds.), *Handbook of New Media: Social Shaping and Social Consequences of ICTs*. Thousand Oaks, CA: SAGE.

Star, S.L. and Ruhleder, K. (1996). "Steps toward an ecology of infrastructure: Design and access for large information spaces." *Information Systems Research*, 7(1): 111–134.

Stock Exchange. (1970). *Stock Exchange Official Yearbook*. London: Stock Exchange Press and MacMillan.

Strange, S. (1986). *Casino Capitalism*. Oxford: Basil Blackwell.

Strathern, M. (1992). *After Nature: English Kinship in the Late Twentieth Century*. Cambridge: Cambridge University Press.

Strathern, M. (2005). *Kinship, Law and the Unexpected: Relatives Are Always a Surprise*. Cambridge: Cambridge University Press.

Streeck, W. (2014). *Buying Time: The Delayed Crisis of Democratic Capitalism*. London: Verso Books.

Streeck, W. and Thelen, K. (2005). *Beyond Continuity: Institutional Change in Advanced Political Economies*. Cambridge: Cambridge University Press.

Swedberg, R. (2003). *Principles of Economic Sociology*. Princeton, NJ: Princeton University Press.

Swedberg, R. (2005). "Markets in society." In Smelser, N. and Swedberg, R. (eds.) *The Handbook of Economic Sociology*. Princeton, NJ: Princeton University Press.

Symonds, M. and Pudsey, J. (2006). "The forms of brotherly love in Max Weber's sociology of religion." *Sociological Theory*, 24(2): 133–149.

Tapscott, D. and Tapscott, A. (2016). *Blockchain Revolution: How the Technology Behind Bitcoin Is Changing Money, Business, and the World*. London: Penguin Books.

Tarde, G. (2010). *Gabriel Tarde on Communication and Social Influence: Selected Papers*. Chicago: University of Chicago Press.

Taylor, S. and Lyon, P. (1995). "Paradigm lost: The rise and fall of McDonaldization." *International Journal of Contemporary Hospitality Management*, 7(2/3): 64–68.

Thelen, Kathleen. (2004). *How Institutions Evolve: The Political Economy of Skills in Germany, Britain, the United States, and Japan.* Cambridge: Cambridge University Press.

The Stock Exchange. (1923). "House on sport." Unknown publishing.

The Economist. (2009). "Rise of the machines: High-frequency trading." July 30.

The Stock Exchange. (1976). "Rules and regulations of the stock exchange," London.

The Times. (1901). "The Stock Exchange Art Society." July 9.

The Times. (1907). "Concerts." March 22.

Thevenot, L. (1984). "Rules and implement: Investments in form." *Social Science Information*, 23(1): 1–45.

Thomas, A. (2016). "'Mart of the World': An architectural and geographical history of the London Stock Exchange." *The Journal of Architecture*, 21(5): 816–855.

Thompson, E.P. (1967). "Time, work-discipline, and industrial capitalism." *Past & Present*, 38: 56–97.

Thompson, E.P. (1971). "The moral economy of the English crowd in the eighteenth century." *Past & Present*, 50: 76–136.

Thornbury, W. (1878). *Old and New London: A Narrative of Its History, Its People, and Its Places.* London: Cassell, Petter, Galpin & Co.

Thorpe, C. and Shapin, S. (2000). "Who was J. Robert Oppenheimer? Charisma and complex organization." *Social Studies of Science*, 30(4): 545–590.

Thornbury, W. (1878). *Old and New London: A Narrative of Its History, Its People, and Its Places.* London: Cassell, Petter, Galpin & Co.

Thrift, N. (1996). "A phantom state? International money, electronic networks and global cities." In *Spatial Formations.* London: SAGE.

TLH. (1917). "Property. Ownership of stock quotations. Ticker service. *University of Pennsylvania Law Review and American Law Register*, 65: 482–485.

Townsend, T. (1774). "Debates of a political society." *The London Magazine*, January.

Traflet, J. (2003). "Own your share of American business: Public relations at the NYSE during the Cold War." *Business and Economic History On-Line*, 1.

Traflet, J. (2013). *A Nation of Small Shareholders: Marketing Wall Street After World War II.* Baltimore, MD: Johns Hopkins University Press.

Treasury Committee. (1996). *Minutes of Evidence: The London Stock Exchange*, London: Her Majesty's Stationary Office.

Treleaven, P., Brownbridge, D.R., and Hopkins, R.P. (1982). "Data-driven and demand-driven computer architecture." *ACM Computing Surveys*, 14(1): 93–143.

Truell, P. (1986). "Britain's 'Big Bang' sputters in practice, starts next week." *The Wall Street Journal*, October 20.

Ugolini, L. (2007). *Men and Menswear: Sartorial Consumption in Britain 1880–1939*. London: Ashgate.

US Congress. (1990). "Electronic Bulls & Bears: US Securities Markets & Information Technology, OTA-CIT-469." Office of Technology Assessment, Washington, DC.

US Congress. (2000). "Competition In the new electronic market: Hearing before the subcommittee on finance and hazardous materials of the Committee on Commerce, House of Representatives, One Hundred Sixth Congress, Second Session. Washington: USGPO

US v. Coscia. (2015a). "Indictment." United States District Court, Northern District of Illinois, Eastern Division.

US v. Coscia. (2015b). "Motion for acquittal." United States District Court, Northern District of Illinois, Eastern Division.

US v. Coscia. (2015c). "Memorandum opinion order." United States District Court, Northern District of Illinois, Eastern Division.

Vargha, Z. (2014). "Clocks, clerks, customers: Queue management systems, post-socialist sensibilities, and performance measurement at a retail bank." In De Vaujany, F.-X., Mitev, N., Laniray, P., and Vaast, E. (eds.), *Materiality and Time*. London: Palgrave Macmillan.

Veblen, T. (1965). *The Engineers and the Price System*. New York: Kelley.

Veneri, C.M. (1998). *Here Today, Jobs for Tomorrow: Opportunities in Information Technology*. Washington, DC: US Department of Labor.

Wah, E. (2016). "How prevalent and profitable are latency arbitrage opportunities on US stock exchanges?" Social Science Research Network. Accessed May 12, 2016, https://papers.ssrn.com/sol3/papers.cfm?abstract_id=2729109

Walker, D.A. (2001). "A factual account of the functioning of the nineteenth-century Paris Bourse." *European Journal of the History of Economic Thought*, 8(2): 186–207.

Walras, L. (1880). "La bourse, la spéculation et l'agiotage." *Bibliothèque Universelle et Revue Suisse*, 5: 452–476.

Walras, L. (2003). *Elements of Pure Economics: Or the Theory of Social Wealth*. London: Psychology Press.

Waring, J. and Bishop, S. (2015). "George Ritzer: Rationalisation, consumerism and the McDonaldisation of surgery." In Collyer, F. (ed.), *The Palgrave Handbook of Social Theory in Health, Illness and Medicine*. London: Palgrave Macmillan.

Waters, R. (1990). "Exchange considers the next stage of its electronic revolution." *Financial Times*, December 8.

Weaver, D. and Hall, M.G. (1967). "The evaluation of ordinary shares using a computer." *Journal of the Institute of Actuaries*, 93(2): 165–227.

Weber, M. (1978). *Economy and Society*. Berkeley: University of California Press.

Weber, M. (1993). *The Sociology of Religion*. Boston: Beacon Press.

Weber, M. (2000 [1894]). "Stock and commodity exchanges." *Theory and Society*, 29: 305–331.

Weber, M. (2013). *The Protestant Ethic and the Spirit of Capitalism*. London: Routledge.

Weeden, D. (1971). "Statement before the Securities and Exchange Commission." Hearings on securities market structure, October 19, Washington, DC.

Weeden, D. (2002). *Weeden & Co. The New York Stock Exchange and the Struggle Over a National Market*. Tempe, AZ: Ironwood Lithographers.

Weiss, D. (1992). *After the Trade Is Made: Processing Securities Transactions*. New York: Penguin Books.

Wells, W. (2000). "Certificates and computers: The remaking of Wall Street, 1967 to 1971." *Business History Review*, 74(2): 193–235.

Werner, W. (1971). "The certificateless society: Why and when?" *The Business Lawyer*, 26(3): 603–609.

White, H. (1981). "Where do markets come from?" *American Journal of Sociology*, 87(3): 517–547.

Whyte, H. (1924). *The Stock Exchange: Its Constitution and the Effects of the Great War*. London: Pitman & Sons.

Williamson, O. (1981). "The economics of organization: The transaction cost approach." *American Journal of Sociology*, 87(3): 548–577.

Williamson, O. (1983). *Markets and Hierarchies: Analysis and Antitrust Implications*. New York: Free Press.

Winner, L. (1980). "Do artifacts have politics?" *Daedalus*, 109(1): 121–136.

Wissner-Gross, A.D. and Freer, C.E. (2010). "Relativistic statistical arbitrage." *Physical Review E*, 82(5).

Yanagisako, S.J. (2002). *Producing Culture and Capital: Family Forms in Italy*. Princeton, NJ: Princeton University Press.

Yanagisako, S.J. and Delaney, C.L. (eds.) (1995). *Naturalizing Power: Essays in Feminist Cultural Analysis*. London: Psychology Press.

Yanagisako, S.J., Junko, S., and Delaney, C.L. (1995). *Naturalizing Power: Essays in Feminist Cultural Analysis*. New York: Psychology Press.

Yates, J. (2005). *Structuring the Information Age: Life Insurance and Technology in the Twentieth Century*. Baltimore, MD: Johns Hopkins University Press.

Young, M. and Wilmott, P. (2013). *Family and Kinship in East London*. London: Routledge.

Zaloom, C. (2006). *Out of the Pits: Traders and Technology from Chicago to London*. Chicago: University of Chicago Press.

Zaloom, C. (2018). "A right to the future: Student debt and the politics of crisis." *Cultural Anthropology*, 33: 558–569.

Zelizer, V. (1988). "Beyond the polemics on the market: Establishing a theoretical and empirical agenda." *Sociological Forum*, 3(4): 614–634.

Zelizer, V. (2009). *The Purchase of Intimacy*. Princeton, NJ: Princeton University Press.

Zelizer, V. (2010). *Economic Lives: How Culture Shapes the Economy*. Princeton, NJ: Princeton University Press.

Zelizer, V. (2012). "How I became a relational economic sociologist and what does that mean?" *Politics & Society*, 40(2): 145–174.

Zelizer, V. (2017). *Morals and Markets: The Development of Life Insurance in the United States*. New York: Columbia University Press.

Index